THE BEST OF THE ATHLETIC BOYS

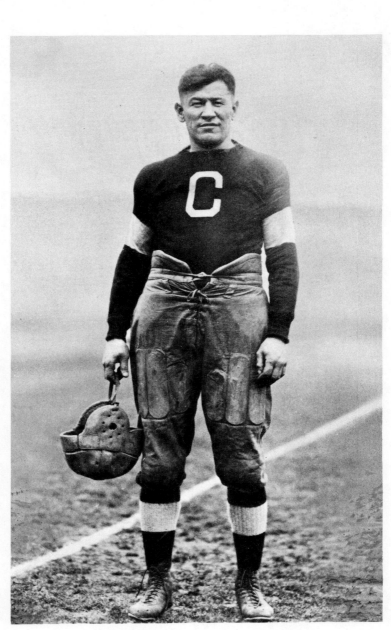

JIM THORPE, SAC AND FOX

The Best of the Athletic Boys

THE WHITE MAN'S IMPACT ON JIM THORPE

JACK NEWCOMBE

1975
Doubleday & Company, Inc., Garden City, New York

ISBN: 0-385-06186-2
Library of Congress Catalog Card Number: 74-33657

To the Sac and Fox

PREFACE

THE BEST OF THE ATHLETIC BOYS

I met Jim Thorpe not long before he died in 1953. He was in New York with his third wife on one of those relentless personal tours she managed, combining her own campaign to get his Olympic medals and trophies returned with a promotional enterprise of some kind. It may have been an announcement of Thorpe's connection with an all-girl softball team or a job for him as trainer for the Israeli national soccer squad. A young reporter, I was the only one who had responded to the invitation to the press to meet him in his midtown hotel suite. It was a day of heavy summer heat in the city and there was no air conditioning in the rooms. Thorpe sat on the bed, gripping the edge of it with a surprisingly white hand, smiling and nodding at me occasionally as his wife did the talking. I wondered who was the more uncomfortable, he or I, as the public relations recital went on. I remember watching his hand, which never relaxed its hold on the bedspread, and thinking that at least I would get a chance to shake it again when I left.

It was the decisive image I would have of this famous Indian until much later when I became interested in the environment he grew up in as a boy in Oklahoma Territory, the special circumstances of the Indian emergence in U. S. sports early in the century, and his own development as an all-around athlete—the best America produced in fifty years according to a wire service poll.

There were, of course, great distances between the man at the end of his life when I met him and the familiar, legendary pieces of his career. I learned that there was little public awareness of

the actual role he served in American sports—a pioneer both in
and outside the arena—and little appreciation of the short, dis-
tinctive Indian athletic presence in America at the turn of the
century. It was an ethnic flowering similar to that of the blacks
later on in the 1900s.

In this book I have attempted to trace the phenomenon of
Thorpe (and his Indian teammates) through his background as
a mixed blood in a Sac and Fox allotment home on the North
Canadian River and through his experience in the Indian education system in Oklahoma and Kansas and, most particularly, at
the Carlisle Indian School in Pennsylvania, a school he attended,
off and on, for nine years. It is also the story of a long, failing
experiment by the U. S. government to educate and assimilate
the reservation Indian—although at Carlisle it did produce strik-
ing individual successes and some very winning football teams.
For Thorpe and many of his talented teammates it offered a
practical route into the white world where there was good payment for their athletic services.

In reconstructing the past on the Sac and Fox reservation and
at Haskell and Carlisle Indian schools, I had help from many individuals who care and know about the Indian. I am particularly
indebted to the staff at the Shawnee Agency of the Bureau of
Indian Affairs in Oklahoma, members of the Indian Archives at
the Oklahoma Historical Society, at the Archives of the United
States in Washington, D.C., and at the Cumberland County Historical Society in Carlisle, Pennsylvania. The book needed the
encouragement and advice of members of the Thorpe family,
particularly daughter, Grace, and sons Carl, Richard and Jack;
Thorpe's close friends Lee and Celia Blanchard; and that of his
former Carlisle teammates, Henry Roberts, of Pawnee, Oklahoma, and the late Albert Exendine of Tulsa, Oklahoma.

CONTENTS

THE BEST OF THE ATHLETIC BOYS

I   PLACES OF THE SAC AND FOX

The Moccasin Highway

The old section-line road, now state Route 18, shoots a nearly straight course out of Shawnee toward the Cimarron, making its wide, reddish-brown sweep across the northern length of Oklahoma. Not far beyond the city limits, just before the highway and the tracks of the Santa Fe railroad cease sharing the same ridge of land, the Moccasin Trail—or Moccasin Highway, as it is identified locally—signals a right-angle turn easily missed in the seventy-mile-an-hour traffic flow. It is a highway in the vernacular only, opening on blacktop and unraveling soon enough into pickup-truck dust which, when the wind is down, hangs in the sky as a rusty veil across the top of Pottawatomie County. The road leads through one of the few remaining clusters of Indian trust land in the area, part of the final reserve of the Sac and Fox after they had been removed by one more treaty from their acres in Kansas to a narrow north-south strip bordering the Creek Nation in Indian Territory.

It is, at the beginning, a graceless track, rolling but unswervingly constant through the sandy earth patched with blackjack oak and cottonwood. This the daily shuttle of school buses, carrying children to and from the low-cost Indian homes, and the run of the bright-toned pickups is the current transit pattern for what was once the methodical beat of wagons, hooves and feet. A few miles along the road is an obscured turning that leads to one of the last significant traces of the Sac and Fox presence of nearly a century ago. Here beyond a hillside, tribe members gathered periodically to worship the change of seasons. The earth, once packed smooth with the drumming of moccasins, is still shaped with the gradual mounds where the Indians sat around the ceremonial dance ring. But much of the once-restricted land spreading far beyond the camp grounds and dance ring, allotted and placed in trust when the government decided in the late 1880s to bestow the benefits of private ownership on the uninitiated Indian peoples, has long since been leased, subleased and sold off to whites. To the south of the Moccasin Highway where the land breaks out agreeably on the thickly grown path of the North Canadian River, the prosperous bottom land fields of the ranchers mock the intent of the severalty policy which evolved, clumsily enough, from the white man's own guilt over his voracious appetite for Indian-held territory.

The broad lands leveled by this old plains river, luxuriant looking even during the arid drone of Oklahoma summer, had an appeal to humans long before the Sac and Fox learned what it could bring on the market place. In 1832, as the Sac war chief, Black Hawk, was making the last major Indian stand against the white take-over of the upper Mississippi, Washington Irving made a tour of the Oklahoma prairies with a casual government military mission. As he approached the North Canadian River near here he enthused over the discovery of "a beautiful camping ground . . . On the edge of the prairie and in a spacious grove of trees which overshadowed a small brook, were the traces of an old Creek hunting camp." While Irving puzzled over the erotic charcoal hieroglyphics the Creek hunters had left scrawled on tree bark, the rangers responsible for bringing in the daily meat supply were learning how well discovered the area was. "The hunters returned with indifferent success," Irving wrote. "The game had been frightened away from this part of the country by Indian hunting parties, which had preceded us. Ten or a dozen wild turkeys were brought in, but not a deer had been seen. The rangers began to think turkeys and even prairie hens were deserving of attention; game which they had hitherto considered unworthy of their rifles."

Some forty years later this ragged general course of the North Canadian became gradually populated with the bark lodges, log houses, dogs, horses, hogs of the remaining bands of Sac and Fox of the Mississippi, survivors of the Black Hawk War, pestilence, dislocation and a long chafing with an alien life-style. In one Sac and Fox cabin, built between the river and the present Moccasin Highway, Jim Thorpe was born, although there is no more significant reminder of that 1887 birthplace than there is of the ancient Creek hunting camps scattered through the area. On the Thorpe section today an efficient farmer manages his strong acres of alfalfa, wheat and a small ridge-land peanut crop. In his hangar-sized equipment shed, which looks out on the patch of meadow and trees where the Thorpe family cabin stood, he often works at reconditioning his single-engine sport plane whenever the weather turns too foul for outside farming. Only the imagination can fill in the woods that once stretched to the river edge and where the Thorpes did their easy hunting (not all of the wild turkey, quail and small game had fled before the Creeks) and where Jim played children's chasing games with his brothers. When young Thorpe broke away from school discipline, which he did with practiced defiance, he made his run back to this stretch of the North Canadian. Thorpe kin, products of his half-breed Irish father's adherence to Indian polygamy, lived up and down the river area. They traded at the nearby small communities and stage stops which developed quickly after the whites moved in: Bellemont, sometimes given as Thorpe's place of birth although he was born a few miles away and four years before the town started; Econtuchka, which was on the river and took its name from the Seminole "surveyed line." The North Canadian bottom land in the vicinity is still admired as that "good old Econtushkee soil." Both towns have vanished now—general stores, cotton gins, blacksmith shops, hotels and all.

For any historical acknowledgment of the final domain of the Sac and Fox, one has to turn north from the river, which set the lower boundary of the tribe's original reserve, to Prague, a market town with a strong Polish strain in its early population and a broad, sloping main street that once might have inspired Western movie-set designers. A dozen miles beyond Prague on Route 99, in splendidly open Deep Fork River country near Stroud, an official roadside marker places the site of the Sac and Fox Agency, the tribe's commercial, political and social headquarters in the Territory. The metallic words of the state historical society read: "Sac and Fox Indians came from Kansas to new lands here in

1870. The agency was built soon; a brick building for the Boarding School was erected and opened in 1872. The old house of Moses Keokuk stands two miles west of here. Sac and Fox Country was opened to White settlement, September 22, 1891."

Thorpe's early years were bound inflexibly to the land around this historical marker, some twenty miles from his home. His first distasteful encounters with education came at the Mission boarding school located under the old water tower on the high ground to the east. Today cattle graze near the broken foundations and the wind brings the sounds of tire whine from the distant highway and the rhythmic squeaking of a drilling rig of the Sac and Fox unit of the Tenneco Oil Company, working ground still held in tribal trust. (The Sacs and Foxes did not make the happy scores in oil and gas that the draw of the land brought to the Osages and other Indians.) On Thorpe's personal map the Agency became a custodial center, as it did for many Sac and Fox children after their parents died, processing his status as an Indian ward. The agency superintendent served him for a time as legal guardian, banker, realtor and, when Thorpe went off to Carlisle, kept him advised of his small accumulation of private capital through lease shares and tribal annuities.

Although Thorpe's links to the tribe slackened as he grew older, as family allotment shares were sold off and his personal course kept him away from Oklahoma for longer periods, all that he was to become, for better or for worse, must have been set in that early experience as a half-breed with the Sac and Fox. There is no certain documentation of the influence; on the current, officially approved tribal rolls, Thorpe's degree of Sac and Fox blood is listed as only one eighth, an arbitrary bureaucratic measurement that indicates he is "of the blood" and assures his direct descendants of their place in the tribe. His father, the son of an Indian woman and an Irishman, was born and brought up on the Sac and Fox reserve in Kansas when it was still a ragged edge of the frontier. From his part-Indian mother, Thorpe would seem to have a more direct blood line with the Potawatomi, a tribe that shared a long association, in battle and in peaceful hunting, with the Sacs and Foxes. There is no Thorpe family marker in the Sac and Fox graveyard on the hilltop above the agency, appropriately concluding one man's narrative of experience with the tribe. (Just off Route 99 there is a wooden road sign beckoning motorists to the "Jim Thorpe Memorial Pow Wow Grounds" for the tribe's annual summer festival.) But the Sac and Fox and Thorpe have sure claims on one another and any search for connecting points in a family heritage, for the source of deep-seated personal traits or an aggressive Indian pride, leads back through the odyssey of decline of the Sac and Fox nation, which was the general route of march of all Indian peoples.

Ruin at the Bad Axe

It is largely because of Thorpe's prominence in American sports through the first of the 1900s and the small battle glories and defeats of that intractable old resistance leader, Black Hawk, more than a century earlier that the Sac and Fox nation has kept a certain hold on the public imagination. Surely without Black Hawk the log of the two relatively small allied tribes that grew to strength along the upper Mississippi would be of interest only to members, Indian historians and scattered ethnologists. Black Hawk remains a romantic symbol of the last holdout against the cajolery, document signing, forceful eviction and bribery with which the new Americans removed the Indians from their lands; it was his provocation, at the advanced combat age of sixty-five, that set off the flurry of hit-and-run skirmishes with U. S. troops and militia in northern Illinois and Wisconsin which acquired a name to preserve in the minds of school children—the Black Hawk War. The aggression, started in the spring of 1832, turned into a cruel retreat and defeat three months later for a small band of Sac and Fox at the hands of an overwhelmingly larger (if militarily naïve) force of white soldiers and volunteers. The war drove Black Hawk into final retirement as a white fighter, but only after he had become a P.O.W. hero in the East where he was put on tour like some curious strand of freshly unearthed Incan royalty.

Today many Sac and Fox show an eagerness to trace their tribal links back to the lodge of Black Hawk, rather than to one of the more progressive and compliant chiefs—a geneological urge similar to that of all Americans who claim posterity with the tiny boatload of pilgrims who landed at Plymouth. Thorpe identified with Black Hawk, accepting the suggestion that through his father he had a blood relationship to the warrior. But the line of kinship turns tenuous and then speculative as it approaches the compact family of Black Hawk, and without appropriate tribal documents and census rolls it rests heavily on hearsay— and a repetition of claims made in Thorpe folklore. Black Hawk and Thorpe do share the same Sac and Fox clan relationship— Thunder clan—which, in the small tribe, is link enough. Thorpe's father, who was born about a dozen years after Black Hawk's death, represented the mixed-blood change in the composition of the tribe, which the war chief would like to have prevented. But there are similarities in the pure-blood Black Hawk and half-breed Thorpes, father and son, that are notable; that is, if they are not laden with too much significance. They shared unusual physical strength and stamina; they were stubborn—damned determined—about winning; when angered or sharply provoked they could unload an enormous ferocity. They could appear gloomy and vain, proud and magnanimous. Thorpe never approached Black Hawk's grandiloquence, but as a famous Indian athlete, stuck with all those pidgin phrases and grunts attributed to Indian athletes by white journalists, he could be convincing and entertaining while addressing young audiences or swapping adult humor with a tongue loosened by drink.

Except for the prominence of the ears and the light facial color—Black Hawk was almost Oriental of skin tone—there was little physical resemblance. The war chief was an unusually noble-appearing figure, as seen in the famous George Catlin portrait of 1832: the narrow features of a handsome face accentuated by a Roman nose and the lack of eyebrows above dark eyes; the head was perfectly shaped and bald except for the stark scalp lock. Unlike other Sac and Fox leaders who acquired a portly, council-lodge appearance, and unlike the heavy-chested, powerfully built Thorpes, Black Hawk was lean, about 140 pounds, and under six feet tall—ideal for the long hunt or ride against the enemy, but not for the white man's games that Thorpe learned to play. There is, in the portraits of Black Hawk and the football poses of Thorpe, a similar bearing, whether it projects a supreme pride, confidence or strain of haughtiness. Thorpe always stuck that chin up, tightening the lines in his Irish jaw, and the football he held, as some ceremonial spear of his forebearers, was securely gripped in the right hand. William Lone Star Dietz, who played with Thorpe at Carlisle and was accomplished enough as an illustrator to become art teacher at the school, complained that the white artist always treated his Indian subjects in a stereotyped way, placing them on canvas with a haughty but awkward pose.

Black Hawk was a Sac (or Sauk), one of the two implacable tribes of Algonquian stock that became closely associated while battling French empire builders in the Great Lakes region. Whites who made early contact with the Sacs and Foxes spoke of their combat bravery and their bright pride when outfitted for war. They were considered extremely tough-minded and fixed on their own beliefs. The Sacs and Foxes were efficient hunters with bow and arrow, traps and of course later, rifles, and became much favored by English and French traders. The Foxes made an early commercial impact as miners of lead deposits discovered in the Mississippi region they called their own. But it was the Sac and Fox warriors, wearing clay handprints on their shoulders or backs and crimson-dyed horsehair roaches, who commanded respect throughout—and eventually controlled—the northern Mississippi. Black Hawk boasted they were "undisputed possessors . . . from the Ouisconsin to the Portage des Sioux," some seven hundred miles in length. Long before he took on the American Army, Black Hawk and other Sac and Fox chiefs had battled the Illinois, the Osages, the Sioux and other tribes over territory. Black Hawk, born in 1767, brought back his first Osage scalp when he was fifteen; three or four years later he was one of a raiding party that nearly wiped out an Osage village. In a campaign against the Chippewas, the Kaskaskias and the Osages in 1802, Black Hawk killed thirteen "of their bravest warriors," by his count and description.

Black Hawk had no hereditary claim to tribe leadership—from

his father he inherited a medicine bag—but he was indisputably a war chief of the strongest stripe. He was also a good provider, as were most of the Sac and Fox warrior hunters. He spent much more time in the hunting areas allotted by tribal council with the guns, powder and traps he had obtained on credit from the American Fur Company than he did riding out in revenge after Osage scalps.

When the Sac and Fox weren't working for fur company agents or acquiring food for their own cache, they lived in comparatively stable bark-house villages on Rock River near its confluence with the Mississippi where they were involved in productive agriculture. In the famous biography that he apparently helped prepare, Black Hawk's description of the rotation of the seasons on Rock River is a vivid reminder of what happened to the tribe's way of life in the yank and haul of only a few decades—to the point where Thorpes and other surviving descendants were trying to make a living in their alien Oklahoma reserve. In front of their village waves of grass stretched to the banks of the Mississippi; behind them lay their extensive cornfields that reached up the side of a bluff and joined those of the Foxes who had their own village nearby. The green land also produced beans, pumpkins and squashes for the Indians. Before the spring corn planting the men came back from their late winter hunt and took care of their business with the fur traders who had followed them into the village. The traders saw that there were always gift kegs of rum for the elders of the tribe—the braves were forbidden to drink. When the women put in the corn and other crops the men feasted on "dried venison, bear's meat, wild fowl and corn [stored since the previous fall] . . . recounting to each other what took place during the winter." Black Hawk, a monogamous exception in the tribe, summed up the traditional work-hard-and-keep-a-low-profile role of the women with the comment: "It is not customary for us to say much about our women as they generally perform their part cheerfully, and never interfere with business belonging to the men." After the planting the women were allowed to join in the feast and crane dance, a celebration that could last two or three days while the young braves selected their wives.

The corn grew to about knee high before the men headed west, beyond the distant Missouri, to hunt buffalo and deer again, and, hopefully, to clash with the Sioux. Their autumn return from the buffalo herds was the time for "the great ball play," rites that the whites adopted in somewhat less vigorous form. Black Hawk, in describing games with three hundred to five hundred on a side, said, "We play for horses, guns, blankets or any other kind of property . . . The successful party takes the stakes. We next commence horse-racing and continue our sport and feasting until the corn is all secured." The Sacs and Foxes, in the best and worst of times, kept up their enthusiasm for games—lacrosse, played with hickory or walnut stick and buckskin ball on fields that could stretch for a quarter of a mile; a similar game called "shinny," played with a large ball and in which the women joined; and later Indian football, which also embroiled community-sized teams. The gambling was feverish and the competition on the field resembled armed insurrection. The Sac and Fox tradition of competing with speed and body contact—and wagering on one's strength and daring—carried down to the reservation and Agency school playing fields.

Black Hawk was inclined to emphasize the more abundant seasons he and his tribe enjoyed along the upper Mississippi valley. "Rock River was a beautiful country," he said. "I liked my town, my cornfields and the home of my people. I fought for them." Historians argue whether he fought, even vaingloriously, more for the Sacs and Foxes and their good lands or because of his old-age anger and frustration over the advancing white line. His anti-American convictions were established on the frontier after he and his "British Band" of warriors had fought, along with the Shawnee chief, Tecumseh, against the U.S. in the War of 1812. (Black Hawk returned from the experience convinced the white man's way of war was idiotic: "Instead of stealing upon each other and taking advantage to kill the enemy and save their own people, as we do, they march out, in open daylight, and fight, regardless of the number of warriors they lose. After the battle is over they retire to feast, and to drink wine as if nothing has happened . . .")

In the succession of territorial treaties that drove the Sac and Fox farther from their environment, the agreement of 1804 offers the clearest cause for the distrust of Americans which became so deep-rooted in the tribe. The treaty, signed by several chiefs under murky—apparently, for the Indians, intoxicated—circumstances ceded Sac and Fox lands largely east of the Mississippi to the United States but gave the Indians "the privilege of living and hunting upon them" until the vague point when settlement had come so close the government would need to claim ownership. It wasn't until later that tribe members learned that the unauthorized deal would deprive them of their richest grounds in exchange for U. S. protection, payment of one thousand dollars a year and the medals and baubles pinned on the chiefs by delighted negotiators. This particular case of the swindling of an Indian tribe by the federal government wasn't easily swept from the minds of either side. It led to a long stretch of bitterness, physical flare-ups, and a few decades later, the Black Hawk War.

Black Hawk, for all his prominence, doesn't accurately fit the shape and temperament of a Sac and Fox leader during this period of negotiation and removal. By the 1820s the major influence in the tribe was a war chief named Keokuk (the Watchful Fox), thirteen years younger than Black Hawk, whose grand oratory and shrewdness in council made him popular with American officials. Tribal allegiance became split between the progressives, who believed with Keokuk that the future should be faced at the treaty table, and those of restless, unconquered—if foolhardy— spirit who, like Black Hawk, had to resist. Keokuk and later his son Moses, whose grandchildren went to school with Thorpe, were prominent negotiators in Sac and Fox land deals for more than a half century, involvement enough to condemn them to generations of discredit from the more radical bands. (The differences cut through tribe members today; some see the headstone of Moses Keokuk on the hillside near Stroud, Oklahoma, as symbolizing the morbid results of "a sellout." Others argue that he eased the inevitable integration of the tribe with the white world, that Black Hawk was, in fact, more anachronism than hero.)

The expulsion of the Sacs and Foxes from their homeland on the Rock River was nearly complete by 1830—after Black Hawk and others had made defiant returns from hunting trips only to find their lodges destroyed, their cornfields plowed under. For a time even Black Hawk and his band seemed overcome by events and the expanding flow of settlers heading West on the newly opened Erie Canal. He surrendered to the authority of Keokuk and appeared willing to remain on the west banks of the Mississippi.

Sac and Fox lore would seem much more pallid to us if the war chief had not, early in 1832, succumbed to the dubious provocation of the Winnebago Prophet—a half-breed with a strong influence on him—the belief he would have support from other tribes, and a false report that his old friends, the British, were ready to help in his campaign to drive the Americans away from Rock River. It was enough to unleash Black Hawk and his enlarged "British band" of about five hundred Sac and Fox warriors (plus their women and children) across the Mississippi, a move that sent alarm clanging through white settlements in Illinois and geared up a huge military force of regulars and volunteers for what one editor called "a war of extermination." As wars go it was one of the more one-sided matches in history. The muster rolls for Illinois list 7,787 men committed to fight against Black Hawk; add Michigan volunteers and other mounted vigilantes and the government force reached about 12,000.

Boldness, blunder and a little terror in the American ranks touched off the fighting. Black Hawk, who had learned he could not count on allied support, was ready to turn back when nervous militia fired on his truce party. Black Hawk angrily struck, routing the militia who in their panic saw waves of attacking Indians. Actually the quick burst of killing was done by Black Hawk and about forty of his men. For the next three months, in grassland, swamp and wood, with occasional contact through raid or fire fight, Black Hawk led the U. S. Army on an agonizing, northerly chase which Private Abe Lincoln remembered for the "bloody experiences with mosquitoes" and a persistent hunger. The Sacs and Foxes suffered hideously from lack of supplies and food. Many of the oldest and very youngest members, unable to survive on a diet of berry, tree bark and roots, died on the trail. The end to the Black Hawk incursion came near the junction of the Mississippi and the Bad Axe River in Wisconsin, with U. S. troops slaughtering warriors, women and children alike as they tried to recross the river. Some of those who did make it to the west bank were hit by vengeful Sioux, adding to the death count. The estimate of Sac and Fox losses during the campaign—fighters and family members—was 450 to 600. The heavy casualties came at the crossing at the Bad Axe. Black Hawk escaped only to be captured by Winnebagos hopeful of the promised U. S. reward of horses and money.

After he had been turned over to the Americans at Prairie du Chien, Black Hawk made the famous farewell speech, the first of a verbose series, which ranged from bitterness and self-glorification to the sublime. Excessive it was but it carried prophetic truth that could be applied to the members of his band who rode with him that spring and to the lines of their descendants who, like Thorpe, were schooled to become one with the white man. Some of the old man's harsh lines:

"An Indian who is as bad as a white man could not live in our nation; he would be put to death and eaten by the wolves. The white men are bad schoolmasters; they carry false looks and deal in false actions; they smile in the face of the poor Indian to cheat him; they shake him by the hand to gain his confidence, to make him drunk, to deceive him, to ruin his wife . . . We are not safe. We live in danger. We are becoming like them; hypocrites and liars, adulterers, lazy drones; all talkers and no workers . . .

"Black Hawk is a true Indian, and disdains to cry like a woman. He feels for his wife, his children and his friends. But he does not care for himself. He cares for his nation, and the Indians. They will suffer. He laments their fate. The white men do not scalp the head; but they do worse—they poison the heart; it is not pure with them. His countrymen will not be scalped, but they will, in a few years, become like the white man, so that you cannot trust them . . ."

The romantic appeal of Black Hawk and his war to the American public, at least in the brick-paved, civilized East, was demonstrated after he and the Prophet were released as hostages from Fort Monroe and escorted home by way of Baltimore, Philadelphia and New York. Huge crowds turned out to examine these famous aborigines, an outburst of American devotion to spectacle (and hero worship) that was repeated for another Sac and Fox after the Olympic Games 70 years later. Black Hawk, unlike Thorpe after his great public moments, was able to slip gently toward his death in his Iowa cabin in 1838. In his twilight stretch of sociability he could sit and talk with attentive whites, enjoy a glass of whiskey now, and help spin out the myth and fact of his life.

If the Black Hawk War was really one aged fighter's last personal tangle with tragedy, the consequences of it spread throughout Indian-white relations and, of course, fell decisively on the Sac and Fox. In the following treaty negotiations, the United States took a hard line, forcing the Sac and Fox to give up a broad, invaluable strip of land along the Mississippi (the eastern half of Iowa) for payments of $20,000 for thirty years. Among the treaty concessions given the tribe was the promised delivery of "40 kegs of tobacco, 40 barrels of salt . . . one additional Black and Gun Smith shop, with necessary tools, iron, steel." The additional blacksmith post was eventually filled by Thorpe's grandfather, Hiram G. Thorpe.

Windows for Whiskey in Kansas

Within a dozen years after the massacre of the Sac and Fox along the Mississippi the tribe was negotiated and prodded out of Iowa. One of the arguments for the sale of the land in the treaty of 1842 (in which the United States acquired "about ten million acres of as fine land as the world can produce," boasted the Commissioner of Indian Affairs) was that removal southwest into Kansas would put them farther out of reach of unscrupulous whites and their infamous traffic in whiskey. It was, of course, also pointed out to the Indians that they were in need of more annuity funds and more credit. The exposure to white ways—or the frontier version of them—and the erosion of their own culture had, as Black Hawk predicted, disastrous effects on the Sac and Fox moral fiber, the Sac and Fox liver and the Sac and Fox sense of direction.

In the early 1830s a visitor to a Sac village had the braves still "proud and haughty, vain and extravagantly fond of amusements of all kinds, such as card playing, gambling, frolicking and dancing. The Indians are kind and generous to strangers and friends, always dividing with them if it is only the last fowl." He did note that the Foxes seemed more inclined to trade for and drink whiskey than the Sacs. But just before their removal from Iowa the agent said, "the whole nation without distinction of rank, age or sex exhibits a continual scene of the most revolting intoxication." He thought the tribe was suffering also because of its open-arm hospitality, that large groups of Iowa and Potawatomi were always visiting the Sac and Fox villages and overstaying through spring and summer, depleting their food stocks. Indian Affairs superintendent John Chambers, in an 1844 report, commented that "their chiefs are men of very high order of intellect and yet they are, without exception, inveterate sots." Which might be one explanation of why they ceded their share of Iowa for $800,000 and the settlement of outstanding debts.

The Sacs and Foxes who moved into their Kansas reservation were only 2,200 in number (there had been 4,500 on the rolls in Iowa, but a large band of Foxes chose to stay behind with other friendly tribes). The agent sent out a buoyant report that the tribe was well located in their new home on the Osage River "beyond the unhappy influence . . . of the white population." There were, however, a noticeably larger number of whites intermixed with the Sacs and Foxes, some through marriage and others who had simply attached themselves to the tribe as a means of making a living on the frontier as traders, blacksmiths, gunsmiths, interpreters or plain opportunists.

The assistant blacksmith was an Irishman, Hiram G. Thorp, who had been born in Connecticut in 1811 and worked his way West as an adventuresome trader well in front of the main line of settlement. (The spelling of the name, with or without an "e," became increasingly inconsistent as it appeared on annuity rolls, legal papers, letters signed by family members through the years. In the earliest Sac and Fox records and on allotment patent deeds it was usually Thorp; when Jim and his twin brother Charles first entered the Indian Agency school in 1893 they were

Thorpes on the class rolls. After that, each teacher chose her own spelling.) The blacksmith was married to a Sac and Fox woman about three years younger named No-ten-o-quah (Wind Woman, literally), whose certain ancestry remains elusive in a tribe where polygamy was the custom and mixed breeds, orphans from friendly tribes, distant relations were warmly accepted into a family lodge as sons or daughters. In an 1853 report on employees and their services, agent B. A. James noted that "Thorp had discharged his duties well, is qualified for the place." His government salary was $240 a year; when added to the quarterly tribal payments which No-ten-o-quah received it provided a better standard of living than many had in the tribe.

There is no remaining evidence of how and where Thorpe and his Indian woman met and married in the custom of the tribe. But the basic structure of their environment in Kansas was as close as the Sacs and Foxes could make it to what they had known on less alien ground. The Indians still shaved their heads, wore their blankets and leggings, resisted the appearance of anyone peddling white religion or education. They built their bark villages, the women planted beans and corn in common gardens and continued the rotation of the harvest, the Change of Season's Feast, of seeing the men away on the summer and winter hunts. In 1847 there had been an encouraging haul of buffalo meat—as much as their horses could carry—even though they had to be wary of the Plains tribes who resented the invasion of strangers from the Mississippi.

But the searing reality of prairie drought struck the tribe in the summer of 1850, with temperatures running between 95° and 110° for weeks, wiping out the six hundred acres of corn that the Sac and Fox women had tilled. The agent laconically noted that there had been six murders from the use of intoxicating drinks since his last report. Far more devastating to the tribe were the epidemics of smallpox and flux which caused about three hundred deaths—even though many of the Indians submitted to inoculation—and sent the despairing night sounds of drum beat and death song rolling through the bark lodges. One of the extra jobs of blacksmith Thorpe was to help in preparing burial boxes or cribbed frames in which the Indians were buried in the sitting position. A long invoice to the government from the Sac and Fox agent in 1853 reads like the death count after a major flood, fire or earthquake:

"To burial suite for Pap e am e quah, consisting
of the following articles:

2½ pt. white blanket	$2.25
1¾ yds. blue cloth	2.18¾
¾ yds. scarlet cloth	.93¾
3 yds. calico	.30
2 yds. ferreting, 1 paper paint	.19
	$5.86½

"To do for Me Kes Sah, same as above
$5.86½

"To do for Paw Ne Ah Quah, same as above, etc.

The cost to the government for burying a Sac and Fox child was $2.85.

As smallpox and other disease cut through the tribe, No-ten-o-quah was caring for a small daughter, Mary, and a son, Hiram P., born about 1850. (Hiram later gave his age to indicate he was born a year later and it is probable that he never knew the date of birth; in most tribes the birth of a child often went without official recognition until a parent gave the name to the agent to be added to the tribal annuity roll.)

Hiram Thorpe was too young to share in the tribe's celebration of one of the last great ego-soaring victories of Sac and Fox warriors, which came in the spring of 1854. It had been a dry, poor planting spring and the tribe's buffalo hunters, about a hundred in all, went farther west than usual, well beyond Ft. Riley and into the Smoky Hills of western Kansas. It was uncertain ground because the Comanches, Cheyennes, Kiowas, Arapahoes and others had vowed to "wipe out" all emigrant Indian hunters from the East. On July 10 a force of 1,500 Plains Indians spotted the Sacs and Foxes in search of the buffalo herds. In one of those apparently unjust contests that became a plot fixture in cowboy-Indian movies, the Plains Indians rode in attack waves against the thin defense of the Sacs, Foxes and a handful of friendly Potawatomi, who had unsaddled and taken position in a small valley. Many of the Plains Indians had not yet acquired an arsenal of white weapons and were still using bow and arrow. The shooting accuracy of the Sacs and Foxes with hunting rifles took such a heavy toll that the Plains tribes withdrew, leaving their dead and mortally wounded on the ground. The Sac and Fox braves rode home with their scalps—and to a victory dance that stirred considerable notoriety and respect along the frontier.

The rout of the Plains Indians quickened the old Sac and Fox impulse for battle. In the next few years Hiram Thorpe and the other children around the Agency watched war parties of brightly adorned braves heading west in search of scalps. The number of the able-bodied fighters was in steady decline, the aims of war more confused, but the small marauding Sac and Fox raised so much havoc (and so many scalps) on the open prairie that even the Comanches became discouraged from taking them on. Possibly Hiram Thorpe's hot-tempered instinct for a brawl—a reputation that grew to legendary size in Oklahoma Territory—was part Irish and partly the result of a boyhood spent in close enough contact to the war-loving bands among the Sac and Fox.

The occasional fights and the hunts for the thinning buffalo herds forwarded pride, but the tribe was increasingly dependent on the annuity and government food and supplies. In the payment roll of 1857 No-ten-o-quah received a $175 share for her household of six children, some of whom were orphans or offspring of relatives. The voucher carried her "X" and the witness signature of H. G. Thorpe. (Annuities depended on the size of the household and it helped to be a chief, even a controversial, U.S.-designated chief such as Moses Keokuk, who had assumed the role from his father; Keokuk drew annuities for himself, two wives and several children and was provided with special housing and a bonus of $500 a year.)

Thorpe resigned as blacksmith in 1860 just as he was about to fall into a generous land allotment. In another deal that stressed the poor bargaining position of the Indians it was proposed that the tribe put about 300,000 acres of their land on sale, since they weren't using it all. The proceeds would pay for old debts and help start a white-style agricultural community—

houses, fences, hens, hogs, cattle. About 150,000 acres were to be allotted in severality in tracts of eighty acres to each Indian man, woman, child; Indian women who married whites were to receive 320-acre tracts. The settlement was most beneficial to the Whistler, Connally, Gokey and Thorpe families. Young Hiram, sister Mary and brother Francis received individual sections. But the attempt to make civilized agrarians out of the Indians was mostly disastrous; many of them went on living in their bark homes, quartered their livestock in the hastily built wooden houses and traded doors and windows for whiskey, which cost about $.20 a gallon at Leavenworth and was priced from $1.00 to $5.00 when it reached the Indians.

Charles Martin, a trader who did business with the Sac and Fox and other Kansas-based tribes, said at the time, "I am more and more inclined to believe the agency system is a failure. The only remedy is to reduce the number and leave the Indian to depend on himself." He saw the preacher, the agent and the soldier as the ruin of the Indian. "Unexposed to them he is a noble fellow, good-hearted, proud, manly, the best kind of neighbor." Most whites who found themselves neighbors of the Indians in Kansas were consumed by the notion of getting them out and acquiring their land, which was being put to unimpressive use. An editorial writer in Topeka, just north of the Sac and Fox reservation, regarded the Indians as "a set of miserable, dirty, lousy, blanketed, thieving, lying, sneaking, murdering, graceless, faithless, guteating skunks."

Before they were removed from Kansas the Sac and Fox finally allowed a token amount of white education to be introduced into the tribe. (The Indians had been so suspicious of white religious teaching that when the agent offered to build a flour mill —to relieve the women of beating meal—they feared that the mill might be a way of sneaking missionaries into their midst.) The first school was started in 1863 by a Methodist minister and his wife but only eighteen or twenty of 230 eligible school-age children attended. The appeal was mostly to the parents of mixed bloods and the names on the class rolls—Hiram Thorpe, Alice Carey, Lizzie Dole, Jane Goodell, Peter Tenon, Robert Thrift— all had a little-red-schoolhouse ring. The teacher, Sarah Duvall, had a frustrating time with this break-through attempt at schooling the Sac and Fox: "We tried to teach them to do right," she said, "but how could they? I have seen them pay $18 for a great coarse blanket at the trading house. We taught the girls to sew and do homework. The boys were not easily managed."

The final trek of the Sac and Fox, from Agency Hill in Kansas to Indian Territory in present Oklahoma, started on November 26, 1869. Behind the tribe was another bitterly accepted treaty which made counterfeit the covenant with the United States of twenty-odd years earlier that had assured the Sac and Fox the headwaters of the Osage River and would provide a perpetual residence for them and their descendants. This time the eviction terms provided for a payment of $1.00 an acre for the diminished reserve in Kansas (about 86,000 acres) and the promise of a large swath of land in Indian Territory, which the government had extorted from the Creeks following thier involvement in the Civil War on the Confederate side. With the cynicism acquired through past treaty rounds, many Sac and Fox openly rejected it and accused Keokuk of being drunk when the papers were signed. One defiant chief, Mokohoko, refused to be removed and for several years drifted around Kansas with his band of about two hundred; others joined the Foxes in Tama, Iowa, or the breakaway Missouri Sacs.

The remaining Sacs and Foxes of the Mississippi who did head south under government escort early that winter were few enough in number to fit into seventeen oxen-pulled government wagons. (Many young warriors had gone off for the winter hunt, planning to join their families in Oklahoma Territory in the spring.) No-ten-o-quah and her household, including Hiram, were part of the group who walked or rode out of the village, leaving behind again the empty lodges, the dead fires in the council center, the worn dance ring where they had gathered for the last prayer songs. Some of the half-breeds still had claims on the Kansas prairie in the form of patents in fee simple.

When the sullen caravan of soldier-driven wagons and uprooted Indians, now so common to the logistics of western expansion, reached their encampment in mid-December snow was falling on the flat red land, which stretched without hope or hori-

zons. But the new superintendent of the Agency, a Quaker named
Enoch Hogue, was soon brimming with government service optimism: "During the winter we engaged in plowing, making rails
for fencing . . . had purchased nine yoke of oxen, wagons, plows
. . . Planted 150 acres of corn, a good crop." In the spring, enrollment for the annuity payment registered 147 males, 132 fe-
males and 108 children—387 had settled in the Mississippi Sac
and Fox reserve from a nation of 4,500 a generation before.

The tribe's land—a seventeen-mile-wide strip that reached
from the Cimarron in the north to the North Canadian forty miles
to the south—had been described as "very rich" to the Sac and
Fox in Kansas. But except for the river bottoms the sandy soil
was most resistant to plow and seed. Only about one tenth of the
reserve was considered arable. The Indians watched their basic
crops wilt in the earth baked by rainless summers; the fish
seemed to desert the lowering streams and a new buckskin for
the winter often came easiest by trading with Indian friends to
the north. Whites who drifted into the Agency deplored the Sacs
and Foxes lack of self-sustaining agrarian know-how, their disinterest in cattle and their devotion to horses and dogs—and happily fleeced them of their annuity payments.

The tribal splintering and the relatively tiny population that
had settled in Indian Territory did allow for a generous sharing
of funds. The second-quarter payroll for the tribe, in June 1871,
was $15,912. No-ten-o-quah received $100 for herself, husband
and two dependents. Somewhere in this vicinity of time Hiram
G., now in his late fifties, and No-ten-o-quah ceased sharing the
same household in the Agency records; in the last payment of
1874 he was allowed $35 as a single male and she was given $175
for herself and four dependents.

The Indian way of marriage, in which the husband could be
as polygamous as he chose, and easy separation for either party
left a trail of geneological confusion behind many Indian-white
relationships. (Probate court hearings later in the 1900s did
drag out a few family truths.) In the case of Hiram P. Thorpe,
the proliferation of his wives and children spread a bewildering
line of ancestral stock in Oklahoma Territory. By 1874 Hiram,
now in his early twenties, had married the first of at least five

women, fathered a child and received his annuity of $105 from tribal funds. His wife was a Shawnee, Mary James. When Hiram's older sister, Mary, married an Ottawa half-breed and missionary named Isaac McCoy, an enduring, stubborn, Indian-Irish imprint was laid heavy on the land that became Oklahoma.

II   SONS OF HIRAM

Birth and Death on the Allotment

Hiram P. Thorpe's own involvement in the raucous gestation of the state added appreciably to the early population and also to its renown as a cauldron of men with a casual regard, at best, for the accepted rules of society. Long before the Dalton brothers and other well-postered outlaws began shooting their way to glorious notoriety across the countryside, the Indian lands offered opportunity for whiskey running, a little horse, cattle or hog stealing, and even the heisting of supplies from a government freighter coming down from Kansas City. When Hiram did get caught and charged for introducing jugs of whiskey into the scene at the Sac and Fox Agency in the middle of payment day, he was hellishly indignant about it. His reputation by then was vivid enough: he was a tough man to beat in a wrestling match or any test of physical strength; he was a discouraging challenge in a horse race; he could be dangerous when temper or whiskey or both got to him. In his choice of sport—shooting out farmers' lanterns while doing a little night riding—there was the reminder that violence came easy to him. A formal studio portrait of Hiram shows the hard image he cared to project: a swarthy, strong face beneath high-crowned hat, his dark hair hanging at Indian length; clothes and boots might be those of a conscientious cotton farmer but the gun belt was unmistakably that of a man of independent mind and action. He was muscular enough for most challenges—over six feet and about 225 pounds.

Hiram fathered nineteen legally identified children (and possibly others who died soon after birth) by five women. He and

Mary James had four children, including a son, Frank, born in 1878, who as an older half-brother became a buddy and comfortable bulwark for Jim, and a daughter, Minnie, who occasionally provided shelter for him and his brothers and sisters after they were orphaned. (Frank grew up with little use for his father or his ways; Jim obviously admired him for his physical abilities, the ease with which he hunted and handled horses.) Hiram ruled a crowded household—actually two—in those early years of Sac and Fox presence in Indian Territory. While married to Mary James he lived with a second woman, a Creek named Sarah La-Blanche, whom he also evidently married in the Indian custom. They had one daughter. Both women fell out of favor with Hiram, or vice versa, at approximately the same time in 1880 or '81. They left him and shared a wagon ride together out of the Sac and Fox reserve and east to Okmulgee.

It was still very much a vacant land where Hiram and his Indian women brought their half-breed children into the world. Except for the Agency and the usual components around it— the schoolhouse with quarters for the physician, Chief Keokuk's brick home, Rankin and Gibbs trading store, and the bark lodge and tepee villages spread nearby in the horseshoe bend of the Deep Fork—the reserve was roadless, fenceless and apparently endless. The land rush that would leave instant towns in its wake and transform Indian Territory into a white man's domain was still a few years away. The last cattle drives, with herds of four thousand or more, were using the soon-to-be-abandoned West Shawnee Trail, which originated in southern Texas and passed just north of the Agency en route to the railroad at Junction City, Kansas. Cattlemen could bargain with or bribe an Indian agent or a chief to graze their herds on the open range, offering early evidence that the land was far better suited for livestock than for dirt farmers. Hiram Thorpe found it easy enough to bring down antelope, prairie hens and turkeys with his guns. But the Sac and Fox buffalo hunters, still clinging to their seasonal cycle of westward search for meat and hides, were coming to the end of a supply that so shortly before had seemed unlimited in the great salt plains of northwest Oklahoma.

The Sac and Fox agents—and the Indian Affairs bureaucracy strung out behind them—were attempting to remove other familiar indulgences from the Sac and Fox in the headlong "civilization process" now underway on the reservations. A ban was placed on gambling and horse racing in the apparent hope that the Indians would stop wasting their annuity money and their time so frivolously and get pointed in more constructive directions—such as raising crops and hogs and chickens and sending their children to the unpopular mission school. For generations the Sac and Fox had enthused over a game of bowl and dice which, with eighteen or twenty players involved, could provide lively action and stakes. The gambling injunction was about as successful as if the Indians had been told it was unlawful to sit cross-legged under the shade of a cottonwood tree. The agents even made futile attempts to discourage the Sac and Fox from carrying on with their feasts, dances and other heathen ritual (the passage of time and fusion with the white world eventually did take care of these traditions).

Although the tribes had been placed in Indian Territory in well-defined reserves, there was a constant shuttle of visitors across the boundaries, Indians exchanging gifts, finding reasons for three-day powwows, going on hunts together, acquiring new friends, and—to the irritation of white officials—picking up omens or messages from tribal prophets that could suddenly rearrange their lives. The Sac and Fox, in the middle 1880s, fell under the incantation of an old Shawnee prophet who had instructions from the Great Spirit that they should return to the former life-style that had served them so well. Hiram Thorpe exhibited another result of the commingling of the Indians in Oklahoma. When Mary James and Sarah LaBlanche departed he took a third wife with another tribal background. Her name was Charlotte Vieux (which became anglicized to View) and she had been brought up as a Potawatomi, the daughter of a Frenchman and tribe member and an Indian woman, Elizabeth Goslin, who had both Potawatomi and Kickapoo blood. Charlotte, who mothered Jim Thorpe and ten other children by Hiram, was about 20—she was born in 1862—when she married.

Charlotte Vieux bore the strong French-Catholic influence which had been implanted in the tribe generations before. The Potawatomi and Sac and Fox were old allies (Potawatomi warriors served with Black Hawk in 1832), buffalo-hunting partners and neighbors in Kansas, but they had some markedly different characteristics. The Potawatomi were unusually receptive to inter-marriage with other tribes and whites, and their easy relationship with the French in the 1670s had produced a Gallic strain that expanded into predominance in some bands. By 1890 there were thirty-two members of the Oklahoma Potawatomi named Vieux. (Frank Thorpe eventually married into the family—Angeline, a niece of Charlotte—and started his own branch of Sac and Fox-Irish-Shawnee-Potawatomi-French Thorpes.)

Jacob Vieux, Charlotte's father, was one of a small "enlightened" group in the progressive tribe who, in 1884, had gone to court in Kansas and applied for citizenship papers and patents to their lands; some 1,400 eventually satisfied the court that they could manage allotments and their own shares of tribal funds. They became known as Citizen Potawatomi, a status that technically denied they were any longer wards of the state and left numbers of them easy prey for land swindlers. The Potawatomi (the state of Oklahoma was later to insist on the official spelling as Pottawatomie) were also soft targets for whiskey dealers, Baptist, Methodist and Catholic missionaries. The liquor peddlers and the Catholics ended up with the most business, and when the tribe was removed to Oklahoma members donated 640 acres of tribal land (about eighteen miles south of present Tecumseh) so that an abbot from Burgundy, France, could build the Sacred Heart Mission in 1876, which with church, convent and a free day-school became the educational and religious center for Indians of several nearby tribes. Charlotte Vieux and Hiram were, according to relatives, married at Sacred Heart by "white man's law" following an Indian ceremony, although there are no church records to confirm it. (Hiram managed to go through life—and wives—without leaving such paraphernalia as marriage certificates, divorce papers or wills behind him.) The French-Potawatomi devotion to Catholicism of Charlotte Vieux, passed on to eleven children, steered Jim to the Catholic Church and Catholic youth clubs when he was required to make a choice at Indian boarding school. The three women he married were Catholic, and although he could hardly have been considered a man of the church, he occasionally attended mass later in his life. His

funeral in the Baptist-spired city of Shawnee was at the only
Catholic church.

An old Thorpe family friend testified in probate court years
after the fact that he was a visitor when Hiram brought Charlotte
Vieux home as his wife and that it was at this climactic point
when Mary James and Sarah LaBlanche packed and left. Charlotte was an imposing woman in her own right—she grew to be
well over two hundred pounds after rounds of chores and childbirth. She, too, was tough minded, and it may be that only this
sturdy Indian-Gallic composition enabled her to endure for as
long as she did—with but one or two recorded separations from
Hiram—the tumult of that marriage. Hiram brought his new
woman into a one-room log cabin, built with cottonwood and
pecan trees, close to the North Canadian (they later moved
nearby to a somewhat larger house when tribal allotments were
selected). A number of Sac and Fox families had broken away
from the Agency trading center and the village clusters to settle
twenty-odd miles away along the river bottom land where the
grass grew thicker for the livestock and crops had a reasonable
chance of survival. Hiram was keen on raising horses, acquiring
horses, trading horses—it was said that he liked to keep a match-
ing team and two women at all times. There is no evidence that
he became heavily engaged in the trial-and-error farming Indians
had started in the red river bed, except to raise the essential alfalfa and kafir corn for the livestock and enough garden vegeta-
bles for meals. The Thorpes ate as well as most Sac and Fox
families who used the river-flattened land, their traps and hunting
rifles and their credit at the Agency to maintain a comfortable
larder.

From the beginning of the marriage Charlotte Thorpe was occupied with the births and tenuous infancy of children. George
was the first, and a little over a year later, in the early winter of
1883, she produced twin daughters, Mary and Margaret. Mary
died the following summer; her twin sister lived less than four
years. There are no records explaining why the girls' life-spans
were so brief, but the cycle of birth-life-death was often completed in a matter of months in Indian Territory.

On May 27, 1887, just before the death of the surviving daughter, Charlotte Thorpe gave birth to twin boys, James and Charles, both of them robust babies. The Indian name given James or James Francis was Wa-Tho-Huck (Bright Path), which later acquired inflated significance in Thorpe folklore as a kind of verification of his Indian background. Charles' Indian name was more easily lost in memory. By the time the twins were ready to enroll in the Sac and Fox mission school as six-year-olds, the campaign to erase the Indian names and require the use of English names was being aggressively conducted by school authorities. If a boy or girl arrived at school as an orphan or was the child of a full blood and had only an Indian name, the school or agent took over the naming responsibility. The agent at the time had his own method for naming the children; first he used the succession of U. S. Presidents, and if he needed more first names he turned to the Vice-Presidents; if that supply ran out he selected from the names of his favorite prominent citizens.

While James and Charles were first experiencing the English-speaking, Indian-toned Thorpe family life, there were, in 1890 and '91, events under way far removed from their North Canadian River cabin that were to have direct and oblique effects on their future. By the summer of 1890 the Ghost Dance movement—which was to end in a flow of disillusion and hopelessness for many Indian peoples—had spread through the plains regions, igniting the spirit of reservation Indians who were eager to clutch at any nostalgic cause. The movement had leaped from the prophecy of a Paiute seer in Nevada who testified that the whites, with all their ways, would soon depart and that dark herds of buffalo and other game would populate the plains again. The Ghost Dance, as whites called the religious dancing and singing that erupted in tribes throughout the West, would hurry the miraculous return. The Ghost Dance faith grew strongest among the northern buffalo Indians; it caused nervous tremors among whites living nearby and led to the massacre of the Sioux at Wounded Knee. The vision of the Paiute medicine man shot a glimmer of belief through the Sac and Fox in Oklahoma that they, too, might be able to restore the long westerly buffalo hunts and justify a few more valorous fights with the plains tribes. But the movement—and any hope of clinging to the past—ended with disheartening abruptness for the Sac and Fox, who found themselves facing the realities of a congested new existence in Indian Territory.

In 1890 the Superintendent of the Census said he could no longer fix a line—in the states or the remaining territories—marking the frontier. The wilderness, along with the buffalo, had vanished and even the arid, unpromising tract of the Sac and Fox was about to fall into the hands of surveyors and claimers. At the Sac and Fox Agency near the Deep Fork tribe members were advised that they were entitled—that is, obliged—to take 160 acres (a quarter section) for their own to live on, grow crops, raise livestock. In effect, they were to get off their haunches around the trading center and show a little white-style, civilized initiative as landowners. Forget, they were told, your traditional regard for the land as a gift of nature to be used communally; it is time you became proprietors and held title deeds of confirmation. The controversial General Allotment Act of 1887 had been applied to other tribes before it reached the Sac and Fox, a majority of whom opposed the policy. A tribal delegation made a futile journey to Washington to protest. Many of the Indians had little conception of what a 160-acre square looked like and no idea of what to do with it, but allotment distribution pushed ahead and by the summer of 1891 over five hundred tracts had been assigned to tribe members under a trust patent for twenty-five years (renewable thereafter). Each Sac and Fox was given $250 in cash as a downpayment on the sale of the tribe's unallotted lands.

For the Thorpes and other mixed bloods who had long ago drifted toward white, independent lives, land allotment served their needs well enough and eventually enabled them to realize small income from the lease or sale of family holdings. The fractioning of ownership in a Thorpe-size family did not allow for any grand distribution to heirs; after Hiram died Jim acquired a $\frac{1}{15}$ interest in his real property. The Thorpes chose to live on Charlotte's 160 acres (Sac and Fox allottee #240, in township 11N, Range 5E, which straddled four sections along the North Canadian just east of Econtuchka). Hiram's own allotment (#239 on the tribal rolls) was a few miles up river, closer to present Shawnee. Jim's allotment, north of his mother's, brought him $250 in annual farming and grazing fees during his last year at Carlisle.

Some twenty-five years after the Thorpes first occupied their original allotment a lease application offered this unenthusiastic description of the property, which included about thirty-five acres of timber and thirty-five of pasture: "the tillable land is very sandy and is best suited for cotton, corn, peas, peanuts."

The Thorpes' new log and timbered farmhouse had a separate sleeping loft, which was rapidly filled by the expansion of the family. In 1889, daughter Mary was born and although she was later scarred and handicapped by a wagon accident she, too, grew to Hiram-like proportions and developed her own local reputation for strength and combativeness. The death rate among the children of Charlotte and Hiram suggests that only an unusually tough constitution led to survival. Son Jesse, born in the fall of '91, died before his first birthday. Daughter Rosetta lived seven years after her birth in 1893. Charles was only ten when he died and left a lonely and confused twin brother.

The Sac and Fox allotment holders did not even have time to fell trees and fire a few stumps for their future gardens before the surplus lands on their reserve were opened to settlement, an act that brought overnight change—better for some and for others considerably worse. Although there were more openings later—the Cherokee Outlet in '93 and Kickapoo lands in '95—the empty Indian prairie was largely parceled away at $1.25 an acre at the start of the 1890s when Congress decided to establish Oklahoma Territory. The Run of September 1891 on the Sac and Fox lands (and also the Potawatomi and Shawnee strip to the south) was a somewhat less thunderous re-enactment of the phenomenon of two years earlier when more than 50,000 people took advantage of President Harrison's invitation to help themselves to unassigned ground in the central part of Indian Territory. Still nearly half that number burst into Sac and Fox and adjoining lands—and uncounted gun jumpers, who had hidden out a day or two ahead, beat them to their chosen quarter sections.

The Thorpe children were too young—and too well insulated on their wooded allotment where their mother was very close to the birth of another child—to respond to the strange disquiet that the opening brought to the reserve on a late September day. On the Cimarron River boundary above the Agency the line of land-hungry pioneers stretched for miles waiting for the volley of gunfire that would send them plunging into the water, which was mercifully low at the time. Sac and Fox tribe members watched the dusty chaos that followed the noon start of the race with a mixture of amusement and disbelief. Grasslands suddenly bloomed with claim stakes, streamers, blankets, fluttering Army-issue tents. An eight-year-old Sac and Fox girl who lived a few miles north of the Thorpes recalled the confusion she and her family felt: "We didn't know the land was being opened to whites, but we began seeing an unusual amount of wild animals all seeming to be headed in one direction . . . and later groups of men with families in wagons and surreys. Some of them acted as if they were crazy. All of a sudden they would stick a pole into the ground and hang something on it. Many set fire to the grass after they had done this."

The flurry of commerce that quickly broke out after the Run in the vicinity of the North Canadian River east of Shawneetown, as the tent and covered wagon settlement was known, produced a post office and store in Bellemont (in 1892) about three miles from the Thorpes. Jim and Charles took their early wagon rides with their father for supplies to Bellemont and, later, to nearby Econtuchka where they could watch the arrival of the stage out of Sapulpa, the terminus of the Frisco railroad. Although the stage went on to Shawneetown and there was a well-beaten trail from there northeast to the Agency, Hiram was limited in his reliable wagon routes in the early '90s. The river required selective fording; the land above it rose and fell unevenly. "I don't know which was worse," said a freighter who worked the area, "the bottoms or the hills. Lots of times we had to double up teams we got so bogged in the bottoms."

At E. J. Brown's store, the merchandise hub near Econtuchka, Sac and Fox and Seminole Indians came to trade along with the white settlers who learned they could occasionally talk an Indian out of a government-issue blanket, clothes or men's (never women's) shoes in exchange for whiskey, staples, even a kettle of white man's stew which stimulated the taste of some Indians. Sharing the same uncultivated neighborhood took some rapid adjusting by both whites and Indians. A homesteader riding toward Shawneetown was startled one day by the sight of his Indian neighbor, struggling through a patch of stumps with

a borrowed plow, and wearing a bright red shirt with a vest buttoned full over it, a pair of new boots—and that was all. Not
far away along the North Canadian in a new settlement called
Keokuk Falls (because it occupied an allotment of Chief Moses
Keokuk), white culture was erecting the first pleasure dome of
what became known as the Seven Deadly Saloons of Keokuk
Falls. It was named the Black Dog, and it was located just over
the territorial line from the Creek Nation in order to circumnavi-
gate the treaty pledge given the Indians that there would be
strict laws in the Territory against the "introduction, sale, barter
or giving away of liquors and intoxicants of any kind or quality."
To the delight and convenience of Hiram Thorpe, the Black Dog
was an easy six-mile ride downstream from his cabin.

Champion Fly Killer at the Agency School

As with most of childhood that is not racked by the extremes
of poverty or disease, Thorpe's early years have been pleasantly
glossed with each occasional recounting. The meat and hides
from those early hunting efforts with his father, which were forever successful, the fish taken out of the North Canadian and
smoked and stored, the free-running children's games, have a
way of mounting up as among the best-remembered times of all.
For Jim and Charles the allotment acres stretched into wilderness
enough; freedom before being sent to school was playing follow-
the-leader in wood lot and dry creek bed, kicking a path through
the patches of cowslips and bluebells for a dip in the river when
the water was down on the red banks, or watching an Indian
neighbor use his buffalo skin raft to ferry himself and trade goods
across to the other side. There were wild plums and grapes for
easy picking, and the pecan trees, which had not yet been leveled
for logs for houses and barns, were heavy with fruit.

Apparently from the start Jim was the more enthusiastic of the
twins in learning how to set traps for small game. Hiram taught
him how to make a figure-four snare to catch quail, which were

plentiful in the area. When he was about eight he made over-night camp alone and when he brought down his first deer his father showed him how to pack it out by horseback for the long return to the cabin. That early acquaintance with horses and dogs —even the wild ones that roved in packs through the area—led him into a long loyalty to both animals.

But whatever the pastoral quality of life along the North Canadian in the 1890s, it was, of course, edged with harshness. Children, as well as the adults, had to cope with the drought and flies of summer, the inadequate barriers against the short, bitter cold spells. They shared some of the responsibilities for keeping the herds of livestock and horses from running loose across the unfenced allotment and being stolen. Until the Anti-Horse Thief Association was formed about 1900, Sac and Fox farmers found it difficult to maintain enough animals to run their farms. With the rush of white settlers came the night riders who made off with the best of the herd for sale across the Creek Nation line; the rustlers often slaughtered cattle and hogs, took the meat they wanted and left the rest on the ground. It was useful to the farmer to have Hiram Thorpe's reputation as a dangerous man to rout out of his cabin with a rifle. The neighboring Wakole family, who with the Thorpes were among the earliest Sac and Fox members to build cabins near the river, were so troubled by rustlers attacking their large herd of horses that they took turns at night-long guard duty. Young Allie Wakole, who had been taught by his grandfather not to shoot to kill, not even horse thieves, became adept at running them off with gun-shot wounds in the arms and legs.

Horse thieving was sometimes a casual, part-time occupation for marginal farmers who had moved into Sac and Fox lands. One of them, George Brown, who married an Indian, recalled that he and his half-breed partners, Milford Growing Horn and Dave Bad Fish, gave up horse stealing as a risky business after they learned that the Light Horsemen, a group of mounted, mobile Seminole police, were after them. Punishment for those caught by the Light Horsemen—lashing—was about as frightening a prospect as a hanging. Even more discouraging to the rustling enterprise in the Sac and Fox area was the experience of six horse thieves at the hands of Tom Washington, an Indian who lived across the North

Canadian from the Thorpes near Econtuchka. When Washington discovered the loss of seven of his animals he rode out to track the thieves and closed in on them enough to exchange gunfire. Apparently the rustlers thought they had frightened the Indian off by their numbers because they eventually stopped and made camp for the night. Washington waited for hours in nearby cover and then efficiently shot all six rustlers, one by one. In the morning he put their bodies in a wagon and hauled them to Tecumseh where he announced to the sheriff, "I bring some horse thieves." Washington later gave the details of his efforts to protect his livestock and his livelihood to a jury and was acquitted.

Horse thieves and gunmen were not the most disquieting reality in Thorpe's youth. That came at the age of six when he and Charles were told they were being sent to the mission boarding school at the Agency. During the next few years Jim's rebellion against the bonds of Indian school education sent echoes rattling from the banks of the North Canadian to the horseshoe bend of the Deep Fork. A Sac and Fox schoolmate and neighbor of Jim and Charles remembered being startled one day by the piercing shrieks that came from a wagon rolling toward his house. The wagon, he recognized, was the one used by the Indian police to round up runaway or reluctant school children; the shattering human sound came from the rear where Jim Thorpe, his face dark with rage, was lying on his back screaming his protest to the trees. The neighbor thought Jim looked so funny in captivity he forgot, momentarily, that the wagon had also come for him.

Jim's opposition to schooling was an easy inheritance. In the early 1890s the Commissioner of Indian Affairs listed the Sac and Fox with the Apaches, Cheyennes and a few other tribes as "most resistant" to white education. When the government completed the first small brick schoolhouse on the rise above the Agency, an attempt was made to impress tribe members with the idea of education by holding a feast on the grounds and offering each boy of school age two suits of clothes. The promotion filled the appetites but did not shake the doubts of most full-bloods about white teaching; the mixed bloods, several of whom like Hiram Thorpe had been exposed to the Methodist reservation school in Kansas, were more inclined to turn their children over to the authority of the new Sac and Fox school.

It was modeled on the rigid, manual-labor boarding school con-
cept which the government decided was the only way to educate
the Indian, a necessity, as one Indian agent put it, "for the more
civilized and intelligent they are the fewer vagabonds and crim-
inals will there be to burden the coming communities with which
the immediate future will populate this fair country." The system,
which took the child away from the home and placed him under
a regimen of tight discipline, simple labor and part-time study,
was but a crude copy of the education program established much
earlier by the Five Civilized Tribes. In the 1840s the Cherokees
had built a male seminary near Tahlequah, Oklahoma (with
money from land sales invested in U. S. registered stocks), that
had eighty-five rooms and offered courses in foreign language,
metaphysics, natural sciences, higher math and music.

Hiram Thorpe believed in formal education—he was listed as
one of thirty Sac and Fox tribe members who in 1892 had the
ability to speak and read English—and he regarded the boarding
school as a convenient means of sharing the burden of discipline,
care and shelter of children in a large, unruly family. The
Thorpes' fourth son, Jesse, had recently died and a new baby
(daughter Rosetta) was about to arrive when Jim and Charlie
were sent off to the Agency school in the summer of '93. There
were Thorpes in the school's dormitories ahead of the twin boys
—Frank and Minnie, children of Mary James, and older brother
George had been attending, all of which apparently offered Jim
no particular reassurance. (Mary Thorpe would be old enough
to enter the following year, but she became speechless after she
fell from a wagon and a corn stalk pierced her vocal cords, a
handicap—along with her deafness—that inconvenienced but
hardly defeated her.)

James and Charlie, as the '93 class roll carried their names,
were placed in a First Primary group, along with Robbie Keokuk,
Walter Mathews, Peter Wyman, Charlotte Pattigua and Shelah
Guthrie. It was for James the beginning of a rambling, discordant
education process that would occupy his life for the next nineteen years. (Shelah Guthrie, a full blood who was registered
with her Indian name, Chi-ki-ka, was sent on to Carlisle three
years later and she was still there in 1911 when Jim had become its most famous football player.) The apocryphal story of

Jim's first days of schooling has him breaking away immediately and racing his father and his wagon back to the cabin, some twenty miles to the south. Actually his distaste for the school that sent him home to face an inevitable beating from Hiram was not evident in the attendance and deportment records until he had been there for two or three years.

The enrollment—mostly Sac and Fox with a scattering of Ottawa, Potawatomi, Iowa and Kickapoo—was about sixty, although the three-story brick building where the boys were housed and the new frame girls' dormitory could accommodate over a hundred. The school consisted of four primary grades and four advanced grades, with few pupils reaching the upper levels before dropping out. The government payroll included a superintendent ($1,000 annually), four teachers ($660), one farmer, one matron and assistant, a seamstress ($450), cook and helper, two laundry workers and three industrial assistants ($60). The farm not only provided subsistence for the school but was used as training ground for boys; the girls' vocational concentration was on sewing and other domestic skills. The school was very much the model of elementary Indian education in the 1890s, a rustic but sufficient incubator for the few who would go on to Carlisle equipped with a background in reading, writing and facing up to a steady discipline.

"Our lives were just one bell after another," said Stella Reuben, a Sac and Fox girl who left the school during summer vacation and got married. "We got up by bells, ate by bells, went to class by bells. Everything was routine work and much different from our free life on the reservation. That is why so many children hated the school. The blanket Indians often came to school asking to visit their children. Few of them could speak English, so one of us girls had to act as an interpreter. Some parents camped for months at a time along the creek at the Agency so as to be nearer their children."

The rule forbidding the use of the tribal language was intended to widen the gulf for the minority of full-bloods between the school and its civilized routine and their parents' circumstances at the creekside camp. Other school requirements—uniform clothing, work details, learning the words in *Gospel Hymns* #5—were no doubt just as uncomfortable a transition for half-breeds like the Thorpe boys as for the blanket Sac and Fox. Jim and Charlie, with all the other boarders, were buttoned into government-issue cheviot shirts, anonymous dark suits (with vests) and crowned with the ubiquitous black hats. In the long hot season the pupils switched to summer straws for formal assemblies and religious services. Jim's rebellion at the school grew noticeably as he became large enough to serve on more of the work details, which included helping in the farm garden or orchard, chopping wood with a crew of twelve for the school stoves and assisting in the kitchen.

In the classroom teacher Minnie Birch primed Jim and Charlie with McGuffy's *First Reader* and held out the promise of more exciting things to come in *Scudders Short History of the U.S.* and Fry's *Primary Geography*. At the other end of the school day, only half of which was given to reading and writing, Isaac McGladish, a hard-voiced industrial teacher, waited to portion out discipline along with his instruction on the use of farm tools. (Not all industrial teachers at the school were as severe as McGladish; a successor was discharged because he allowed the boys "to chew tobacco and to spit on the floors and stove hearths." He also was caught playing cards with the boys in the hayloft—a violation of paragraph 239 of Indian Rules, prohibiting card playing.)

If the farm projected the horror of heavy labor for the boys, it also occasionally provided enough excitement to puncture the school's drab daily cycle. The birth of a calf, the slaughtering of livestock for food, the discovery of the death of a cow in the sandy pasture were enough to fire the imaginations of the pupils. (Since the animals, as well as the children, were the government's responsibility a dead cow required a solemn report from Superintendent Holmes and Teacher McGladish, swearing that death occurred "through causes unknown and not through negligence or want of foresight.") For scheduled diversion the boys and girls were offered a combination of the games teachers thought they should be playing or those carefully specified by government regulations; it was only in their own free time that they could turn to happier, improvised sport.

An observer of the reservation school recreation period recalls being depressed by the sight of a group of boys playing horseshoes. "They were dressed in ill-fitting black clothes; weighted down with those enormous black felt hats peculiar to Indians. Their movements were slow and hesitant, each handling his horseshoe as if it were dangerous. I asked their overseer about it, and learned that these boys would not play the games provided unless forced to do so. No wonder! I asked if he had tried Indian games; with a blank look he said the government rules specified what games were to be played. Perhaps it never occurred to him that Indians had games of their own."

A Sac and Fox schoolmate of the Thorpes, who in his late eighties lives in an Indian home a few miles north of the old Agency site, says that there was no ball playing, no Indian ball (lacrosse, which tribe members still played with enormous abandon), that the height of fun was the running and jumping games they made up. Jim was quick for his age and could use his legs better than most; in the scuffling and wrestling competition—the Indians' favorite test of strength and stamina—he was a rough match. He liked the idea of being leader in follow-the-leader, making bold use of trees, fences and hen-house roof, and always promoted the paddling line which was the doom of those without the courage or strength to follow him. Sometimes his daring sent him so far ahead of the rest that he became a leader without followers. Fox and Chickens, or Fox and Geese, was another favorite of the primary-age pupils. Baseball, introduced by the whites as soon as they settled in numbers in Indian Territory, had not yet made an impact on the isolated boarders at the Sac and Fox school.

In the summer of '96 the school reports on Jim and Charles reflected their physical similarities and suggested that their temperaments were very much their own. Both were listed as nine years old. Charles, who had darker skin, was fifty inches in height and weighed sixty pounds; Jim was just over fifty inches and weighed four pounds more. Charles' deportment was considered *good;* Jim was marked *fair.* Nearly everyone in his age group—including friends Ira Walker, Clara Ellis, Sadie Ingalls, Shelah Guthrie and Orlando Johnson, who joined him at Carlisle—received good behavior comments. Only Jim, Ester Bigwalker and Daniel Kirsho-ka-me, a Kickapoo boy who had attended just fourteen days, were less than satisfactory. Jim's re-

port also showed an attendance gap of two weeks when he ran
away from school. Hiram returned him—along with a sharp memory of a hiding—to Superintendent Holmes. One can assume that
there was more than just the tug of freedom, the defiance of
school authority that drove Jim out of the ugly, awkward-looking
brick school building and onto the path toward the North Canadian. There must have been doubts enough darting through his
mind of what he would find when he reached home, or what
might happen if he didn't seek an answer. At about the time he
and Charlie were sent away to school his father left his mother
and took up with another woman, Fannie Groinhorn (or Mc-
Clellan). Their son, William Lasley, born in 1893, was later
known as "Little Jimmie" because of his attachment to his older
half-brother. (As a student at Haskell, where he became the
school's best printer, the boy used both names, William Lasley
Thorpe and Jimmie Thorpe.) After Hiram left her, Charlotte
applied for a divorce but it was never granted. Sometime in late
1894 or early 1895 they "remarried" and started living together
again.

Jim was hardly alone in his rebellion at the Sac and Fox school.
Runaways were a steady part of the disciplinary flow, and it was
not unusual to have ten or twelve turn up missing each month
from the boys' and girls' dormitories. Jim's cousin, Esau McCoy,
walked out of school at the end of classes one day after announcing that he was leaving for Coffeyville, Kansas, and Osage country where he said he wanted to live. Most of the runaways (including McCoy) were returned, but in the more conservative
bands of the tribe parents often made no effort to turn their children back for more education. In his desperation to break the
truancy, Superintendent Holmes requested the use of federal
troops in the spring of '96. The Commissioner turned him down,
suggesting that he might add two or three policemen to handle
"the turbulent element." Holmes tried compulsory attendance
for a while, but it failed. He blamed it on the long distance from
the school to the Indian villages, the close proximity of "that
harbor of refuge," the Creek country, and the reluctance of the
Sac and Fox police to offend their own people.

Jim's reputation as an obstreperous, restless pupil was sharpened by the contrast in personalities of the twins. Charlie was

"sweet, gentle" in the memory of his teachers; Jim was "an incorrigible youngster." (Years later Mary Thorpe would chide Jim with "why couldn't you have turned out like Charlie?") Harriet (Hattie) Patrick, daughter of the Sac and Fox agent Frank Patrick in the early '90s, was their teacher for a couple of years and found them dismayingly different, with Charlie showing the softness that endears pupil to teacher and Jim the restless child, "uninterested in anything except the outdoor life," always challenging her discipline. He was a poor student, she said, because he went out of his way to absorb himself in anything but his lessons. Once he devoted his time in class to testing his marksmanship—with a piece of rubber—on flies, of which the school had an overabundance. Miss Patrick gave him the assignment of exterminating flies, but his interest in the job ran out long before the target supply.

If the twins were as different as "night and day," according to teacher Patrick, they had grown quietly close as brothers. There were no sure bonds between Jim and George, who went on attending the Sac and Fox school after Charlie had died and Jim had dropped out. For some time Frank, nine years older than Jim, served the big brother role, which occasionally yanked at his patience and understanding. On a summer marketing trip to Prague with Charlotte, Jim and Frank began teasing and testing one another on the dusty main street. Jim pulled out a coin his mother had given him and flashed it at his brother. "Why don't I get one?" Frank yelled. "Because you can't do this," Jim said. He farted loudly, took a quick little run down the road and did a full somersault in the air.

In the late winter of '97 illness and epidemic disease, which seasonally seeped through the tribe as members tried to cut themselves off from the cold in overheated lodges and cabins, reached the boarders at the school. Measles was rampant and a few pupils were struck down with pneumonia and other respiratory problems. (The outbreak was not as severe as the one the next fall when roseola and confluent variola—smallpox—became epidemic and so many frightened Indians ran away from the quarantined school that it was closed for over four months.) One of the pneumonia victims was Charles, and when his condition worsened Hiram and Charlotte were asked to come to the school. Harriet

Patrick, then the principal teacher, who had been attending Charles and dozens more of the sick, turned over the bed watch and fire-stoking to his parents when they arrived so that she could get some rest. When she awoke at 5 on the morning of March 10 she found the Thorpes asleep, the fire down and Charles near death. Parents and teacher called for the school doctor and put the boy's feet in hot mustard water, "but he just lay back and died in my arms," Harriet Patrick said.

The death of Charles was the fourth among the children of Hiram and Charlotte. For Jim it was the first time he had lost a playmate and a brother. He was taken out of school that spring —or maybe in his grief and confusion he insisted that he stay home—and didn't return until the fall. By his eleventh birthday, the following March, he was among the fifteen pupils who had recently run away from school.

The Gunslingers of Keokuk Falls

Beyond the range of the Sac and Fox school dormitory bell the near countryside was going through the jarring, sometimes deadly upheaval of pre-statehood days, an untidy transition for the Territory and adjoining Indian lands that even the younger pupils could sense in the dust clouds of wagon traffic around the Agency and in the stories brought back to school or picked up in gossip around the trading center. By early summer of '95 Shawnee had emerged out of the oak forest as an eager town of 2,500, and the Fourth of July celebration for the hurried completion of the Choctaw Coal and Railway Company brought an excursion train from Oklahoma City and such crowds of curious Indians that the editor of the Shawnee *Quill* was moved to comment:

> To very many the presence and hearty interest of hundreds of well-dressed Indians was a big surprise and the more thoughtful saw in the commingling of the

races and the mutual enjoyment of the holiday, a sensible and happy solution of the vexed Indian question. Enjoying the rights and privileges of a citizen and freed from the various domination of autocratic satraps, styled agents and the spoilation of buccaneering marshals the Indian quickly responds to the demands of good citizenship and is as loyal and patriotic as his white brother.

While the good citizens and not yet citizens were hailing the arrival of progress in the shape of the Choctaw railway engine, a less glorious Fourth of July episode was threatening the holiday mood forty miles away in Oklahoma City where an outlaw named Jim Casey jumped the jailer, grabbed the keys and set free "the notorious Christian brothers," who disappeared into the safety of the thicket along the North Canadian. The Christian gang did not gain the lasting reputation of the five Dalton brothers, who had been frequent visitors to the area, but they unleashed a certain amount of concern whenever they were reported in the vicinity. Their return to a lawless livelihood was one of those unsurprising events of the day that fitted into the conversation at the new Union Avenue Hotel and in the saloons Hiram Thorpe frequented in Keokuk Falls, along with such functional topics as the need to plow wide fire guards for the windy season ahead, the price of watermelon (six for a nickel), the coming ball game between Shawnee and El Reno.

If the names and cold-blooded reputations of the active gunmen around the Territory—among them, the Christian brothers, the Cook gang, Zip Wyatt, White Horse Doolin, Cherokee Bill (a mixed breed named Crawford Goadsby, who had once attended Carlisle)—did not filter down to the school children, the climate they created was very real to them. Cora Smith, a Sac and Fox who was twelve in 1895, commented, "You could not tell a good man from a bad man unless you knew him personally. Almost everyone carried a gun." The "bad men" were not all gimlet-eyed adults; nor were they necessarily men or boys. That August, several miles north of the Sac and Fox Agency, a sheriff's posse ran down two gun-wielding girls—Jennie Medkiff, sixteen, and Annie McDoulet, fifteen, who admitted they had been selling whiskey to Indians. A few weeks later the girls, dressed in boys' clothes, were arrested as horse thieves. Justice, as it was served in the middle of Oklahoma in the mid-1890s, did not always come swiftly to the side of the Indian in trouble or under suspicion—a condition that periodically threatened to touch off an uprising in Indian villages. In July '95 a sheriff in El Reno killed Red Lodge, a Cheyenne accused of assaulting a white woman, and the expanding rumor in the white community said that about four hundred Cheyennes, with the help of the Kiowas, were about to avenge the death. Indian police, given uniforms, weapons and authority to keep order among their people, often proved to be more trigger nervous than white law officers. Alex Sanders, an Indian doing a little trading in Shawnee one January day in 1896, was stopped by a Seminole Light Horseman who accused him of carrying whiskey. In the argument that followed Sanders was shot dead. The suspicious bag held a head of cabbage.

With hostility and bloody revenge constantly piercing life's daily rounds, the Shawnee *Quill* tried hard to get some of the better tidings out to the public: Sac and Fox student William Jones was heading East to finish his education at Harvard and would be taking seven young Sac and Fox pupils to enroll at Carlisle on the way; local cotton farmers shipped four thousand bales out of Shawnee in 1896; white folks were encouraged to witness the marvels of Indian baseball ("with 50 players on a side!"); in Shawnee's 5–3 victory over El Reno—in white man's baseball—an Indian named Alford "made the fly catch of the day." And if people doubted that the most gracious of living was not available in Shawnee, they should regard the holiday menu in the dining room of the Union Avenue Hotel, offering blue point oysters, mock turtle soup, Philadelphia capon, lake trout, a rich assortment of pies and puddings.

Hiram Thorpe's social preferences ran in the direction of Keokuk Falls, which was close enough to his land so that when the wind came in from the East he could practically smell the sour mash that was dumped behind the distillery run by Ed Thomlinson and Mike Rooney. Keokuk Falls, in all its community consciousness, tried to develop into a legitimate town, but the reason for its existence (beyond one grist mill) was its location adjacent to the territorial line marking the "dry" Creek Nation.

Even if a man did not choose to drink in Keokuk Falls, he knew of its Seven Deadly Saloons, the feuding and shoot-outs that established them and the fact that it took a special breed to develop a sense of well-being in the town. It is difficult to say whether Hiram Thorpe's reputation was unfairly colored by his attendance in the saloons of Keokuk Falls or whether it was more a case of the town suffering handicaps as it struggled toward normalcy because of his presence and that of others like him. In its brief stay on the maps (it was doomed by statehood prohibition, the decision by railroad builders to avoid it and the vagrant tendency of the North Canadian), Keokuk Falls became as notorious as any stage stop in Oklahoma. The stage driver took delight in announcing to strangers on board as he pulled up to the Keokuk Hotel, "Stay for a half hour and see a man killed."

The gun play in town was not all of the Main Street, Hollywood shooting-gallery variety. Aaron Haring, who took over as owner of the Black Dog saloon and aroused the anger of Doc Stutsman, a gambler and proprietor of the Red Front Saloon, was murdered in bed in the summer of '97. Stutsman was tried and found guilty but later retried and acquitted. Distillery owner Ed Thomlinson, a friend of Thorpe and respected as a town booster and leader, also received a favorable verdict from a jury after he killed the town marshal in a dispute over his daughter. Testimony given at the trial indicated that the marshal had pulled his gun first. (Thomlinson was later shot down by Felix Grundy, "a none too reputable gunman" and bill collector, on an occasion, witnesses said, when the distillery owner had chosen to walk unarmed.)

The story that flavored Hiram Thorpe's notoriety in the area of the Falls involved a saloon shooting on a heavy drinking night —an argument between two men at the bar, a scuffle and then a gun shot that left one of them dead on the floor. In the uneasy silence that followed the assailant drunkenly waved his gun at the crowd in sure gesture of challenge and defiance. Thorpe walked over to the body on the floor, stuck his finger in the fatal wound and then held up his hand, dripping with the dead man's blood. The gunman backed off—and the story of the incident was into Territory tradition the next day. A more realistic—or

more common—view of Hiram in Keokuk Falls sees him downing
the last glass of whiskey from the long bar of bridge planking at
the Black Dog and heading for the residence of Perry Johnson,
the hotel owner and justice of the peace. Hiram preferred the
relative ease and safety of Johnson's front yard to sleep off a
long night's drinking rather than to attempt to make it to his
cabin several bends up the river.

Hiram, now close to fifty, was still stretching the size of the
family. Daughter Adaline was born in September 1895, and another son, Edward, arrived three years later. But the relationship with Charlotte had not mellowed with age and experience.
By 1899 the Sac and Fox annuity roll listed them as "separated,"
and they were not enrolled again as husband and wife by the
time Charlotte died in the early winter of 1902 (although they
certainly lived together part of that time, and in the spring of '02
Hiram went to the Agency to draw Charlotte's annuity payment
as her legal husband.)

There was no inconsistency in Hiram's attitude toward Jim
and his failure to stay put at the Sac and Fox boarding school.
When Jim ran away again during the year following Charlie's
death Hiram told him, "I'm going to send you so far you will
never find your way back home." Through the Agency he arranged to have him enrolled at Haskell Institute in Lawrence,
about three hundred miles to the north. It was two months after
Jim had been removed from home, boarding school and friends
and sent to Kansas that Hiram was caught running jugs of
whiskey into the reservation, causing an uproar at the Agency
below the schoolhouse and arousing the wrath of Lee Patrick,
the new agent. (Hiram's open defiance of the prohibition in-
flamed the incident; most whiskey peddlers went to inventive
extremes to get their merchandise into Indian hands at $1.00 a
pint. Some, posing as egg and poultry buyers, used wagons with
large hollow axles that held several gallons each.) Agent Patrick's
formal appeal to the U. S. Attorney's Office in Guthrie read:

Hiram Thorpe, a Sac and Fox Indian, did on the 5th
day of November 1898 introduce onto this reservation
one gallon of whisky and gave same to Naw-mil-wah,
Henry Miller, Parkinson, Sam Brown, Sac and Fox In-

dians. On November 6th 1898 he did introduce upon
this reservation one gallon of alcohol and gave same
to Naw-mil-wah, Sam Brown, John Logan and Wish-ke-
na-etal, Sac and Fox Indians. I have the jug in my possession . . . This liquor was introduced during the Sac
and Fox payment and created much disturbance. He is
very defiant in the matter and I respectfully request that
you have him immediately apprehended and prosecute
him to the full extent of the law.

There is no indication that Hiram's contempt for the law or
his drinking habits were diluted by the experience.

III   AN EXILE AT HASKELL
       AND CARLISLE

In the Company of Chauncy Archiquette
and Thaddeus Redwater

From the Sac and Fox Agency, Haskell was a wagon ride to Guthrie, then the train to Arkansas City across the Kansas line and another train trip to Lawrence just west of Kansas City, a discouragingly long way from everywhere for the eleven-year-old Thorpe. The school, which had been operated by the Indian Education Department since 1884, was patterned after the older Carlisle, with emphasis of manual training, military discipline and classroom education in about that order. When Thorpe was brought to Haskell Institute in early September the superintendent had released with great satisfaction the production figures for his 600 students during the last school year: from the wagon shop, 50 farm wagons and five spring wagons; the tailor shop turned out 350 uniforms; the school bakers averaged 500 loaves of bread a day; the farm had a corn crop of 2,500 bushels.

If the announcement somehow reached Jim's consciousness, it could only have come as a ringing threat that Haskell was going to be more work than enjoyment. Haskell loomed as one larger trap in a system that had him ensnared, and the loneliness and discomfort he felt in that uniformed crowd were either to be endured or resisted. Characteristically, he endured it for a time and then went his own way. Haskell did provide him with some useful training for the Carlisle years ahead: he learned how to stay in military step and keep a low profile in the ranks of the privates. He had more exposure to reading, writing, numbers—even if he did not bother to come to grips with those subjects at the time.

Haskell acquainted him with football. The school had taken up the sport two years before he arrived and in the fall of '98 played six games, including two with Purdue and one with Denver. On the small boys' playing field Thorpe felt for the first time the sting and delight of running into a mass of tangled bodies in the crude scrimmages. Football for the small boys, according to Henry Roberts who was at Haskell with Thorpe, was a matter of kicking or throwing an improvised ball around—sometimes just a stocking stuffed with rags or grass and tied at the open end. Roberts, who became a Haskell football captain and then joined Thorpe on the famous 1911 team at Carlisle, said, "One of the disciplinarians took us aside and taught us a few basics of the game. We played in our regular hickory-cloth work shirts, jeans and heavy shoes. Sometimes we had to fatten the ball by stuffing more grass into it. Football was new to most of us. Baseball was the big game at Haskell then and we could play that."

The sure impressions that remain of that long ago schooling are of assembling in front of the four-story gray stone dormitory in the late fall twilight and marching to the dining hall in company formation. Outside the dining hall the students stood at attention, removed their military caps at the command "uncover" and the school band played "The Star-Spangled Banner." One marched to the dining tables, stood behind the chair and sang the "Doxology" before sitting down to the mounds of hominy, potatoes, the unbuttered bread. From reville at 5:45 each morning until taps at 9 P.M. the students moved to the call of student officers, the dinging of disciplinary bells and tried to avoid the penalties for using any Indian words their parents had taught them, for being tardy at morning assembly or study hour or evening roll call, for leaving their rooms in disorder—for slipping into almost any of the habits that had shaped their lives before they had been packed off to boarding school.

The regimen at Haskell did give way to the spontaneity of the country's celebration on New Year's Eve 1899, when Lawrence—and all the other towns that had sprung out of the prairie or forest within easy memory of many of its residents—let go its whistles and peeled its church bells for the new century ahead. The Haskell band formed on the campus walk and boomed its music to the students. For Thorpe, Roberts and all the others pressed around the windows of the small boys' dormitory it was a pin point of time that would remain with them and grow in significance when much of their experience at Haskell had been washed away; it placed them, momentarily, in that world of infinite possibilities that waited beyond the campus grounds and the fields of the school farm.

Several days later, on January 12, those vague opportunities became more realistic when the Carlisle football team stopped at Haskell on its return from a three-week trip to play an "East-West" championship game on the Pacific Coast. The game, which ended with a narrow Carlisle victory over the University of California, was of small matter compared with the enormity of the occasion, the longest trip taken by a football team for one game. The Haskell students held a dress parade and inspection for their guests and at a breakfast served in the domestic science rooms, supervisor Wright complimented both "Carlisle and Haskell, the two best schools in the Indian service, the two best schools in the United States! . . . Today I saw the best thing at Carlisle and the best thing at Haskell—the Carlisle football team and the cooking class at Haskell Institute." The Carlisle players trailed excitement through the halls, particularly among the small boys who had heard or read about the eastern team and the names that had made Walter Camp's All-America selections. There was Isaac Seneca, the dark, chunky halfback who had been picked on the first team All-America because of his open-field running; the tackle, Martin Wheelock, an Oneida, was a second-team All-America; Carlisle's quarterback, Frank Hudson, a Pueblo, who stood only five feet, five inches but could drop kick goals with astonishing accuracy. Towering over his teammates in their red turtlenecks with the large C in front was the most impressive of the Carlisle players, Thaddeus Redwater, who at six feet, four inches was one of the tallest Indians they had ever seen.

At the Cheyenne reservation at Tongue River, Montana, Thaddeus had been known by his Indian name, Redwater Bull Owl. Because of his size and a few memorable demonstrations when he had been drinking, Redwater became the focus of attention wherever he appeared. On one game trip that fall, Pop

Warner physically had to sit on Redwater after he had consumed a bottle of whiskey and then tried to add to his consumption at each stop. Before he finished his course at Carlisle he was expelled, after he had played one ferocious last season as end for Warner. Redwater wanted badly to make something of himself and so he entered Haskell in 1901, played football and took a business course which he failed. He returned to his reservation and became an interpreter, occasionally writing letters East offering "to do any thing for the dear old Carlisle Indian School." In November 1911, when the former Haskell small boys Thorpe and Roberts had become famous players at Carlisle, Redwater did return in minor triumph. He was asked to accompany and speak for four chiefs of the tribe—Charles Noyak, Charles Toe Ball, William Bighead and Little Sun—who visited thirty Cheyenne students and the superintendent. To show his old friends at Carlisle that he had acquired new habits with his responsibilities, Redwater took the chiefs to a drug store in Carlisle and introduced them to their first milkshakes.

When the Carlisle players talked to the Haskell students about the game in California they spoke of having to play on a field covered with sand that was too soggy for Frank Hudson's drop kicking. They discovered that the football used on the Coast was heavier and more balloon-shaped. They had named it "the California pumpkin." Warner had made them work on the long train ride to and from San Francisco—on the way out he had the team jog alongside the train as it crawled up some of the steeper Rocky Mountain passes; during the return trip through the Southwest they stopped over in Phoenix for a game in the desert heat against a new government school.

Haskell had its own football hero at the time, a quarterback named Chauncy Archiquette, and while he had received scant attention from Walter Camp or other eastern football influentials, he had a colorful reputation in the Kansas-Nebraska area. Thorpe was one of the Haskell boys who watched and admired Archiquette and remembered him later as the first player he identified with. Archiquette was a superior student as well as a busy athlete; he played on the school's early basketball teams, was catcher on the baseball nine, sang in the choir and was prom-

inent in the literary society. After he finished at Haskell it was
no surprise to find him playing under Pop Warner at Carlisle.

In the late summer of 1901 a classmate came to Thorpe with
word that there was a letter in the school office from his father,
saying that he had been shot in a hunting accident and was sending money so that Jim could take the train home. "I never did
find out why they didn't give the letter to me," Thorpe told
friends years later. "So I took off on my own." Henry Roberts recalled that he missed Thorpe when shops, classes and football
resumed in the fall. "But it wasn't unusual for boys to go away
for the summer and not show up again. Years later he told me
he had taken French leave, that his father had become sick and
the school wouldn't help him."

Thorpe left Haskell in his work clothes, walked to the railroad
yards in Lawrence and crawled into an empty box car of a freight
train that was being made up. When the train rolled out of the
yards, it headed for Kansas City and not south toward Ottawa,
the old Sac and Fox lands in Kansas and the Oklahoma border.
After he realized his mistake Thorpe jumped off and started
walking, occasionally hitching rides on freighters and farm
wagons. It took him two weeks to reach his home on the North
Canadian.

He found his father recovered and his mother, heavy into another pregnancy, handling a family that had not seemed to di-
minish in size or responsibility. His sister Rosetta had died at
the age of seven while he was at Haskell, but Adaline was now
six and his baby brother, Edward, nearly three. Whatever
Hiram's reasons for wanting Jim home after the accident, they
were overridden by his anger at the boy's desertion from Haskell
and his realization that it would be that much harder to send
him back—or to any other government school. He gave Jim a
beating for his show of independence, which was enough to
turn him away from home again. This time Jim headed out of
Indian Territory for the Texas border. The timing and length
of his runaway are unclear—Thorpe once said he was gone for
much of a year. If so, he would have been away when his mother
gave birth on January 8, 1902, to her eleventh child, a son named

Henry who lived only three days. His mother never recovered from the complications of the childbirth and she died at Dale, where her family had an allotment home, with Hiram at her bedside, on January 24 of that year. She was forty. Her burial was in the cemetery at Sacred Heart, all that remained of the abbey, the monastery and the academy after a fire had destroyed the mission a few months before. Two weeks after the service for Charlotte at Sacred Heart, Hiram married a white woman named Julia Hardin.

Thorpe found work on the Texas cattle range for a few months, repairing fences and helping with the horses. There were always jobs on the expanding ranches for young drifters who were strong and hungry enough. Thorpe was willing to take on heavy work —the experience on the Sac and Fox and Haskell school farms had not been a complete loss—and he cared and knew about horses. In the tales woven around this period of his boyhood there were attempts to link Thorpe and Will Rogers—who later became friends on the West Coast—as two Indian adventurers who roped and rode together on a Texas ranch. The scene is an appealing one: America's favorite humorist of the 1920s and its finest athlete practicing rope tricks and boosting each other's young egos after work hours along the Brazos. Rogers, who was born nine years before Thorpe in northeastern Oklahoma and had much more Irish than Cherokee in him, did go to Texas in 1902. But if his path crossed that of young Thorpe the event made no ringing impression on either of them. Rogers explored well beyond Texas, booking passage on a cattle boat and working as a cowpuncher in Argentina for a time. Thorpe stayed in Texas long enough to save money for a team of horses. "When I came home," he said, "my father took a look at the horses and decided to let me stay."

Jim agreed to return to school, but this time to the one-room public school that had recently opened at Garden Grove, a crossroads about a mile from the Thorpe allotment. While he had been away the nearby town of Bellemont did about all the growing it could—the population was up to 114, by the 1900 census, and another cotton gin, general store, a small hotel, a new blacksmith shop joined the cluster of wooden buildings. There

was enough vitality in and around the town to generate a baseball enthusiasm that produced pickup games on dusty diamonds
trampled out of an abandoned wheat field, games that began after school and on Saturdays with four or five boys in overalls
and Thorpe in the middle of the infield cranking his arm as he
had seen the pitchers do at Haskell. He could throw harder than
others his age, and often enough when the game was stopped to
hunt for the ball that had been hit into the timber that rimmed
the outfield, it was the fifteen-year-old Thorpe who had
rounded the bases for a home run before joining the search.

Baseball was relief from public school—when he attended—
from the small farmhouse where he had to help with Adaline
and Edward while the stranger and stepmother carried her first
child by Hiram. (Jim held onto his older-brother concern about
his sister and small brother. At Carlisle, later on, he worked to
get them both enrolled; Edward did attend and became one of
the band's leading trumpet players.) In mid-April 1903, Hiram
sent a familiar birth announcement from Bellemont to the Sac
and Fox Agency:

> I have another little boy down here and I wish you
> would put him on the payroll for me if you please he
> was born on the 10 day of May and his name is Ernest
> Thorpe. Yrs respectfully, Hiram Thorpe.

With another family started, Hiram was anxious to settle some
of his backlog of responsibilities and aggravations which evolved
from his marriage—marriages—to Charlotte Vieux. When her
estate (the allotment and its improvements) was partitioned
by the court in the summer of 1903 he and son George took fifty
of the developed acres in common, which they immediately sold
for $1,602, and the remaining 110 acres were set off for Jim, Mary,
Adaline and Ed.

Soon after the land sale was approved, Superintendent W. C.
Kohlenberg at the Sac and Fox Agency received a letter from
Bellemont, urging that Jim Thorpe be sent away to school again,
the greater the distance the better. Because of its clumsy mis-
spellings and error in Jim's age, the letter reads as if it had not

been written by Hiram, even in full rage or full of Keokuk Falls whiskey. It may have been dictated by him, or sent as the sum of his—and their—sentiments by one of his freshly acquired relatives:

Bellmont OT
Dec 13th 1903

U.S. Indian Agent
Sac & Fox Agency OT

Dear Sir— I have a boy that I Wish you would Make rangements to Send of to School Some Ware Carlyle or Hampton I dont Care ware He went to Haskill but I Think it better one of the former plases so he cannot run a way—he is 14 years old and I Cannot do any thing with him So plese at your Earlest Convence atend to this for he is getting worse very day—and I want him to go and make somthing of him Self for he cannot do it hear—

Respectfully yours
Hairm Thrope
Bellmont OT

His Name is James Thrope

Captain Pratt's Route to Civilization

With his transportation, via the Frisco Railroad, arranged through the Sac and Fox Agency in Oklahoma, Thorpe arrived at Carlisle in early February 1904 as the warm wind of a welcome thaw was draining the snow from the Indian School campus, which managed to keep an orderly presence in most lights and weathers. The strings of icicles that had formed on the wisteria vine at the superintendent's residence had disappeared overnight and around the two-story small boys' quarters games of marbles were breaking out on the fresh brown patches of earth. The school, located at the edge of the southern Pennsylvania town on a knoll patterned with walks and tree-lined parade green, had none of the forbidding, institutional stone appearance of Haskell or the Sac and Fox Agency schools Thorpe had attended. The grouping of wooden Federal-period buildings suggested a military academy for the sons of Cumberland Valley squires, rather than the ultimate conversion center in the government's Indian education program where impassive, reservation children came for the civilizing process that promised to turn them out as useful—acceptable—members of society. (The twenty-odd acres where Carlisle Barracks stood had served the people in less-tranquil times. It was originally the site of a rude fort where the nearby citizenry could take refuge in case of Indian attack. During the Revolutionary War captured Hessian soldiers had built a powder magazine on the hill which the school used as a guard house. Carlisle was the Army's first cavalry post and a Civil War target for one of Jeb Stuart's commanders who shelled the town and burned down the barracks.)

The school was approaching its sixteenth commencement later in the month, a time when the academic societies, gym drill teams, class speakers and industrial shops were being tuned for the streams of outsiders, including Department of Interior and Congressional visitors. The band, which the Indians joined with enormous enthusiasm, rehearsed passages from *La Traviata* for the exercises; the physical culture classes perfected their calisthenics and mass demonstrations on the gym floor (dumb-bell drills by the girls, wand drills by the boys); the basketball team tried to put the leather ball through the hoop that hung discouragingly high above them (at basketball the Indians were adept at getting into position to shoot and could outscramble opponents for the ball, but their poor marksmanship suggested there was something alien about the object of the sport). The Invincible Debating Society received special compliments from superintendent Pratt for its performances of selections from *Hamlet*. (The audience took delight in seeing Albert Exendine, the big end in football who was later named to Walter Camp's All-America team and became a successful college coach, in the role of one of the clowns and grave diggers.) The school publication,

The Red Man and Helper—which carried the slogan: "There Is Only One Way: To civilize the Indian get him into civilization; to keep him civilized, let him stay"—noted that enrollment just before graduation was up to 599 boys and 470 girls. It applauded "the good wholesome rivalry between young ladies and young gentlemen as to the order of their rooms" at Sunday morning inspection.

Thorpe was better prepared than most new arrivals for the tightly structured student life at Carlisle. He was older (nearly seventeen) than many of the starting students who had been committed by parents, guardian or agent to spend at least five years at the school. He had already been turned away from home, or bolted from it, often enough so that the pinch of resentment or loneliness he might feel was a condition as familiar as the stiff buttoning of another military-cut tunic. He had responded to the commands and numbers, the call of the bells at Haskell, and acquired a background, spotty as it was, in reading and writing and figures. More important to him, he had been out on his own and had proved he could handle himself in the rough and tumble. After facing up to Hiram, drunk or sober, the physical penalties he might be required to take at Carlisle could not have loomed as very terrifying.

The Indian school's acquaintance with Thorpe began with the spare details in the descriptive statement accompanying all pupils transferred from tribal Agency to the school. Nowhere in the report of the Sac and Fox physician, Dr. F. W. Wyman, is there the hint of Thorpe's physical potential or any positive or negative projection at all, except that the blank spaces seemed to assure that his general health posed no immediate danger to himself or to the school. The form:

Indian name: (blank)
English name: James Thorp
Blood: Half
Nation: Sac & Fox
Band: (blank)
Father's name and rank: Hiram Thorp
Father: Living
Mother: Dead

Sex: M
Age: 17
Height: 5 ft. 5 in.
Forced inspiration: 32½
Forced expiration: 29
Remarks: (blank)

The descriptive statement was completed and signed at the Agency in Oklahoma on February 4, 1904. Looking at pictures now of Thorpe taken within two years of his entrance at Carlisle one is inclined to fill in the blank space next to "remarks" with impressions such as "appears young for his age," or "vulnerable" or "exceedingly placid and withdrawn around strangers."

The Sac and Fox group which Thorpe became a part of at Carlisle was one of the smaller tribal representations, seldom more than eight or ten in number, compared with the hundreds from the Sioux, Chippewa, Oneida nations. But the experiences of the Sac and Fox children who were at the school when Thorpe arrived or came soon after—among them, Margaret Bigwalker, Linda Greyeyes, Shelah Guthrie, Sarah Mansur, Sadie Ingalls, Ira Walker, Orlando Johnson, Robert Davis, Bill and Emma Newashe, Stella Ellis—formed a composite of the best and the worst that young Indians encountered at the school. Some of them were kept, despite their plaintive protests, for ten years or more before being allowed to return home; some were counted as "deserters"; one girl was expelled for unspecified "immoral" reasons; a few adjusted easily and graduated with superior academic honors. Bill Newashe, who developed into an excellent college-level baseball player, was encouraged to stay on at Carlisle in order to keep his bat in the lineup. When he did leave he became a victim of ill health and obscurity in the minor leagues. Thorpe's exceptional abilities were recognized early by the Sac and Fox girls—long before the public had any claim on him at all—and they wrote letters to parents or guardians in Oklahoma, proudly calling attention to "our football boy from home, James Thorpe." (In the idiom of the day, and particularly at Carlisle, to be identified as "one of the football boys" or "one of the athletic boys" commanded as much respect as one could hope to find around the age of twenty.)

The collection of football boys who were gathered at Carlisle in the early 1900s arrived there by chance, design, selective recruitment or, as in the case of Thorpe, through a parental determination to send the boy off in hopes that the school might make something of him. Carlisle did have an existing network of recruiting agents on the reservations scattered across the country who were periodically reminded of the school's need for a steady flow of new students and its particular interest in enlisting the well-developed, athletically inclined Indians. Col. R. H. Pratt, the founder and still superintendent of the school when Thorpe arrived, made an appeal to Sac and Fox Agent Patrick in 1899 to be on the lookout for the physically gifted, as well as the normally qualified young Indians:

Have you not a small number of exceptionally good boys and girls to send to Carlisle this year?" he asked. "No students sent should be under 12 years nor over 20. They should be in good health and of good character, and advanced at least to the fourth grade, though I do not make that last a condition.

Incidentally, if you should by chance have a sturdy young man anxious for an education who is especially swift of foot or qualified for athletics, send him and help Carlisle to compete with the great universities on those lines and to now and then overcome the best.

A few of Thorpe's teammates came to Carlisle because an Indian agent had discovered they were "especially swift of foot" or they had shown promise at Haskell or Sherman Institute (California) and were quickly drafted by Pop Warner. But some were there simply because of their own eagerness to learn a trade or get an education. Albert Exendine and Gus Welch, two of Thorpe's most influential friends, pushed their own cases in order to reach Carlisle.

For Exendine (or Ex as he was, of course, called) getting into the school was of such great moment the memory of it was fixed sharply for the rest of his life. Ex, three years older than Thorpe, was the son of a part Cherokee father and a full-blood Delaware mother. He spent most of his boyhood in the Lake Creek country of western Oklahoma and attended the Mautame (Presbyterian) Mission school near Anadarko where he and his closest friend, a Cheyenne named Joe Tremp, spotted an announcement: "Students Wanted for the Carlisle Indian School." They made a pledge that somehow they would get to the eastern school. "That summer I was working in a hayfield," Exendine said, "and Joe Tremp came around looking for me with a team and buggy. He said he was off to Carlisle. I was amazed and excited. But I was afraid to ask my father's permission to follow Joe so I had my older brother approach him. It took my father six months to say, yes, he would talk to the Indian agent at Anadarko—he didn't like the idea that I would have to stay for five years in order to get a free education and free transportation to the school and back.

"It was near Christmas 1899, when I left alone for Carlisle. I had never been on a train before and it was an experience. I remember a strange sight as the train moved slowly through Kansas City—there was a chain-haltered hog grazing in front of a beautiful home. Father let his hogs run loose up and down Lake Creek and they thrived with little feeding attention. As we were leaving Kansas City, passing through a residential district with many three-story homes, I saw how well citizens were housed but found no answer on what they did to make a living. The people once were immigrants and the Indians had owned, hunted and stomp-danced on that ground. But this is civilization, I thought, and the way the Indians must learn to live.

"I arrived at Carlisle around 9 at night and asked someone how to get to the Indian School. He said the trolley would take me right out to the gates. When I got off I saw this large building that still had lights on and there a woman greeted me with, 'You're a new student?' Yes, I said. 'You are in the girls' quarters now,' she said. 'There are the large boys and the small boys. We had better take you to the large boys' quarters.' I was asked if I knew anyone at the school and I told them about Joe Tremp. 'He is one of our top boys,' I was told. At the dormitory they called for Joe Tremp and I heard his feet hit the floor above me. He came down and we ran up and hugged each other we were so glad to be at Carlisle together.

"The next day I was given a tour of the shops and told I would have to pick one. Joe told me about the military way of life and quickly showed me how to march, left-right, left-right. I was determined to accept the system. I chose the baker's shop first and learned how to make bread their way.

"It wasn't too long before they discovered that Joe had tuberculosis and it was decided that he should return to Oklahoma—where he died a year or so after that. When Joe took the train out of Carlisle I couldn't face him to say good-by."

Like Exendine, Gus Welch became an achiever in class and athletics. He also went on to Dickinson Law School and into a long college coaching career. Gus pushed his way into the attention of the football team in order to get admitted to Carlisle, no easy matter because he lived deep in the lake and lumber country of northern Wisconsin. The scrawny son of an Irish logger and the full-blood daughter of the chief of the Lac Court Oreilles band of Chippewas, Gus was raised by an apparently imperishable grandmother after both parents had died of tuberculosis (the disease also took two brothers and two sisters). The woman could portage a canoe when she was one hundred years old and still took her furs from traps to the market in Duluth. Gus often went with her, and on one trip he saw a notice of the coming football game between Carlisle and the University of Minnesota in Minneapolis (the schools played three games in the successive years, 1906-8). Gus was excited by the advertisment because both the game and the distant Indian school appealed to him. He had been introduced to football—in the unpredictable shape of a leather ball stuffed with grass—at school in Hayward, Wisconsin, and although he was scantily equipped for hard contact he was exceptionally quick of feet and mind. (As a quarterback at Carlisle, 1911-14, Welch never weighed more than 150, but he was the team's intellectual leader and was about as spectacular as a breakaway runner as his buddy, Thorpe.)

In November 1907 Gus took the bounty money he had received for trapping a wolf, put on a baggy overcoat that had belonged to his father and went to Minneapolis a few days before the game. At the hotel where the Carlisle team was staying Gus asked to talk to the Chippewas in the group—end, George Gardner, and center, Peter Jordan, were both tribe members. Gus told them he wanted to join the team. They arranged for a one-man try-out, and although Gus had never handled or kicked a real football before he impressed Pop Warner enough to be encouraged to enter. Gus, who was not yet sixteen, said he would like to wait until the next summer when his younger brother, Jimmy, would be old enough to go East with him.

When Gus and his brother were put on the train the following September their grandmother supplied them with dried fruit, apples, wild rice and bottles of spring water and told them to eat and drink nothing else. They walked through the train and were surprised to see people sleeping in beds in the Pullman car. "When do we sleep here?" Gus asked the conductor.

"You have a reservation?" the conductor asked.

"No, no," Gus said. "We're not from a reservation; we live with our grandmother."

Gus overcame the language problem, learned to live among —and compete against—white people with a great deal of winning flair. But brother Jimmy could not make the adjustment that Carlisle demanded of him; he longed for the way of life he had known in Wisconsin, and he virtually refused to give up his native Chippewa and learn English. He soon left and went home.

The Carlisle way, which nearly broke Jimmy Welch at the age of twelve and which trained—for far richer than poorer—Gus Welch, Albert Exendine, Jim Thorpe and other prominent Indian athletes, was the personal creation of Richard Henry Pratt, an Army captain when he started the school with Department of Interior support in 1879. When Pratt left in 1904, having lost his war with the Army, the Indian Bureau in Washington and some less well-entrenched opponents, he was a brigadier general and such a dominant part of the lives of the students that many, including Exendine, counted his forced retirement as a personal tragedy. Carlisle moved on to a new administration without any jarring wrench in the system; the major changes were an accelerated emphasis on athletics and the military trappings that surrounded the school's daily routine.

But there was no replacing the personal infusion of Richard Henry Pratt at Carlisle because it came from a man whose idealism (detractors called it fanaticism) on the need for equality of human beings and his conviction that he had the answer to "the

Indian problem" permeated the school's system. Pratt felt an affinity for both the Negro and Indian minorities; his first command as an Army lieutenant was with an all-Negro cavalry regiment in 1867; at Fort Arbuckle, Indian Territory, he led units of Indian scouts. Later he spent three years as jailer, counselor, instructor for seventy-two Kiowa, Comanche and Cheyenne prisoners at an old Spanish fort in St. Augustine, Florida, where he experimented with his ideas of a civilization program.

Pratt's conversion of his Indian prisoners caught the attention of government officials—he had taught them to speak English, adopt white man's clothes and habits, even march with guns over their shoulders—and enabled him to be assigned to start a school at the abandoned barracks at Carlisle. He was certain that if he could train (i.e., civilize) enough Indians at enough Carlisles far removed from the influence of the reservation, the race of people might eventually be able to compete with the white man and assume an equal place in society. In his call for equality among the races Pratt found himself at times on a deserted platform, but he refused to temper his convictions—or his criticism of those who opposed his methods. When Pratt's set of rigid guide rails in Indian education got in the way of his own compassion for individuals floundering in the system, his rules usually took over.

"In Indian education I am a Baptist," Pratt said soon after coming to Carlisle, "because I believe in immersing the Indians in our civilization, and when we get them under holding them there until they are thoroughly soaked." In one of the Carlisle student publications, which Pratt used for propaganda and occasional debate on education, a comment under the heading, "Why Not Let the Indian Boy Keep His Long Hair and the Girl Her Dress?" reached the core of his belief: "There is a great amount of sentiment among Indian teachers but in the work of breaking up Indian customs there is no room for sentiment."

Pratt started Carlisle—and his great crusade—by personally recruiting most of the first group of students at the Pine Ridge and Rosebud agencies of the Sioux nation. In his hurried roundup in the fall of 1879, he overcame the suspicion and doubts of tribal chiefs Spotted Tail, Milk, Two Strike and White Thunder with an impassioned speech: "You have many children. Give me some of them and let me take them to Carlisle and teach them our language, how to read and write and do business as we do, so that they may come back and help you in your position as chief of this people . . ." He left Dakota with eighty-four children. En route to Carlisle by boat and special railroad cars, he introduced his recruits to their new way of life by buying up the supply of cigarettes from a trader who had been selling to most of the Sioux boys. Pratt took some for himself, distributed the rest to the young smokers and said, "We will all have a good-by smoke on the boat and railroad and when we reach Carlisle we will all quit." Pratt had arranged to have two local barbers cut the boys' hair as soon as possible after their arrival at the Barracks, and most of them silently submitted to this early step toward civilization. But for the first few nights of the school's existence from the boys' quarters came a loud, eerie wailing, the traditional sound of mourning over a personal loss.

The framework of the Carlisle system, which lasted in much the same shape for as long as the school did, was set quickly by Captain Pratt for the Sioux children and the fifty or so others from a half-dozen tribes. Boys and girls were organized into companies with student officers responsible for their conduct in formation, in dormitories, and to and from classes. The daily schedule consisted of a half day of work, a half day of school and an evening study hour. Practical journeymen mechanics, not industrial arts instructors, were hired to teach the trades. The class requirement was fixed somewhere between grammar and high school grades (although after Pratt left, some business-college level courses were offered). There were to be no fads, no catering to the children because they were Indians, no other medium but English. To break down tribal habits and attachments, children from various tribes were placed as roommates.

Neither the school nor the first entering class of Indian children were really prepared to pursue Captain Pratt's dream in that October of 1879. Luther Standing Bear, one of the young Sioux recruits the captain had returned with from the West, later wrote down his impressions of the beginning experience:

"When our interpreter told us to go to a certain building he pointed out we ran very fast expecting to find nice beds like those the white people had. We were tired and worn out from the long trip . . . but the first room was empty. A cast iron stove stood in the middle of the room on which was placed a coal-oil lamp. We ran through all the rooms but they were all the same. No fires, no beds. We had to make the best of it so we took off our leggings and rolled them up for a pillow. All the covering we had was the blanket each had brought. We went to sleep on the wood floor . . .

"When we marched into the schoolroom we were given a pencil and slate. We were seated at single desks. We discovered that the pencils made marks on the slates. So we covered our heads with our blankets so the others would not see what we were doing. We would draw a man on a pony chasing a buffalo, or a boy shooting birds in a tree or it might be one of our games . . . When we had finished we dropped our blankets on the seat and marched up to the teacher to show what we had done. Our teacher, a woman, bowed her head as she examined the slates and smiled, indicating that we were doing pretty well.

"We had to learn to write our names. Each pupil was required to select a name from a long list on the blackboard. Our teacher had a lot of patience with us—she first wrote my name on the slate for me, and then by motion indicated that I was to write it just like that."

There was, in those first years of strange encounter by the pupils and missionary drive on the part of Pratt and his small staff, an innocence and candor on both sides that were soon swallowed up by the system. Captain Pratt encouraged the students to publish their own newspaper in the early 1880s—a modest monthly called *School News*—and it was at the beginning relatively free of the slickness, heavy doctrine, Indian success stories and editorial defensiveness of later publications. Some student notes in 1880 and early 1881:

> • Capt. Pratt's birthday came on December 6th. The band boys went up to his house and played several tunes for him. He was very glad. In the evening all the boys and girls went to his house and sang a hymn before his door. That made him more glad.
> • On the trip to Philadelphia I saw a picture of William Penn and an Indian man shaking hands. They looked like alive, the hands shook all the time.

• The snow is perfectly removed from us.
• On May 30th some of the students at the Carlisle School took part in the parade in town. The sun was very hot when we were marching around the town and in the grave yards.

Pratt had concluded long before the arrival of his first students that only part of the job of educating them could be accomplished in the classroom and shops at Carlisle; that a practical living experience must come by placing students in white homes where they would learn housekeeping, practice a trade, earn wages and, most important, "imbibe in the best of civilization." The Carlisle Outing became the most famous element in the Pratt system—"the great monument of his life work," in the words of Commissioner of Indian Affairs Francis Leupp, whose views on Indian education tended to collide harshly with Pratt's. The Outing was, incidentally, Thorpe's first major encounter with the Carlisle curriculum in the spring of 1904. It turned into a small Thorpian disaster.

All students during their tour at Carlisle were pulled into the Outing program, usually for stretches of three months in the summer and occasionally for longer periods in the winter. The selected patrons were generally farm families in Bucks County or New Jersey, Quaker, or Pennsylvania Dutch homes in the area between Lancaster and Philadelphia. The Outing code—there were many rules that patron and student were obliged to follow under the periodic inspection of an Outing field agent—stated that "pupils are placed in families to learn English and the customs of civilized life." Patrons were not allowed to hand over more than one-half the wages to the pupil and were to encourage the boy or girl to save most of that. The balance went to the student's interest-gathering account at school. Pratt and successive superintendents were forever tallying the remarkable accumulations of money the Outing system had produced for the students' benefit: "In 1903 there were 948 boys and girls placed out and their earnings amounted to $31,393.02!" But the wages, sometimes only $5.00 or $6.00 a month, were hardly half what the patrons would be paying white workers, and while it can't be said that all the good farmers and middle-class American families who participated in the program regarded it as a welcome source of cheap easily exploited labor, it must have occurred to them that they had hit upon a handy economy.

Pratt, with all his idealism, looked at the Outing children as "helpers" and participants in family life. In his set talk to the students who were to go to the country he said: "When you boys and girls go out on jobs you don't go as employees—you go and become part of the family." But the girls often found themselves mopping up in deserted Pennsylvania Dutch kitchens, the boys up to their elbows in the onion fields or eating with the other hired hands off a tin plate on the back porch. The patron was required to keep a monthly disciplinary report, answering such concerns of the superintendent's office as: "Does pupil bathe as often as rules require [once a week]? How does pupil use evenings and Sundays? Has pupil used tobacco or spiritous liquors in any form? State what pupil bought with money expended . . ."

Thorpe's first outing, which followed an introductory course in the school's tailor shop, began in mid-June 1904, on a farm in Summerdale on the Susquehanna River not far from Carlisle. The patron, A. E. Buckholz, put Jim to work cleaning the house, helping out in the kitchen. He was also required to eat in the kitchen, an arrangement which, along with the $5 monthly wage, left him humiliated and increasingly mutinous. He complained that he wanted to work outdoors, and when he was kept on as a plain scullion he broke off the Outing tour and returned to Carlisle. Thorpe, who was sent out three more times in the next two years, ran into other conflicts with the Pratt system of learning manners in the country homes of white families. Yet many of his schoolmates—particularly the girls who easily developed family attachments—counted their Outing time as exciting relief from confinement on campus. (The program must have been a hard piece of logic for the Sac and Fox students to accept; the government, in settling its land debt to the tribe, was sending them quarterly payments that made the Outing wages appear most uncivilized.)

Gus Welch, who worked for a Pennsylvania Dutch family when he first came to Carlisle, found that the steady supply of apple pie just about overcame the salary deficiency. Albert Exendine got more out of the Outing experience than Pratt could have possibly imagined. Exendine was sent out to a farmer in Tullytown, Pennsylvania, who put him to work in the potato fields. "I had never seen a man work so hard and fast digging up potatoes," he said. "I tried to keep up with the farmer until some college boys he had hired as summer help took me aside. 'Slow down,' they told me. 'Be steady and don't miss any potatoes.' It was my first great lesson at Carlisle—do your work right; dig out all the potatoes. One day one of the students said, 'Today let's debate the immigrant question. Resolved, that further legislation be enacted to restrict immigration.' I looked up from my row of potatoes in astonishment. I had never heard such words used before. I listened hard to the debate that went on while we worked and then finally participated myself. I remember the conclusion: that there were enough laws on the books already to restrict illegal immigration. Let's not have new laws that might be unconstitutional and unnecessary. I had a great education that summer in the potato fields."

IV   ONE WHITE MAN'S
FOOTBALL TRICKS

The Hunchback Who Embarrassed Harvard

During Thorpe's early months at Carlisle a string of unrelated events brought an atmosphere of gloom and doubt to the school, and although Jim was too new to share the students' concern he had a sorrow of his own to carry. On April 24 Hiram died of "blood poisoning," a medical definition that covered a range of mortal ailments of the time. It was reported that he had been bitten by a snake, hardly a unique experience for him, and that this time the poisoning could not be controlled. He had died in his early fifties, with his new wife pregnant again, with the children from other marriages scattered through allotment farm houses and at government boarding schools in Oklahoma, Kansas and Pennsylvania. Hiram was buried in a small sunburnt cemetery in Garden Grove, across the road from the school house Jim attended and a short distance from the North Canadian. His first wife, Mary James, who outlived him by fifteen years, was later buried in the same plot.

For Jim there was the cold bureaucratic passage of acquiring a guardian to handle his interests in Oklahoma, which now included the annuity, the rent on his allotment, the fractional shares of his mother's—now his father's—land holdings. But he alone would have to settle the bitter differences with his father and puzzle over the depth of their similarities. He would, of course, be reminded often enough about the streak of Hiram in him. In Thorpe's last year at Carlisle, Sac and Fox agent Horace Johnson commented on rumors of the athlete's heavy drinking: "If he does drink," Johnson said, "he comes by it honestly. I knew his father quite well and he was notorious as a booze fighter." (The booze fighter's death while he was still within his prime may have eased evening tensions along that strip of the North Canadian from Keokuk Falls to Shawnee, but old reputations ran deep in the red soil and as long as there were Thorpes in the vicinity there was an edge of fear in many households. George Thorpe wasn't about to let the legacy slip through his hands. Six weeks after Hiram's death his widow sent a panicky message to the Agency: "Those Indians George Thorpe, Jose Mc-Combe and one other man we did not know came to our place and gave us a fearful scare. We are afraid for our lives. They swear they will settle matters. We ask them what matters they only swear. They only are awful drunk.")

At Carlisle, Thorpe's early emersion in the Pratt system went on without pause for the distant death of a relative. He took his anonymous place in company formations, went through the required daily half hour of gymnastics and sat with the other young apprentices in the tailor shop. The break in the regimen that set him and a few of his Indian friends apart, and in which he must have found reward, came on Sunday morning at 9 when everyone else was lining up in front of dormitories for the regular school religious service. He and a group of Catholic boys and girls were taken into town to the Roman Catholic Church for mass; Sunday evenings at 6 the sisters from St. Katherine's Parochial School came to the Barracks to give them individual instruction. On Easter Sunday, in early April, Father Mahoney led the Indian children in singing the high mass.

The two announcements at school which had such an ominous impact on the older students involved first Pop Warner and then Superintendent Pratt. Warner, who in the four previous years had made the football team known from New York to San Francisco, said he was returning to his own school, Cornell, to coach. Then came the report that Pratt was being forced to retire—he had become too outspoken for his enemies in the Indian Service. "The best friend the Indians ever had," Warner said of Pratt. There was little question about the way most of the young Indians at Carlisle felt. Despite his fast rules, his unshakable opinions, he had provided a human element at the school which fortified students during their long stay. "The gloom was awfully thick that spring," Exendine said. "They were strong personalities, Pratt and Warner. The first time I met the superintendent he looked at my size and said, 'Do you play baseball, football?' I told him I had seen some baseball but didn't know anything about football. 'You'll learn, you'll learn,' Pratt told me, and the way he said it I knew I would.

"First I was on the bakers' team, then the blacksmiths'. I was big but crude and they kept yelling at me, 'Get down, down lower.' I worked at it until I finally decided to approach Warner—it was August and Pop always had the team out ahead of the others—and ask if I could try out.

" 'How much do you weigh?' he said.

" '165 pounds.'

" 'You should have come out last year.' That's all he said. But he turned me over to his brother Bill, who was a great lineman at Cornell and was helping out that summer. He was big—he must have weighed 270 pounds. The first time I tried to block him out, he threw me way back. I went at it again, and again in that hot sun and got thrown back. Slowly I learned to turn my shoulder, use it and take him that way. When we finished we were both wringing wet. Bill walked over to Pop and said something. I was in uniform the next day."

Warner left only to be lured back to coach the famous Carlisle team of 1907 that Exendine and Thorpe both played on and the teams of Thorpe, Welch and Joe Guyon later on. But it was Pratt who, in his zeal to get the Indians into the mainstream and out front in athletics, gave football its early impetus at Carlisle. He often talked up its value of providing travel experience for students, of broadening their exchange with other people (actually the Indian teams on the road kept much to themselves); he also valued the attention it drew to the school from a wide cross-section—congressmen who liked to support success, newspaper editors looking for happy Indian stories, the general public which had feelings of revulsion and guilt about Indian reservations. He also hoped football would counteract the stereotype Indian in the entertainment business, the costumed, monosyllabic sideshow Indian.

Pratt was wary about football when it was first played informally at the school. He was concerned about injury and the intended violence built into the sport. One small Indian-white riot around the goal posts could set his civilization program back to its origin. In 1890 a Carlisle pickup team was scrimmaging Dickinson College, located across town, when Stacy Matlock, a large Pawnee boy, suffered a broken leg. Pratt was so distressed by his experience of helping carry Matlock from carriage to the hospital operating table that he ordered an end to all outside football games. The following year about forty of the prominent athletes, accompanied by the school's best orator, a descendant of Logan, the famous Mingo chief, went to Pratt's office and presented their case for playing intercollegiate football. The combination of the orator's fine-spun argument and the intense appeal in the forty sets of black eyes behind him were too much for Pratt. He said he would agree, with two conditions:

"First, that you will never, under any circumstances, slug. That you will play fair straight through, and if the other fellows slug, you will in no case return it. Can't you see that if you slug people will say, 'There's the Indian of it. Just see them. They are savages and you can't get rid of them.' . . . If the other fellows slug and you do not return it, very soon you will be the most famous team in the country.

"My other condition is this. That, in the course of two, three or four years you will develop your strength and ability to such a degree that you will whip the biggest football team in the country. What do you say to that?"

"Well, Captain, we will try," the speaker said.

"I don't want you to promise to try. I want you to say that you will do it. The man who only thinks of trying to do a thing admits to himself that he may fail, while the sure winner is the man who will not admit failure. You must get your determination up to that point."

Pratt's rousing pep talk did not produce giant-slaying Carlisle teams right away, but it launched a winning program, first under volunteer coaching and then under Warner's professional hand. As for the edict against slugging, it was observed well enough to avoid serious warfare. The Indian teams did become targets of heavy aggression—there were particularly notorious efforts by Princeton, Navy, Bucknell—but they grew capable of cloaked retaliation. In a loss to Princeton—the Big Three school won the

six games played over a fifteen-year period—Carlisle was sub-
jected to threats and obscenities from enraged coaches who ran
along the sidelines urging their players to "Kill the Indians." A
Bucknell-Carlisle game grew so heated Bucknell players took to
working over the Indians with their metal nose guards.

Bemus Pierce, Carlisle's best and largest player in the 1890s
and team captain in '96, served as volunteer police chief for the
team. He was a full-blood Seneca from New York and his in-
ordinate size, about 230 pounds, compared with his lithe, mod-
erately framed teammates gave him a mountainous, commanding
appearance. When his brother Hawley, about twenty-five pounds
smaller, complained during a game of being belted in the face by
a Brown University player, Bemus called time. He grabbed Hawley and walked up to the Brown team still in position on the
scrimmage line. "Which one did it?" he asked. Hawley walked
the length of the line and shook his head. He couldn't decide.
When the referee's whistle ended the time out Bemus yelled at
Hawley, "Keep your eyes open and find out. I'll take care of him
after the game." Brown was very rules-conscious for the rest of
the afternoon.

Bemus later became outspoken in his belief that Indians
should be coached by Indians (he did coach at Carlisle during
Warner's short absence), but as a student and team captain he
was not given to speeches or speaking much at all in front of his
peers. At the football banquet after the '96 season his teammates
and girl friends (this was one of the special school occasions
when the boys were encouraged to select a girl as dinner guest)
prodded Bemus to make a captain's speech. He refused until the
clamor embarrassed him. He stood on his feet in silence for a
time, shifting his heavy frame from foot to foot, looking out at
Superintendent Pratt and the tables of his teammates and their
girls. "I have a confession," he began. "When we played Wisconsin in Chicago [a momentous event held under electric lights before 15,000 dazzled people], I noticed a big fellow who kept slugging our boys. I waited for a chance to tackle him and when I did
let go with the elbow like this"—and Bemus took a fearful swipe
at the banquet room air—"and he yelled 'What's *that* for?' I told
him, 'I just tackled you, that's all.'" Bemus sat down to loud applause.

Superintendent Pratt may have been unrealistic in asking his football boys to refrain from slugging back, or slugging their way through the wedges and crushing mass plays that were then such a part of the game, but he seemed to be reassured by the newspaper comments about the exemplary play of the team. The superlatives and headlines were clipped and often reprinted in the school paper:

• The game was one of the cleanest ever played (a victory over Duquesne).
• The play was full of dash and vim . . . the Indians' wedge work was fine and all their plays were quickly started, so they seldom failed to gain when they secured the ball (Lehigh game '94).
• That's the kind of football I dream of. It's bred in those men (Penn coach George Woodruff).
• A more gentlemanly set of young men than those from the Indian School at Carlisle have never visited Pittsburgh, nor a faster lot of football players (first Pitt game).

Captain Pratt couldn't have been more gratified by a press notice than he was after the Columbia game, a 45-0 victory in New York, and this comment in the Sunday edition of the New York *Herald:* "Carlisle's Indian football team walked up Broadway last evening on their way to the theatre with a stoicism worthy of their ancestors. Some of our college teams who indicate by their behavior that victory is an excuse for rowdyism would do well to emulate this dignified conduct of men they are pleased to consider semi-savages, who had just administered a crushing defeat to Columbia University."

During the formative, pre-Warner years of Carlisle football, players and students were excited by the discovery that Indians could become quickly skilled in a sport that most of them had heard little or nothing about before they arrived at the school. Early coaching and guidance from Vance McCormick, a volunteer who had played at Yale, acquainted them with the game's basics, with the cohesion needed in team play, but it was their

Indian facility at copying and absorbing the essence of the talents of others and perfecting them in their own fashion that accelerated the growth of football at Carlisle. Their size worked against the Indians in this era of muscular face-offs, of the mass-momentum plays and the guards-back formation in which guards were pulled out of the line and used as battering-ram interferers for the ball carrier. There was so much emphasis on mass rather than open football that 200-pound linemen became a recruiting priority at the universities that took their football seriously. Carlisle often found itself woefully out of its weight class. So the Indians leaned on speed, their quickness off the line, and on their field-goal kicking—a goal had a rugby-size value of five points then. The Indians produced a line of excellent drop-kick and placement kickers, probably because of their fascination with a skill that required timing, strength and dexterity of leg and foot. Jonas Metoxen, a short, broad-shouldered Oneida, set the standards in the mid-'90s that first Frank Hudson and then Thorpe would improve upon. Thorpe's long field goals were from placement and subject to the ball-handling quickness of the holder. Metoxen had the entire school drop-kick conscious because he practiced constantly the year-around—in the gym with parallel bars as goal posts and during the outdoor season with any available target he could find. His successor, Frank Hudson, also gave full-time attention to the drop kick, and he became proficient with either foot. Hudson was probably the best there ever was at this antiquated method of scoring points from the field, a risky business for anyone who could not control the bounce of the ball off the grass turf. Goals had to be kicked from the scrimmage point—wherever it was—and often the angles were discouragingly oblique. Hudson became uncanny at chipping the ball through the posts at forty yards or less, and his kicks were rarely blocked. After a long scoring drop kick he made against Yale he and his teammates were welcomed back from the game as victors (they lost 18–5) and pulled around the parade grounds in a large herdic by exuberant students. A local Carlisle jeweler presented Hudson with a gold ring in honor of the feat.

The appearance of Glenn Scobie Warner in 1899—actually he was always called "Pop" from the time he was an overage twenty-one-year-old freshman at Cornell—guaranteed the achievement of Carlisle's restless ambition to play and beat the best in college football. Superintendent Pratt had promised his football boys that he would in time ask Walter Camp to recommend the foremost young coach in the country to come to Carlisle. Warner was the choice, even though Pratt had to pay the "almost impossible figure" of $1,200 to get him, a salary that grew with the rapid rise of football revenue at the school. Warner's coaching reputation was based on two seasons at Cornell, two at the University of Georgia and experience at Iowa State College in Ames where he taught football to the farm boys for a month beginning in mid-August (at $25 a week) and then took the train to Georgia to coach the university for a full season (at $34 a week).

Warner, a 200-pounder in his late twenties with a bushy "football" haircut, did not appear to fill Pratt's requisites for a teacher and molder of highly civilized men. He had been a greenhorn plunger at the trotting tracks in northern New York State before he entered Cornell (at Carlisle he became a dedicated market player). He was a hard, profane loser and drove his players without compassion. He started out by scrimmaging with them as part of their instruction but gave it up because of the injuries and wounded egos he left behind. At Georgia he startled the candidates for the team by getting them out at six o'clock each morning for five miles of road work. When he first came to Carlisle he learned to moderate his language somewhat because the Indians took his indignities personally and began staying away from practice. Behind the profanity and gruffness was an exceedingly fertile mind capable of the enterprise that Pratt needed from a coach-athletic director-public relations coordinator. Warner, who had earned money toward his law degree by peddling his own water-color landscapes, developed into a master salesman at Carlisle, broadening schedules, hiking up game guarantees, persuading Indian athletes who had finished their education elsewhere to come to Carlisle and then keeping them on by arranging for paying jobs or a chance to prep for law school. He learned when to prod or ease up on the Indians and was generally more effective in handling Thorpe than the scholarly, quick-minded quarterbacks Jimmy Johnson and Gus Welch.

Warner, after forty-four years as a coach (he was at Pitts-

burgh, Stanford and Temple after Carlisle), is remembered less
for his fine teams than for his innovations. He coached from
football's Stone Age into the modern era and probably had as
much to do with the game's rapid evolution as anyone. The
three-point sprinter's stance for backs, the blocking sled, fiber
padding in uniforms, the double-wing or double-flanker formation, the cross-body block, pulling guards or tackles for interference (on wide plays Carlisle had so many men in front of the
runner they were known as Warner's "cloud interference"), and
the perfection of the spiral pass and spiral punt for accuracy
and distance were some of the Warner originals or polished
improvements.

Warner's contributions to Carlisle football came impressively
fast. With such excellent Indian athletes as Isaac Seneca, Hugh
Wheelock, Frank Hudson on hand in 1899, Warner was able to
defeat Penn, the most popular rival, for the first time, which assured the students that their football team had reached the
big time. The Harvard game turned encouragingly close when the
Indians scored with a thirty-five-yard drop kick by Hudson and
Thaddeus Redwater pulled in a loose ball and ran eighty yards
for a touchdown.

Under Warner's prodding the Indians acquired a facility for a
variety of deceptions which made it difficult for the crowded
defenses to follow the ball. The crisscross, the reverse with the
tackle or end handling the ball, double and triple passes in the
backfield, began to characterize the Carlisle game. They were
particularly slick with the double pass in which the quarterback,
crouched under center in the original T formation, handed the
ball off to a halfback moving laterally who, in turn, passed it back
to the quarterback. Carlisle's quarter, Jimmy Johnson, fast with
his hands and feet, called his own signal with great success.

But nearly all of the Indians' mastery of the game during
Warner's first term was upstaged by one *coup de theatre*, a ma-
neuver that astonished the football public—or, rather, delighted
the people so much that they would drag descriptions of the play
into their conversations for years to come. Part buffoonery, part
ingenuity, it became immortalized in vaudeville skits and was
written into Joe E. Brown comedies in Hollywood. The Indians
loved it; Warner was embarrassed by the attention it drew; the

1903 season, in which the weekend death rate on the field challenged later auto fatalities, was badly in need of its comic relief. Warner introduced the play to the Indians, the ultimate in hidden ball stunts, at the start of the season. Because the ball was hidden in the most logical of hiding places, the back of a player's jersey, it became known as "the hunchback play." From the first rehearsal the Indians took to it so enthusiastically Warner had to restrain them from springing it too early. In practice it was a welcome antidote to Warner's hard blocking and tackling drills and the Indians rehearsed it daily. On kickoffs the receiving team dropped back into a wedge or broad V in front of the ball carrier—that is, whenever the ball was kicked high and deep enough. Unlike the mobile five-man picket line the colleges and pros use today the wedge involved the entire team. It provided, Warner discovered, enough congestion and poor visibility for the kicking team so that the receiver surrounded by the wedge could stuff the ball up the back of his own jersey or that of a teammate. It required some slick hand work, a little stagecraft, a means of securing the ball under the jersey to prevent a tragic fumble when the runner was heading surreptitiously for the goal line—and it needed a perfect kickoff by the opponents. Warner had the tailor shop sew heavy elastic bands into the bottom of two or three jerseys. The Indians rehearsed the fake show until they had perfected the quick formation of the wedge. Chosen for the hunchback role was Charles Dillon, a tall guard who at 184 pounds was the heaviest Indian that year. He was a strong, straight-ahead runner but hardly as shifty as Johnson, the best return man.

The play was to be saved for the Penn game. But it was late on the schedule that year and so mighty Harvard became the Indians' choice as victims. There was, as usual, a preponderance of confidence and a large weight advantage at Cambridge that season. When Carlisle came to Cambridge, the Harvard football community was, quite frankly, looking ahead to the Penn game the following week, preparing for the week of lively betting on the stock exchange. The firm of Thibault, Pennington & Coldet had put up $8,000 even money on Harvard, a large part of which was soon covered by Pennsylvania supporters over the wires of Dick Bros. There was little action on the Carlisle game, but Harvard substitutes were busy collecting a pool of $250 which they intended to bet against Penn.

On Friday morning before the game Pop Warner took twenty-four players to Philadelphia for the all-day ride on the Colonial Express to Boston. After checking them into the Copley Square Hotel he led them in a walk through the darkened Back Bay streets and they talked about the play and the conditions required for trying it. Harvard was capable of long deep kickoffs, one happy advantage. The Boston papers that week had reported that "the Indians have a whole bag full of tricks to spring in the game," a warning that apparently did not strike terror into Harvard hearts. Their practices were described by reporters as "shiftless" as they prepared for their "light but sandy" opponents. It was one of Warner's lightest teams, yet it had won five of six games before meeting Harvard. The center, an Eskimo named Nikifer Shouchuk, weighed just over 160 pounds; he had an effective low charge and a face so indescribably homely that it made opposing linemen edgy. Captain Johnson, "an artful dodger and a corker at running in punts," according to the week's press notices, was Warner's finest quarterback. (In his retirement Pop named Johnson ahead of all the others he had coached. *Colliers Weekly* selected him as first-team quarterback on its 1903 All-America.) Johnson, a Stockbridge Indian from Wisconsin, was moody and brilliant. After leaving Carlisle and his field command in football he graduated from Northwestern, married a Carlisle girl and earned $4,000 a year as a dentist in San Juan, "with profit to himself and relief to the natives"—a success story that was constantly cited as an example to the students.

Early in the game Johnson's kick returns fooled Harvard's large ends and he was able to break free for long runs. Johnson had perfected the bluff of holding out his arms as if to catch the ball and then moving quickly under its path and taking it in full flight. Harvard was pestered by other unfamiliar Indian maneuvers. Warner had the muscular Exendine drop into the backfield and take a hand-off from Johnson while a halfback faked to the outside (the offense was not required to have at least seven men on the line then). The Indians gained with a simple fake-punt-and-run and used a wing shift, moving two backs up on the line at Johnson's signal, which confused Harvard's stereotype defense.

Carlisle advanced close enough for a Johnson field-goal try and when he made it the entire squad rushed up to the captain and pumped his hand. Carlisle was given no chance to pull the hunchback play in the first half—although Dillon made sure his jersey was pulled out over his pads—but it held a rare lead over Harvard.

The crowd of 15,000 at old Soldier Field—the 35,000-seat Harvard Stadium was opened in late November for the Yale game—included a turnout of nonpartisan Bostonians who had come mostly to be entertained by and to root for the Indians. They stood and cheered when Johnson led the small red-shirted team back onto the field for the Harvard kickoff. Exendine recalled the rise in nervous tension as they lined up to receive the ball. "The stubby referee Mike Thompson raised his arm. Were we ready? Yes, we were. Dillon and Johnson dropped back a little deeper (the field was then 110 yards long and kickoffs started from the 55). The kick was hard and somewhat low, and it went to Jimmy Johnson near the goal. Instantly we realized the kick was made to order. We raced back to form the wedge for Jimmy and Dillon. When Jimmy yelled, 'Go!' we knew he had the ball in back of Dillon's jersey and we spread out temporarily. Harvard spread with us, looking for Jimmy with the ball. Dillon headed straight up field, his arms pumping. Johnson tripped and fell and a Harvard man went down on top of him, then another and another. We could hear the crowd roaring."

For most in the crowd awareness that they were watching an absurd—a brilliant!—piece of football mischief rose with each of Dillon's long determined strides toward the goal 103 yards from where he or Johnson or both had received the ball. At first Dillon looked like a solitary blocker, perhaps assigned to get rid of Harvard's captain Andy Marshall. But his unswerving course, the bouncing hump at the back of his jersey! Arms pointed to Dillon and Marshall, the only Harvard man to take up the chase. The Harvard captain did haul Dillon down after he crossed the goal but by then Carlisle teammates had raced down field to pull the ball from Dillon's jersey and make sure it was in his hands for a proper touchdown. Harvard coach John Cranston, with appropriate indignation at seeing his team fall for such a stubble-field ruse, protested to the officials. But they had been briefed by

Pop Warner before the game, who assured them that Johnson would be stuffing the ball into Dillon's shirt from the side to avoid the penalty against a forward pass on a kickoff return.

Warner's trick play earned a just place in football folklore, but it did not win the game for Carlisle. Harvard, aroused by the deceit, slings and arrows of the lightweight opponents, scored twice in the second half, enough for a 12–11 victory. But at the game's end, in the growing darkness of a last day in October, Jimmy Johnson had Carlisle scrambling toward the Harvard goal line again.

That final, too-late drive is what Warner hoped would be remembered about the game—"I never saw them play better football," he said. But he underestimated the public's fascination with a stunt he knew he could never get away with again. "Indians Turned a New Trick/Introduced Hidden Ball Against Harvard" . . . "Scant Victory for Harvard/Indians Hide the Ball Trick" were Sunday headlines. Warner chose to talk about the play after the game in such a condescending manner that it could only have removed much of the immediate delight for the players:

"It is an old trick I tried once before when I was coach at Cornell," he said. "It worked all right then and I've had it in mind ever since. It can hardly be considered varsity football, but I think it is all right for the Indians to use. Harvard was caught napping. It's a trick that can be used only once in a great while and it pleased the Indians to get away with it."

It hadn't pleased Warner quite enough. The play did not beat Harvard.

High Jumper from the Guardhouse

It would be three years before the return of Pop Warner to Carlisle and the athletic arrival of Thorpe resulted in one of those fateful intersections, timed surely to serve the interests of both of them. Warner had been away long enough and sufficiently missed to come back with more freedom and power vested in his job as coach and athletic director—a franchise to use his imagination and experience to bring real prosperity to the football program—plus the glory and a little extra funding for the school itself. Thorpe, meanwhile, had completed some of his "civilizing" time in the country, had tentatively involved himself in the shops league and pickup sports at the school and, perhaps as a result of his exercise as an asparagus cutter on a New Jersey farm, had added muscle to his narrow frame.

The first football he saw at Carlisle came in early September 1904, and even if Pop was away on the hillside campus at Cornell, it was very much a Warner production. Indian Field, between dormitories and shops and one of the school farms, was the site of two or three opening games, usually against small Pennsylvania colleges, before the Indians went on the road for nine or ten more dates. These home games were as much festival as football with the townspeople pouring into the grounds to hear the smartly uniformed band greet them with "Great Big Indian Chief Loved a Kickapoo Maiden"; the students signaling the arrival of the team in big maize-colored sweaters over their red jerseys with the school cheer: "Minnewa Ka, Kah Wah We! Minnewa Ka, Kah Wah We! Minnewa Ka, Kah Wah We! Carlisle! Carlisle! Carlisle!"—a cheer that had originality and brevity on its side. Often the football became an incidental part of the Saturday celebration by the students as it did that September in the Albright game when Carlisle scored so monotonously that the time was cut to thirty minutes, with the Albright players behind by one hundred points and very anxious not to miss the train back to Reading. The Dickinson series, which had become one-sided and overheated, was restored in 1905 with a meeting in nearby Harrisburg and the racial expressions were kept in overt good humor: a Dickinson student in cowboy suit scalping a Dickinson student in Indian feathers before the game; a dummy dressed in Dickinson uniform punctured by an Indian arrow each time Carlisle scored. After six Carlisle touchdowns and six goals the dummy was limp from arrows.

Most of the football Thorpe saw, or became involved with, during his first autumn on the school grounds was Tailors vs. Harness Makers or Printers vs. Blacksmiths—the shop rivalries that crowded the playing fields with struggling knots of Indian boys every afternoon around four o'clock. The Carlisle varsity, following the course Warner and Superintendent Pratt had set, was often on the road for three or four successive weeks in November and the students had to depend upon the school paper to keep them in touch with the team's progress. One unusual road game in 1904 fired the interest of nearly everyone at school because it involved Haskell, and many students, like Thorpe, had associations on both sides.

Major W. A. Mercer, the military-minded, football-boosting superintendent who succeeded Pratt, interrupted practice one day by striding up with his walking stick in one hand and waving a telegram in the other. Haskell was challenging Carlisle to a game, he said, to be played at the World's Fair in late November, "for the Indian championship of the world." The major wanted very much to go ahead with it, even if it meant playing the game two days after Carlisle was to meet Ohio State at Columbus. But coaches Bemus Pierce and Ed Rogers, who had been a good end at Carlisle and had gone to law school at the University of Minnesota where he captained the football team, were more restrained. They assumed that Haskell would load up for the game, using employees, former players or even a few full-blooded white ringers. They agreed to the game if they, too, as former Carlisle students, were allowed to play.

Carlisle defeated Ohio State, 23–0, using mostly its scrubs. The game at World's Fair Stadium in St. Louis on November 26 turned into a bitter mistake for Haskell, which had been misled by victories over Texas, Nebraska and Kansas. The eastern Indian school was much farther advanced in football and with Rogers at end and Bemus Pierce and his strong brother Hawley in the backfield, the game turned into a 38–4 rout. Only the kicking of Pete Hauser prevented affairs from getting more completely out of Haskell hands. In their frustration the Nebraska Indians began slugging the Pennsylvania Indians in a brief resumption of the Indian wars of the plains, and several had to be dismissed from the game, including Pete Hauser's brother Emil, a hefty lineman who played under his Indian name, Wauseka. The St. Louis *Globe-Democrat* noted that "while there was no doubt about the Carlisle players being Indian, Haskell had quite a few pale faces."

The game was dropped as a poor idea and the two Indian schools never competed in football again. The experience convinced several of the Haskell players, including the capable Chauncy Archiquette and Hauser brothers, that they were wearing the wrong Indian colors. Within a year or two they were enrolled at Carlisle.

Thorpe's early emergence from the anonymity of the boys' quarters, where one hundred of them were assigned three each to the sparse beds-wardrobe-washstand-and-table rooms, was not in athletics but in a military demonstration called by Major Mercer. The superintendent announced in June 1906 that the new American flag with a forty-sixth star representing the admission of Oklahoma to the Union would be raised in a special dress parade on the grounds. A unit made up of Oklahoma boys was given the honor of presenting and raising the flag with the entire school in attendance. Student Captain Fritz Hendricks and Sergeant Mike Balenti, both football members, led the "regiment" of twenty-eight privates, who had done some extra drilling in order to keep in step for the ceremony. Among the chins-up, tightly tunicked privates were Sac and Fox boys Thorpe, Ira Walker, Orlando Johnson and Bill Newashe.

If Thorpe, after more than two years at the school and in and out of the Outing program, seemed to be tolerating the role, some of his Sac and Fox classmates were that spring suffering the consequences of the boarding school confinement and long separation from their home environment. Margaret Bigwalker, who had been away from home since 1901, was suddenly expelled for "immoral conduct." (Whatever her breach of Major Mercer's moral code, it did not rate the severe punishment later given an Onondaga girl and Umatila boy who were caught having intercourse. They were both locked up in the county jail for seventy days.) Major Mercer sent a wire to all Indian school superintendents advising them that Margaret Bigwalker was no longer eligible to be enrolled at any of the government schools. Margaret said her disgraced, tight-lipped good-bys to authorities and her best friends and none seemed to notice how sick she was. Three months after her return to Oklahoma she was dead of tuberculosis.

Shelah Guthrie who had been away from her Sac and Fox relatives even longer than Margaret—she entered Carlisle at the age
of nine in 1896—finally found the homesickness unbearable. She
wrote Agent W. C. Kohlenberg in Stroud: "Please help me to
go home this summer. As it is I am to discouraged to work at my
studies and to recite them nicely." Major Mercer at first refused,
saying that from what he knew of her Indian home conditions
he thought she should be kept away from such influence. But
with Kohlenberg's assurance that Shelah would return in the fall
he allowed her home leave. Another request to the Sac and Fox
Agency for permission to leave Carlisle came from Linda Greyeyes: "One has been away 12 years now . . ."

Emma Newashe, whose Sac and Fox parents were both dead,
was finishing her first year at Carlisle at age fourteen and she
maintained a cheerful contact with her homeland by writing long
"Dear Guardian" letters to Kohlenberg which she signed "Your
ward." She reported regularly on her brother Bill, the baseball
player, who was in Room No. 8 that spring—"the beginning of
the sixth grade," the class that Thorpe would join later in the
year. She wrote of her daily chores in the dining room, of the
recent night a girl in her quarters had hysterics and frightened
everyone within hearing, and she enclosed a report card full of
"very good" or "good."

Brother Bill was more businesslike in his correspondence. His
letter to his guardian weeks later read:

> Please send me $25.00 before 21 July. I want to buy
> summer suit and shoes. I haven't any at all.
>
> Yours truly,
>
> William Newashe
>
> P.S. We are all well.

In athletics that spring Thorpe was a shops-league ballplayer
and a sometimes spectator as the varsity worked through a long
twenty-five-game schedule. By far the most prominent athlete
in the school was a small placid-faced Tuscarora Indian, Frank
Mt. Pleasant, who was setting records in track that even Thorpe
would not improve upon later. Mt. Pleasant, who weighed less
than 140, came to Carlisle from the New York Agency with an

entry card marked "weak heart." But he was soon allowed to compete in track and football. By 1906 he had run the 100-yard dash in ten seconds, the 220 in 22.6 and broad jumped 23 feet 9 inches. Two years later he became one of the first two Carlisle athletes to be sent to Europe to compete in the Olympic Games.

As usual the football boys worked out informally during the summer, and when August and regular practice arrived the familiar heavy figure of Pop Warner was seen on the sidelines, volunteering assistance to coaches Pierce and Hudson and watching the Indian linemen endure the torture of a new bucking strap produced by the harness shop. There was an unusually large turnout for the team and the school paper, *The Arrow*, warned that those students who were there in order to feed well at the training table were out of luck. Only those who qualified for the first two teams would be allowed to swallow the benefits of the special football kitchen run by the gym instructor's wife and two domestic science girls. Thorpe's first football experience would have to wait a year. On September 14, as the team was preparing for its warm-up exercises with Susquehanna and Albright, he was again sent to the country for several months.

While Thorpe was working on the Harby Rozarth farm near Trenton, New Jersey, for eight dollars a month, agreements were made that would lead to Warner's return to Carlisle at a salary that grew to four thousand dollars—unusual for any employee of a government school—and with additional benefits that most Washington bureaucrats of the day could picture only in their most avaricious dreams. The appointment was probably foreordained, but Warner and Major Mercer actually got together with urging from Albert Exendine, captain of the 1906 team. Following the season in which Carlisle won nine of twelve games, Exendine was a guest at the Army-Navy game held in Annapolis. He was seated in a straight-back guest chair on the sidelines when he felt a thunderous slap on the back and turned to greet Pop Warner. The coach and his greatest lineman exchanged congratulations—Cornell had lost but once and tied two games during the season—and Exendine asked Pop why he didn't hurry back to Carlisle.

"You have coaches," Warner said.

"They're not coaches," Exendine replied. He urged Pop to talk to Major Mercer right away. The major and a prominent Carlisle merchant were at the game, both of them resplendent with huge autumn flowers in their lapels and polished canes in their hands. Mercer was anxious to get a forceful white coach to handle the Indians and build up the athletic program. Warner was the obvious choice. After the game Pop caught up with Exendine before he boarded the train back to Philadelphia and Carlisle. "I want you to meet the new football coach," he said.

In April 1907 Sadie Ingalls, a small full-blood girl who had attended the Sac and Fox Agency School with Jim, commented in her required monthly letter home: "Last Monday the first party of country girls went out. I think I will go out the second party. I am sorry to say that James Thorpe is in the guard house for running away from his country home . . ."

Thorpe had been sent to the country again in mid-March, back to the Rozarth farm in New Jersey, but within three weeks he apparently had decided that the forbidding guardhouse at Carlisle was preferable to the endless vegetable rows that needed planting and the frustration of being absent another spring while Bill Newashe and his other friends were playing ball on Carlisle's neatly groomed diamond. (The runaways among the older boys at or near twenty kept the Outing agent busy; there was also an increasing problem of drunkenness among those sent to the country.) Thorpe's confinement in the guardhouse was just long enough to acquaint him with the dank interior of the old powder magazine, which he and other football boys would visit from time to time. He surely couldn't have spotted the small irony in the fact that by running from the vegetable farm battle at Trenton he had ended up in an impregnable lockup built by mercenaries who had lost the original Battle of Trenton.

This was the spring of the "discovery" of Thorpe, that dramatic turning which the accounts of the lives of most people of great talent seem to require, as if, without the singular occurrence, the world might have rolled them quickly into obscurity. Thorpe's discovery by Pop Warner soon enough became pounded into triteness: the small crudely styled boy, an unknown in work clothes, leaves the coach wide-eyed with an astonishing leap, hit, kick, pass, run, etc. In Thorpe's case it was a high jump, and in his memory of the occasion Warner wasn't there at all. He was crossing an edge of the running track and football field one afternoon to play a pickup baseball game when he stopped to watch the varsity high jumpers trying to clear the bar at 5 feet 9 inches. (Whatever the height of the bar—it was probably a few inches lower—history has set it at 5-9.) Thorpe asked if he could have a try, and when he was waved on he took a couple of short practice sprints and kicks as he had seen jumpers do before. To the surprise of the track members and a few students who were watching, Jim rolled awkwardly but surely over the bar. A friend, Harry Archembald, later reported the incident to Warner who suggested that Thorpe start working out with the squad.

It may have happened as abruptly as that but awareness of Thorpe's grasp of baseball, his high-jumping and hurdling abilities had been spread around the school for some time, just as boys always knew who the tough challenges were in marbles, who to hang clear of in wrestling or tackle football. At the annual Class Day meet on April 26, shortly after he was released from the guardhouse, Thorpe, Walter Hunt and Ed Twohearts were the pride of Mr. Henderson's Class Room No. 9. The track meet was the large excitement in a schedule full of Arbor Day ritual. Each class planted a tree—Room No. 9 chose a shade tree for the road to the greenhouse—and offered speeches extolling nature. Among the orators was a proud Shelah Guthrie, now nearly twenty, speaking for the sophomores. School authorities were anxious that visitors see the ceremony by twelve Hopi Indians who had been taken from that resistant nation in Arizona Territory and brought to Carlisle only three months earlier. None of the emaciated-looking, long-haired boys could speak a word of English when they arrived. They submitted to the immediate haircut, were given uniforms and placed in a special class, below Room No. 1 and even the manual children, and drilled daily in English words. At the Hopi Arbor Day tree the boys lined up in front of their teacher, Miss Anna Goyituey, and dutifully sang two verses of *America*, and then the Carlisle school song, with words written by Pop Warner that were hardly designed to acquaint small illiterate pueblo children with the English language:

> You play another team today,
> Keep a goin'.
> You've been playing pretty well,
> No don't take a breathing spell,
> Give the stands a chance to yell,
> Keep a goin'.
>
> If you strike a tougher bunch,
> Keep a goin'.
> You only need a harder punch,
> Keep a goin'.
>
> Taint no use to stand and whine
> When they're coming through the line,
> Hitch your trousers up and climb,
> Keep a goin'.

The Hopi boys managed to "keep a goin'," despite this handicap introduction to their new civilized tongue, and became a favorite administration exhibit of the values bestowed by the Carlisle system. Before-and-after photographs (before, that is, the boys were shorn, scrubbed, uniformed) were distributed to newspapers and periodicals with commentary: "These 12 Hopi Indians who were crude specimens of a low order of civilization when they came here have been so wonderfully transformed . . ." Among the Hopi singers was a spindly-legged boy named Louis Tewanima who used one of his crude Hopi gifts—the ability to run enormous distances—to go to the Olympic Games in 1912 and prosper briefly as a celebrity in the white world before he returned, as most of the group did, to Hopi life.

In the Arbor Day track and field competition the sixth graders finished second, beating out all of the upper classes. Thorpe won the 120-yard hurdles in 19 seconds, was second in the 220-yard dash and first in the high jump at a height of 5 feet 3 inches, considerably lower than the bar he supposedly cleared in his overalls and work shoes. With classmates Walter Hunt and Ed Twohearts, a promising dash man, he joined the twenty-two-man

Carlisle track squad, the start of a long commitment to the sport that would lead to the Olympics five years later. It became a popular assumption that Thorpe burst into Olympic fame with a token amount of preparation, that he really didn't put his mind or body to it until Pop Warner convinced him he could earn a place on the team in the Olympic Trials of 1912. Actually, from early spring of 1907 he was training and competing in track, often in winter meets and frequently with some irritation because it prevented him from playing more baseball. Since Warner coached both track and baseball, Jim seldom had much choice and he was able to pitch only irregularly for the nine. Track was not one of Warner's major fields of study, but he acquired a general knowledge from texts written by leading coaches. He had some firm ideas about training for events which he tried to apply to Frank Mt. Pleasant, Thorpe and others who felt that the sport did not require their full attention until they took their starting positions in serious competition.

Thorpe had a first chance to test his college-level performance in a meet with Pennsylvania State College. He took a second in the high jump behind teammate George Thomas. In the last dual meet of the season at Carlisle, against Bucknell in a dripping late-May rain, he qualified for his first varsity "C" by finishing second in the 120-yard hurdles. He had scored 9 points in dual competition that spring.

The summer exodus at Carlisle—home leave for a few, Outing assignments for many, the completion of training for others, the band's annual two-month engagement at a New Jersey shore resort—varied the tempo for the boys and girls who remained. They were required to respond to bells and formations but there were walks downtown for shopping and Sunday services, and occasional rides on the trolley to Mount Holly Springs a few miles out of town. For Thorpe the summer of '07 meant a decisive change. He was now one of Pop's boys. The threat of being sent out to the country had been removed; there would be some light football training, a chance to play more baseball and in the fall a new privileged way of life at the school. He was one of the summer students who took up the challenge of an employees' nine in a game that drew a large turnout of women teachers, wives,

Indian girls. They were there to root and squeal a little for Pop Warner, whose popularity soared that June when he invited every small and large girl in school for rides in his new motor car, the focus of enormous local curiosity. In the game Warner, who had thrown his arm out as a pitcher at Cornell, managed to sail enough soft curves past Thorpe and other student hitters to hold the score to 4–4 before darkness stopped play.

Most of the varsity nine had scattered for a summer of baseball, which varied from semi-pro to regular organized minor-league competition. Earning summer ball money was one of the Carlisle athletic benefits that Thorpe eagerly awaited (in another two years school authorities decided that baseball professionalism had become so rampant among the Indians they would have to take action, and they dropped the sport). That June, Thorpe watched football players Pete Hauser and Bill Newashe go to the Hagerstown, Maryland, team and reserve quarterback Mike Balenti to Du Bois, Pennsylvania (Balenti was a quick shortstop who later played partial seasons with the Cincinnati Reds and St. Louis Cardinals). Bill Gardner, the left end, played for Sunbury, and Joe Twin and Titus Whitecrow joined the Williams Valley League. Charles Roy, captain of the previous season's Carlisle varsity, joined Newark. Warner did not discourage the flow of his best athletes into summer baseball jobs, but he was nagged by the concern that one of them might find life on the outside too prosperous and fail to return. Two or three years earlier he had a second-string halfback and talented pitcher named Louis Leroy who was so determined to play professional ball that he bolted from Carlisle several times to join a club. Once after a game against Franklin and Marshall College in Lancaster, Pennsylvania, Warner discovered that Leroy was missing when it came time to take the return train to Carlisle. Pop went back into town to make a search, checking along the way with the manager of the Lancaster pro team. No, the manager said, he didn't have any Indians but he had just signed a promising young Italian pitcher. Pop found the "Italian" entering a local rooming house and took him back to Carlisle to serve time in the guardhouse. After that Leroy was known among the students as the pitcher with the "$10,000 arm and ten-cent head." He finally did play briefly in the majors, appearing in fourteen games for the New York Americans in 1905 and '06.

The appeal of baseball for the Indians had been sharpened by the quick success of Charles Bender who graduated from Carlisle at the age of twenty and went directly to the Philadelphia Athletics in 1903. Bender, a Chippewa boy from Minnesota, was an unusual student with a hunger for books—he attended Dickinson College after Carlisle—and a very strong right arm. He was one of the game's most dependable pitchers for a dozen or more years, winner of six World Series games. He was a fine wing shooter and acquired a professional interest in jewels. On his many returns to Carlisle, where he helped instruct the baseball boys, he was a World Series hero to the students, which was as heroic as they came then, and a most visible, useful Indian school product for the superintendent to call upon.

Thorpe did get a chance to play some outside baseball in July and August, and in at least one game he was playing not for just peanuts but chocolate bars. He went with a Carlisle pickup team to Hershey, Pennsylvania, and returned with a supply of chocolates from the sweets factory that became a popular supplement in his dormitory to the uninspiring dining-hall rations turned out by summer cook, Nikifer Shouchuk, and baker, Goliath Bigjim. After three years of anonymity at the school, Thorpe's baseball activities—even his summer assignment in the school paint shop —began to draw comment in the "arrowhead" gossip columns of *The Arrow*, "a paper devoted to the Interests of the Progressive Indian; only Indian apprentices doing typesetting and printing":

• In a game between Big Chiefs vs. Little Chiefs Johnson made a pretty catch off Thorpe's bat.
• James Thorpe is working hard to make the football squad. If James can equal his track records on the football squad, he will be a star.
• James Thorpe had charge of painting detail during the leave of absence of our painter Mr. Cairns and the skillful manner in which he handled his boys as well as the large amount of work accomplished showed that James is interested in his work.

Thorpe had either encountered his first volunteer publicity director that summer or, perhaps, thought it was time to make up for all those old blots on his Indian school files.

The recognition Thorpe received in his first track season and his short travels outside the school gate as a respected athlete (instead of just an Outing pupil serving time as a common field hand) raised his confidence—and also his need for a few non-government-made extras. In July he sent off his first letter and request to Agent Kohlenberg who shared guardian responsibilities with Hiram Holt of Shawnee:

> Dear Sir: I would like you to do me a favor with you and my gardian Mr Harim Holt. to send me Fifty dollars from my lease money being this is my first letter to you I hope that you will fill out my request Well Mr. Kolenburg I am getting along fine and in good health since I left good old Okla. and to return next summer if nothing happens I hope receive the money in a short time these are the needed articals
>
> suit $22.00
> Pannam hat $5.00
> a watch $15.00
> a pair of shoes $4.00
> spending money $4.00
> $50.00
>
> Oh yes how is my land getting along and what is the amount received from the land.
>
> Yours Res.
> James Thorpe

A month later, on August 14, Thorpe wrote again to the Sac and Fox Agent:

> Dear Sir-:
> Taking the time and interst to drop you a few lines of business.

Mr Kolenburg I dropped you a letter a few days ago
and didn't hear from you.

wether you received my letter or not I dont know.

I wrote the letter for money.

it was Fifty dollars, I sent you the needed articals in
the other letter.

Mr Harim Holt is my gardain

I wished you would make correspondence with him
about this matter of business. I am in need of the money
very bad.

Mr Kolenburg take this matter of business in to hand
right away if you please.

Mr Kolenburg if you send the Money Send it personly
to me.

for you dont I will never see but just a part of it.

If you send it through the head quarters here that will
be what they will do. send it through mail to me if you
please.

I think I have money of my own out there.

Mr Kolenburg what is my interst in my father's land
kindly let me know. This will be all trusting I will hear
from you soon.

                    Yours truly Friend
                        Jim Thorpe.

As a landowner, heir, Sac and Fox tribe member Thorpe had
been accumulating small amounts of capital in Oklahoma and
Carlisle which were kept out of his reach and, as best possible,
away from his attention. That feature of civilized life called
spending or pocket money was one the Indians were introduced
to with authoritative caution. In two of the most recent quarterly
payments to the tribe Thorpe and nine other Sac and Fox children had been credited with annuity checks of $45.35 and $29.20
each, which were deposited in the school bank at an interest rate
of 3 per cent. His own allotment was eventually leased for grazing and crops at $250 a year. The usable bottom land of his
father's property—seventy acres—was being rented for $2.28 an
acre; he shared the small revenue with six others. (The final

approval of the heirship of his mother's real and personal property did not come from the courts until 1915.)

Jim was unsuccessful in his efforts to get his fifty dollars or
even an accounting of his funds. (Sarah Mansur, whose lease
money and Sac and Fox annuities were deposited in the school
bank, inquired of her savings that summer and learned they had
reached $638.) Kohlenberg, as agent and guardian for several
students, had received a warning from Carlisle: "Please do not
send money to students except through the Superintendent.
Every student of 14 years or more, who is in good health, has
under our outing system opportunities to earn money, and, under
the rules, is allowed half of it as required . . ."

Since Thorpe's outing experience the previous fall had netted
him only four dollars spending money a month (for three
months) he undoubtedly was in poor financial shape to acquire
both Panama hat and a watch.

Just before Kohlenberg received Thorpe's second more urgent
appeal for funds in August he had a short letter from Sadie Ingalls suggesting that she and Jim were kept busy at school but
that they were receiving some compensation for their hard work:

> There are about two hundred staying for the summer
> while about 800 are out to the country. Nearly all the
> Sac and Fox boys are out except Ira, James, Orlando,
> Stella and I. We work all day but still we are being paid
> —all the buildings are being painted. Doctor's cottage
> and the new hospital are nearly completed. The old
> hospital will then be the residence of the athletic boys
> and I think James will enter the football squad.

V   PRIVILEGED WORLD OF THE FOOTBALL BOYS

Mt. Pleasant's Lordly Throw

When Thorpe reported for practice in August, still too narrow across his sloping shoulders for the pads and red jersey handed him by Wallace Denny, the Indian trainer and later a harsh assistant disciplinarian, football at Carlisle was at the edge of a transformation. The game itself was being restructured through major changes in rules and had been placed under an eligibility code in the East that would bring a little more order to the jungle competition among the college teams. The rewritten rules emphasized open, offensive play in hopes of discouraging the grinding, mass formations and free-swinging roughness that had caused such universities as Columbia to drop the sport. In a 1905 White House conference called to discuss the grim condition of football, President Theodore Roosevelt had given his sanction to the game but urged that it be cleaned up. (The Roosevelt review of the sport came after his son, Teddy, Jr., a Harvard freshman scrub, had experienced an inglorious afternoon against Yale. The Eli frosh concentrated their attack on the unprepared Roosevelt, giving him a merciless thumping and breaking his nose. Harvard protested the tactic as poor sportsmanship.)

Warner was about to seize the most important new offensive allowance, the forward pass, which had been introduced the previous season with cumbersome restrictions, to give Carlisle a "modern" run-pass attack, the most surprising and effective of its kind in 1907. The sweeping new agreements on player eligibility and the general sterilization effort did not discourage Pop from accelerating his own program. The special football quarters, the training table, first-class travel, clothing allowances and payments to players out of the rising gate revenues, the hired publicity hands, the news-clipping services (to measure the sales impact of the team, to bolster individual egos), payoffs to local police to keep a gentle but close rein on the players—all of the now familiar habits of big-time, university-level football were set in motion by Warner during the 1907 season. Pop didn't invent the system, but he added some bold strokes to it. Unlike the more saintly clothed modern coach he did not turn over the responsibilities for luring and coddling of the athletes to assistants or alumni. Pop took care of everything himself, from diagraming the plays to distributing the fringe benefits. He did, of course, have the advantage of dealing with a captive group of Indian athletes, but he sometimes was forced to take unique measures to keep them close enough to Carlisle even to appear eligible to play.

To join the privileged world of Pop's football boys, Thorpe had to make what Warner always regarded as his strongest team at Carlisle. Better, according to Warner, than the near-national championship team of 1911 because he was so well fixed with talent at each position. Jim had to compete with experienced backs in the squad of about sixty. Frank Mt. Pleasant the small quarterback—the fastest Warner ever had—became an early master of the forward pass. No one in football then could throw spiral passes more accurately. Behind Mt. Pleasant was Mike Balenti, the shortstop and one of the best students at Carlisle. Another Oklahoma Indian, Fritz Henderson, was the right halfback. Warner that fall began placing his blocking back out on the wing to team with the end on assignments, a tactic that bedeviled uninitiated defenses. Albert Payne, a Klamath boy who had learned football in the West, was the starting left halfback Thorpe would have to replace. The fullback was Pete Hauser, the heavy runner and good kicker from Haskell and one of the most muscular Indians Warner came up with. Hauser had fallen into trouble with Major Mercer in the spring—for drunkenness and disobeying company officers—and he and Emil, who had given him brotherly encouragement, were dismissed from school. But they were on the football squad in the fall, which was why they had come all the way from Nebraska. (Three Hauser sisters also attended Carlisle; a classmate of one of them said that she wasn't sure who the tougher members of the family were—the boys or the girls.)

Thorpe drew the first full attention from Warner, line coach Bill Newman from Cornell and backfield coach Jimmy Johnson during open-field tackling practice. Forty or fifty players were scattered through the 5-yard blocks that marked the field that year. The horizontal and vertical markings, the gridiron effect, were to assist with enforcement of the new rules which prohibited the quarterback from hitting the line five yards from where he received the ball (to discourage straight mass plays) and the passer from throwing within five yards of center. In Warner's tackling drill a back was given the ball and allowed to run until brought down in one of the zones by a tackler. Two or three times the 155-pound Thorpe ran through the entire squad, to his delight and the mixed reactions of Warner who could not be sure whether he had uncovered a ball-carrying phenomenon or a horrible weakness in the team's tackling habits. Thorpe could run— Warner had recognized that months before—but he was woefully crude at handling the ball, blocking, tackling and kicking. Warner put Thorpe through the same course he used with other newcomers: he let one of the veterans show him the way.

"I think the Indian athletes learned the correct form of doing things faster than whites," Warner once said when asked to compare the two races. "They were trained through their forefathers, for generations, to be great observers and they learned from watching skilled performers. Take the matter of falling on the ball. The novice would stand around and refuse to try until he had watched older players do it. After he had seen experienced players fall on the ball he would try and do it almost as well as a veteran. The Indians, as a rule, were not fond of work but they did like to play and would devote much time to learning the proper way. They were, I found, more persevering than white boys."

Exendine, who had helped Thorpe with the high jump and shot-put in the track season, was an early tutor. Ex had finished his Carlisle work and had graduated but he was back for one more season under a felicitous Warner arrangement: while preparing for Dickinson Law School he would get some physical relief from the grind and the needed subsistence by playing football. (Walter Camp, apparently unconcerned about where Exendine was getting his education, named him to his second All-America team that fall.) Ex, who had earned great respect at the school as a fearless, all-out end and a conscientious student, took Thorpe aside for blocking and tackling instruction. "Thorpe was a good learner," he said. "He was quick at doing things the way you showed him. He wasn't afraid and I kept at him about being mean when he had the ball or was blocking or tackling." (Pete Hauser had been an unwilling witness to Exendine's ability to turn mean; in the Carlisle-Haskell game Hauser played with a tender carbuncled shoulder, and as soon as Ex found out he made a special point of it in his tackles.)

For kicking models Thorpe had Hauser, Mt. Pleasant and Balenti, who was improving as a placement kicker (in the Navy game the following season he scored all of Carlisle's winning 16 points with field goals). He observed Hauser, a strong punter, stand back as deep as twelve or thirteen yards and as soon as the ball was in the air guide his ends by shouting, "Right, Left or Short." Although Thorpe would not be expected to do much passing, he could copy from the best, Mt. Pleasant, who had learned to spin the ball off his fingers instead of lob or push it as other pioneer passers were doing. Mt. Pleasant could throw forty-yard spirals accurately. Warner taught his quarterback to sprint about ten yards to either side (today's roll-out pass) to enable the receiver to get into position and to make the defense wary of a run. Thorpe's early scrimmaging experience came against seasoned linemen, several of whom had played during Warner's first term at Carlisle. Exendine and tackle Antonio Lubo, now in their mid-twenties, were too strong and experienced for many of their matches. Others, mostly full bloods, in Carlisle's strongest line chose to play under their Indian names, and they left opponents with reeling impressions that they had been through an afternoon of Indian wars. Wauseka (Emil Hauser) was huge for a Warner tackle; Little Boy and Afraid of a Bear often flanked Nikifer Shouchuk, the ferocious Eskimo who was by now far more employee than pupil. Among the reserves were Little Old Man, Two Hearts, Cries for Ribs and Owl, who filled in for Pete Hauser. (As Carlisle rolled over victims that fall, including Penn and Harvard, there were increasing

1. Hiram Thorpe, Jim's father, wore a gun belt for this studio portrait.

2. The Sac and Fox Mission School in Oklahoma where Thorpe began his schooling.

3. A group of incoming students at the Carlisle Indian School before receiving their uniforms—and haircuts. *(Photo courtesy of Cumberland County (Pa.) Historical Society)*

4. The student body at Carlisle Indian School lines up on the campus green. *(Photo courtesy of Cumberland County (Pa.) Historical Society)*

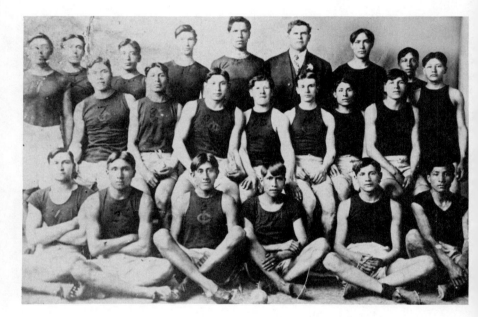

5. In 1907 young Thorpe (second row, center) was on the varsity track team for the first time.

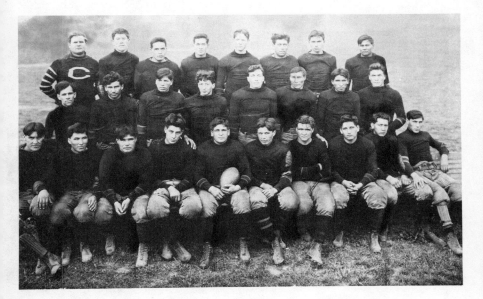

6. One of Carlisle's best teams—1907—with Thorpe (next to Coach Pop Warner in third row) as a reserve halfback. All-America lineman Albert Exendine is in the second row, extreme right. *(Photo courtesy of Cumberland County (Pa.) Historical Society)*

7. Charles Dillon of Carlisle whose hidden ball trick scored a touchdown against Harvard in 1903. *(Photo courtesy of Cumberland County (Pa.) Historical Society)*

8. Gus Welch, Thorpe's friend and roommate and Carlisle's clever quarterback. *(Photo courtesy of Cumberland County (Pa.) Historical Society)*

complaints that Warner had ignored eligibility rules and gentle-man's understandings in his haste to erect an all-Indian power-house by drawing on the best athletes government money could provide forage and shelter for. Warner answered the charges with this accounting: of fifty-four team members, fifty-two were full-time students, five of them—including Exendine and Mt. Pleasant—were taking special courses at the local commercial col-lege, Conway Hall—a Dickinson prep—or Dickinson Law School, which like most law schools at the time had easier entrance re-quirements than the college itself. Forty-seven members were in regular attendance at Carlisle. One regular and one scrub were employees. Two members had played more than four years, the new limit in the East. As for the criticism that Little Boy had been banned from Haskell and all other non-reservation govern-ment schools, Warner didn't bother with a comment. Little Boy obviously deserved a second chance, the same as those players he was using who had run afoul of the discipline at Carlisle.)

Thorpe's immediate reward for making the team of veterans was space in the football boys' quarters, which Warner was in the process of remodeling from its role as school hospital at a cost of about $13,000 (paid out of football income). The boys were given a reading room where they could follow their careers in the pages of the Harrisburg *Patriot,* the Philadelphia *North American,* the Boston *Herald* and other newspapers. There were pool tables for the players' use, even a music box. The foremost luxury was the special kitchen and dining room which assured long relief from the bland, cheerless meals of the school's main dining hall. The students ate a standard breakfast of coffee, oat-meal (no milk or sugar) and gravy that was varied once a week with a meat pie. At dinner there was butterless bread, an abun-dance of beans, pearl hominy or rice and buckets of gravy and occasionally ginger cake. To satisfy their longing for fruit, a taste which many had acquired in the country, the regular students saved their money for the periodic trips to town (one day for the girls, another for the boys) and a chance to stock up at Frank Farabelli's fruit stand on North Hanover Street, the auto-matic last stop on the way back to the campus. For the football boys Pop Warner made sure there was milk, beef and potatoes and butter with the bread on the training table. Some of the older boys acquired such cosmopolitan eating habits on long trips that they regularly ordered oysters on trains and in hotel dining rooms.

The 1907 season started with a customary midweek warm-up game against Lebanon Valley. Thorpe played for the first time, coming in for Payne in the second half with a scrub backfield of Winnie (for Hendricks), Owl (for Hauser), Island (for Mt. Pleasant). Louis Island, an Oneida, was not good enough to push Mt. Pleasant or Balenti at quarterback, but he later went to Haskell and made a football name for himself. Carlisle ran up 40 points in the shortened game played in the rain against "plucky Lebanon Valley," as the papers reported the next morning. Carlisle's real home opener was scheduled for three days later, a Saturday game against Villanova.

Although the early games served as a useful promotional build-up for the team and provided needed conditioning, Warner could regard them as a show of altruism, beneficial mostly to the spirits of the eight hundred or more pupils on campus. They were the only games that didn't make a profit. Pop believed that football, like any commodity, had to be sold to the public, so he hired an aggressive local advertising-promotion agent whose account was Carlisle football. Hugh Miller, a letter-shop owner, built up a "news syndicate" of more than 150 papers and supplied them with everything from florid game reports to Pop's gloomy midweek practice propaganda and misleading injury lists. Later, as client demands for Carlisle football news increased, Miller was assisted by E. L. Martin, the editor of the Carlisle *Evening Herald* and correspondent for the Associated Press and Philadelphia *Evening Telegram.* Warner paid Martin $300 a season plus expenses for the distribution of placards and bills and bought him a $140 box camera to take portraits and game pictures for the newspapers. Miller's success in placing his "news items" with the major press in Philadelphia, Pittsburgh, New York and Chicago would make him the envy of modern sports flack pounding after the same high huckster scores. In 1907 Warner proved that the return on a small ad-promotion investment could be spectacular.

Warner and Miller made a strong effort to sell the Villanova game, one of the surer attractions at Indian Field. Miller reported that there was much local betting on the eve of the game—with odds about even that Villanova (or Villa Nova, as many papers spelled it) would not score; there were descriptions of the Carlisle boys, fit and ready in their new athletic quarters near the playing field. In the advertising scattered around Harrisburg, Steelton, Shippensburg and Chambersburg, the public was reminded there was plenty of room for autos and "no exchange for their admission or parking." In downtown Carlisle the game was billed on a banner stretched above the main street.

The promotion and a clear, cool September 25 brought out a crowd of three thousand, enough to fill the extra seats arranged on the hill east of the field and many watched from their autos parked farther back on the slope. Villanova, which was accustomed to playing a few big teams such as Princeton, Penn and Yale, was unable to contain the Indians' speed or the passing and kick returns of Mt. Pleasant. Pete Hauser scored and kicked a field goal, and then Warner waved in his reserves, giving Thorpe a chance to play briefly before the largest crowd of people he had seen.

As the Indians ran through the early opposition—another midweek game against Susquehanna as well as away games against State College and Syracuse—Thorpe was growing more comfortable in his position. He had learned to take the hand-offs and pitches from Mt. Pleasant and Balenti and to stay behind his blockers until he could break into the clear. At Buffalo for the Syracuse game Carlisle drew a crowd of twelve thousand, many of them Indians from Canada or upstate New York reservations, and when Warner sent in a substitute he was compelled to run through a gauntlet of yelling, shouting Indians who were pressed close to the field. Warner's new offense dazzled the correspondent from the Buffalo *Express,* who wrote: "With all the craftiness and cunning of their race Coach Warner's proteges resorted to trick plays and fake formations. Mt. Pleasant feigned a punt but instead ripped off a pass to Gardner for 30 yards . . ." One of the Syracuse players, Ford Park, recalled later: "They were especially wily because of the pass. The Carlisle ends wore white helmets, the halfbacks red ones and they had half footballs sewed on their shirts [the fake footballs were soon declared illegal].

When one of those high passes descended they all took off and
I had my hands full keeping track of them. I broke up some of
the passes by pushing the eligible receiver. There was no interference then."

On Friday before the Bucknell game, played at Carlisle in
mid-October, press agent Miller and Warner arranged for a Pho-
tographers' Day and representatives from New York, Chicago
and Philadelphia papers came to take pictures of the Indians.
Those who stayed for the game saw a lot of Thorpe at left halfback, playing in a line-up patched with reserves because of the
number of injuries to veterans. Balenti and Island did the quarterbacking and were limited by Warner to the use of three running plays. The correspondent for the Indian paper criticized
them for weak ball handling and, "both seemed anxious to get
into the limelight by kicking drop kicks. Island did succeed in
scoring in this manner. After the first score, made by line and
end rushes, Thorpe made a long run but dropped the ball. It was
recovered by Owl on the bounce who carried it over for the
score. Thorpe did most of the work carrying the ball and proved
to be an excellent ground gainer." Bucknell was beaten 15–0. In
seven years no visiting team had been able to score a touchdown at Indian Field.

In her letters home to Stroud that October, Sarah Mansur sent
reassurance about all the Sac and Fox pupils and called attention to the emerging celebrity in the group:

We are all writing our letters in this room and thought
it would be nice to write you as I think you are very
much interested in us who are away from home getting
the best education the government can give us. We, the
Sac and Fox children are doing our very best to make
less trouble for the employees around here not only for
that but for our benefit. We are very proud of our only
football boy from home, James Thorpe.
. . . I now work in the sewing room and have just finished several hundred of boys' checked shirts and have
begun on the white shirts. It's a rule now, we have to
make button holes ourselves and sew buttons on, just on
the white shirts.

Thorpe's life had become absorbed with football which freed him from paint shop or lessons in Class No. 10 (a grade below freshman) each mid-afternoon, but the school's controlled cycle kept Sarah at her sewing table and others at their shop work; the No. 9 pupils spent the day out at the school farm studying agriculture; the rule breakers, whose violations weren't flagrant enough to put them in the guardhouse, marched their penalty hours around the bandstand with a log over their shoulder. Teachers had to launch a search of dormitory reading rooms and quarters because of the many *National Geographics* missing from the library. Shelah Guthrie was so troubled with granulated eyes (trachoma) that she was kept out of class until early October—a common handicap among the Indian children and one that later sent Thorpe to the hospital. When the fall list of leading students came out, James Mumblehead, a freshman and mandolin player in the band, led the school with a 9.2 average. Right behind was Mike Balenti. At the Susan Longstreth Literary Society reception Exendine was voted the most graceful dancer. On these clear fall evenings students stayed awake after taps just to listen to Stub Felix, new on the night watch, softly singing an Indian love song as he made his rounds.

The Penn game, at Philadelphia on October 26, was the peak of the athletic and social season for the students. They were encouraged to attend, under faculty supervision, but required to pay their own fare, a financial plunge that was hard for most of them to make. When the Pennsylvania Railroad hesitated to offer the special $3.70 round-trip rate many reluctantly decided to stay on campus and watch the Printers (Typos) vs. Blacksmiths. The 160 self-sponsored students, plus the Carlisle band, who went to Franklin Field—and the Penn crowd of 22,500— were witness to an epochal football game, decisively won by the Indians, 26–6, in a style that was to dominate the new game in the years ahead. The immediate impact of Warner's System and the Indians slick application of it was one of astonishment that Carlisle had clobbered unbeaten Penn. The Philadelphia *North American* commented: "Former students who rolled out in their automobiles or hung on to the straps or running boards of trolley cars, sportsmen who never went to college but love the game, the superb beauty show made up of the football girl and her scarcely less beautiful and fashionable companion, the society matron, never dreamed of a redskin victory." The Philadelphia *Press*, "amazed at the score," was lugubrious: "The gloom that the shadows of dusk cast upon the cut and cleat-marked gridiron was not as deep as that which laden the hearts of these loyal sons of Penn." What actually had happened to Penn was that it fell heavy victim to a persistent passing attack from what Walter Camp later called the Carlisle Formation—a T-formation with one back flanked beyond the defensive tackle, an early version of Warner's single and then double wing and not that far away from modern college and pro sets. Carlisle passed sixteen times and completed eight, a reasonable college output today. Most of the passing was done by Mt. Pleasant, but Hauser also passed well. Late in the game Thorpe threw one that went astray. The rule makers who had introduced the forward pass had made it a risky weapon to handle: if the ball fell incomplete, the passing team was stung with a fifteen-yard penalty; but if the pass was handled by the attacking team and then dropped it could be recovered as a fumble. The Indians became very adept at outscrambling opponents for the loose ball. Carlisle's first pass set up a field goal minutes after the game began. "And such a forward pass, the first trial," commented the *North American*. "It will be talked of often this year. No such puny little pass as Penn makes, but a lordly throw, a hurl that went farther than many a kick." Hauser threw to Gardner who caught it on the run for a forty-yard gain, and Penn's confusion mounted as the Indians mixed the pass, run and quick kick with Mt. Pleasant or Hauser handling the ball. They outgained Penn 402 yards to seventy-six, made twenty-two first downs to three. Carlisle's game was not completely guile, speed and wondrous passes— Antonio Lubo was sent off the field for slugging. Thorpe came into the game long enough for a few hard runs and a kick return and the experience of being part of Warner's advanced strategy must have given all the Indians a lift. They had made their own distinct style a part of the game.

The Denver *Express* reacted to Carlisle's one-sided victory over Penn with this burst of sociology: "The Indian on the foot-

ball field stands in the very front rank. Man for man, pound for
pound he has no superior. Through all the years of 'mollycod-
dling' and paternalism on the part of the 'dominant race' the
hereditary trait in the Indian still manifests itself. He can give
and take with the best of them in the severest strain the white
man can put on the athletic field. In such case there is still hope.
There is no 'race problem' to interfere. The Indian who can stand
a grilling on the football field hath his uses in the everyday stren-
uous life."

Against Princeton in New York the following Saturday the
Indians encountered a meteorological problem with their new
art: they found that the pass did not serve well in the rain and
mud (and against a defense that was set for it). In anticipation
of another major victory Carlisle had arranged for a telegraphed
account sent to the school so that play-by-play progress of the
game could be shown to the students at Indian Field. Rain sent
the production into the gym and there through a gloomy afternoon the students waited vainly for the ball indicator to cross
the goal marked "Princeton." Carlisle gave up 16 points for its
first and only defeat that year.

There were rewards from the Princeton game that only
Warner and his financial clerk, William Miller, could immediately
appreciate, although they would soon benefit the whole team.
Carlisle's share of the game receipts was $9,253, the largest
amount entered in the athletic fund since Miller began keeping
books for Warner the previous spring. The Harvard game, before
twenty-eight thousand at Cambridge, brought far more satisfaction (and profit) to Warner. The Indians defeated their most
glamorous rival for the first time, 23–15, proving the effectiveness of the Carlisle system against a much heavier team. Mt.
Pleasant returned a kick seventy-five yards for a touchdown and
set up two other scores with passes of twenty-five and thirty
yards. "The speed of the aborigines on a dry field and the forward pass lowered Harvard's banner," wrote one observer.
Warner was unwilling to interrupt the smooth flow of his attack,
and he left Thorpe and Balenti tense and waiting on the bench.
The conflict between Harvard frustration and bursting Indian
confidence brought on a few slugging matches. Waldo Pierce,

the 205-pound Crimson guard, was thrown out of the game and Captain Bartol Parker, who weighed 230 pounds as the other guard, had to be nursed off the field. This Carlisle team not only looked different to Harvard but it sounded surprisingly cocky, almost boisterous. Quarterback Mt. Pleasant goaded his line with shouts of "Remember last Saturday!" Captain Lubo gave peppery instructions that could be heard by the crowd banked in the steel and concrete horseshoe. "The Indians used to go through a game with a few mumbled comments and grunts," said a Carlisle follower. "If a play was well executed, you might hear an up end grunt; if it was poorly done, they would sometimes give a downstairs grunt."

Back at Carlisle that night the students were allowed to hold a victory parade and snake dance in town. The traditional procession—the boys wore their night shirts, draped pillowcases over their heads and carried flickering torches—brought the townspeople out on their porches and stoops. In the middle of this ghostly promenade a group of Indian boys carried the "remains" of Harvard on a stretcher covered with a crimson sweater.

Warner took his best-of-all Indian teams on the road for its final games, a two-week trip that would win the West where Fielding ("Hurry-Up") Yost, coach of Michigan's famous point-a-minute teams, decried the use of the forward pass and Alonzo Stagg of Chicago had come up with another "peerless" quarterback in Wally Steffen to replace Walter Eckersall, an All-America from 1904 through '06. The trip to Chicago and Minneapolis gave Thorpe and other first-year players a taste of the first-class travel Warner provided his players—and the opportunity to mix a little rowdy pranksterism with the Pullman luxury. Captain Pratt had regarded the train travel as civilizing and broadening for the Indians; they enjoyed it for the dining-car food, the card games, the horseplay, the chance to locate a bottle of beer or whiskey after a game. One of their favorite mileage-killing sports tested their self-control: after "Indian counting" the player who was "it" was required to stand in the aisle while twelve or fifteen more pressed closely around him; he bent over and closed his eyes while one of the group gave him a lusty swat on the rear end. The victim then straightened up and tried to guess who in the crowd of impassive, unsmiling faces was guilty. Thorpe was made to suffer as victim of a run of pranks—the shoes he was told to leave in the hotel hall for a shine were returned without laces or mixed with someone else's, he was locked out of his room, handed fake messages in the lobby, left clothesless in his Pullman berth. The Indians tried all of the heavy-handed practical jokes that have sustained traveling athletes for years—and enjoyed them enormously.

In Minneapolis for the Minnesota game, Carlisle entertained curious Indians from reservations in the Dakotas and Wisconsin (including Chippewa Gus Welch), who had been drawn to the football spectacle, by winning with the forward pass—one touchdown coming on a fake field goal with Mt. Pleasant throwing to Captain Lubo on a tackle-eligible play, the other a forty-five-yard scoring pass from Mt. Pleasant to William Gardner, Carlisle's left end. In Chicago 28,000 jammed Marshall Field to see "these masters of modern football give an exhibition of its possibilities that will not be forgotten" (Chicago *Tribune*). Mt. Pleasant had broken his thumb in the Minnesota game and Balenti started. He let Hauser do most of the ball carrying, field-goal kicking (three) and some of the passing, including one of thirty-five yards to Exendine for a touchdown. Chicago, losers by 18–4, protested that Little Boy, an ineligible receiver, had actually caught the ball but the Indians made sure it was Exendine, very eligible at right end, who raced across the goal line with it. When Gardner was injured and dazed, Thorpe got off the bench hoping to get into the game, even at unfamiliar end, but the veteran refused to leave the field.

Warner and the team headed back to Carlisle for Thanksgiving, having made believers out of the public and press in the Midwest and having boosted the athletic fund by $16,960 from the Chicago game alone—the highest ever for one day's receipts. In five major road games Carlisle had taken home over $50,000, and football was no longer just a popular activity that paid the costs of other games at the school; it was big business.

Whatever lingering innocence Thorpe and others still held about playing football for the mere competitive sport of it and the applause and respect it brought was removed during the tri-

umphant 1907 season. Superintendent Pratt had started the policy of rewarding the football boys not only with their varsity
"C" but also with practical gifts of a $25 suit of clothes and a
$25 overcoat. Warner, in control of the expanding football prof-
its, was in a position to do more than that to keep his players
content—and to keep them enrolled at Carlisle. During the 1907
and 1908 seasons they were given cash payments totaling $9,233.
Some of it was in regular $10 and $15 monthly amounts for expenses (in the modern athletic department vernacular it became
"laundry money"). Some of it was distributed in the form of
"loans" that were not expected to be repaid (when distance runner Louis Tewanima began representing Carlisle in major invitational meets in the East he rated loans of $350). There were
direct cash bonuses to the regular football players. Thorpe received a total of $500 during 1907 and 1908—better reward than
he found playing minor-league baseball in North Carolina a year
later.

This Warner system, which escaped the attention of the amateur athletic watchdogs who pounced on Thorpe's baseball professionalism, at least avoided the hypocrisy of shielded alumni
pay-offs and procurement deals adopted later by the major football schools. Warner chose pragmatism—the football fund was
booming because of the players; why not let all members of the
association share in the proceeds? At the end of the season
Warner wrote out a check, drawn on the account of the association—in December 1908 it amounted to $4,283—and the pay-
ments were made to the football boys.

The athletic association, which Major Mercer and Warner for-
mally organized (it was later incorporated), was composed of
the superintendent, athletic director, a treasurer and all of the
boys who had won a varsity C. As president of the executive
committee, Warner served as grand disburser. The association
made such financial scores through the '07 season it was decided
to invest some of the money in Northern Pacific and Reading
Railroad bonds, worth about $30,000 at par, purchased below
that and sold at a pleasant profit.

The surge in athletic prosperity scattered benefits throughout
the school and, to a minor extent, enriched the lives of Carlisle

civil servants and townspeople. Warner's own residence, a two-story cottage on the school grounds, was built with $3,400 of fund money—and the utilities were covered. Bills for canned food for the training table from the Springfield Canning Co., which Warner had interest in, were paid with association money. So were tutor fees for football boys trying to qualify for entrance to Dickinson College or the law school. The fund took care of such incidentals as the $5.00 worth of weekly courtesy to the local minister who conducted Sunday afternoon service at the school (the churches, all except the Catholic, alternated each week); the $2.00 payment to the local police every time they caught a student in town without a pass and the more unusual $10 tip to the sheriff for arresting a troublesome girl of loose morals in Chambersburg. There were major campus improvements involving nearby labor—remodeling the school dining hall, new lighting in the boys' and girls' quarters, a print shop and an art studio—that probably would never have found authorized approval in the bureaucratic maze of the Department of Interior.

To the Indian athletes benefiting from the special considerations, the gifts and cash hand-outs, the policy should have seemed a most normal part of their relationship with the whites who had them in their charge. This time, however, they were being paid for services rendered and not simply for relinquishing more land. Many of the football boys were still receiving fractional payments from tribal funds set up by the government; some were getting lease monies on allotments they hadn't seen in years. At about the time Thorpe was receiving his first season-end allowance as one of Warner's established players, he received notice the first week in December 1907, that he and eight other Sac and Fox members at Carlisle were getting credit in their account for quarterly annuity shares of $45.35. For the time being Jim's position in the Carlisle athletic hierarchy removed the necessity of writing another urgent financial message to Agent Kohlenberg in Oklahoma. He could afford his own new hat or ask Warner to write out a voucher to Mose Blumenthal, the local haberdasher. Soon enough he would be awarded more watches than he could conveniently stick in the pocket of his new suit.

In a Swift Crowd of Redskins

The difference between the priveleged football boys and the other Indian students, a gulf that widened with each more successful season, is explicit in the letters Fannie Keokuk sent from Carlisle to the Sac and Fox Agency in the early winter of 1908.

Kind Friend:
Well well I have waited and waited and I am just indignant. I don't see why you keep me waiting so long for my money here I have not had a cent to spend during the Holidays have spent most of my time at the Hospital. I am just going to give up trying. I want you to sell my piano and send the money to me for I do not expect to be home any more. Now really Mr Kohlenberg I have got to have some money. I have a lot of work to be done with my teeth and we have to pay our own expenses with dental work. I remain,
                              Fannie Keokuk

Dear Friend & Guardian:
    You have not sent me any money since I have been here I have been in the hospital the last few days. My but it was lonesome. There was a boy died yesterday of pneumonia fever.
    I never had any money during the holiday. I felt awful cheap. They furnish us only with uniform and work clothes. I am ashamed to go to the dances and stay home Saturday because I have no shoes. I remain your discouraged friend,
                              Fannie Keokuk

Fannie's second letter was written on the eve of a large Saturday reception given in the gym by tribe members from Oklahoma, saluting their new state. Exendine, an impressive figure in dark suit and tie, gave the welcome address and then waltzed across the floor with Texie Tubbs, one of the smoothest dancing partners in the school. Mike Balenti, looking more white than Oklahoma Cheyenne with his hair neatly parted in the middle and slicked down, was busy with Shelah Guthrie on the committee that prepared the refreshments and program of events (which included the singing of a state song to the Civil War tune, "Tramp, Tramp, Tramp"). Pete Hauser limped around the gym, having recently given up the crutches that supported him during his recovery from a leg injury. Thorpe had no role but he was there with the 250 other students for the refreshment and dancing, an activity that was beginning to hold appeal for him. Two weeks later he was back in the gym for his first varsity awards night, the most elaborate banquet of the social season. (A critic of the school remarked that of the top priorities at Carlisle, football ranked first, the band second and commencement third.) Warner and his boys celebrated the awards ceremonial surrounded by red and gold streamers, red and gold candles on red and gold tables where they were served ham, roast turkey, Waldorf salad, nuts, bonbons, coffee by fortunate young waitresses recruited from the older girls' quarters. Pop congratulated Thorpe for winning two varsity C's, in football and track.

The retirement from the Army of Major Mercer in March brought in a new superintendent—and soon a change in the atmosphere—to Carlisle. Moses Friedman, a civilian who had taught in schools in Cincinnati before joining the Indian Service in Arizona and at Haskell, took over the administration. One of the first pupil problems that came to his office was a plaintive request by Fannie Keokuk that she be sent home to Oklahoma. Friedman refused to let her go but he did arrange to have the Sac and Fox Agency transfer $70 to her school bank account. He let her have $5.00 of the sum for spending money. The decision apparently lifted Fannie's morale, even if it didn't do much for her purchasing power, and she celebrated by inviting three of her Sac and Fox girl friends to a card party in her dormitory room.

Thorpe considered the spring of 1908 as the significant beginning of his athletic career at Carlisle, with his membership in

the football brotherhood officially recognized and the apprentice-
ship and impatient bench-sitting behind him. Success for him was
not limited to the playing field—he was drawing approval from
his academic teacher, the shop instructor and the disciplinarian
who monitored students' conduct in the dormitory. In April he
received an academic marking of "excellent" for his elementary
grasp of history, civics, grammar, literature, form & numbers
(geometric design and common fractions). Painting was still his
industrial major (the school offered plain house painting and
fancy carriage painting) and he rated "good." His dormitory
neatness and conduct were also considered "good." With the arrival of spring and the track and baseball season he was back
at the training table in the athletic dorm, avoiding parts of the
school drudgery that stretched from the rising bell at 5:45,
through the morning and afternoon work whistles, the daily recalls. The academic turn at commencement time in April advanced him to a freshman, now nearing the age of twenty-one,
senior to most of his classmates but not as old as several friends
in the athletic quarters. His exalted position as an athlete—
in his white-dominated Indian community the twentieth-century
equivalent of the warrior who had proved himself in campaign
—prompted Miss Wood, the freshman academic teacher, to turn
the class over to him when she was absent for a day. Thorpe took
the responsibility seriously and several pupils said he made "a
fine teacher," a development that surely would have astonished
his early instructors at the Sac and Fox Agency School. It would
have appeared that he had at last found a sort of a home—one
that offered a means for achievement, growing fame, respect, a
little money in his pocket. It was enough to hold him for another
year before he would make a break from Carlisle that nearly became permanent.

Warner entered Thorpe in the Penn Relays at Philadelphia on
April 25 and confirmed his belief that he could compete against
anyone in the high jump. Thorpe won by clearing 6 feet. *The
Arrow* saw in the feat "evidence that the Indian is not just a specialist in football." Although Thorpe managed to score 26 of the
freshmen's 28 points in the Class Day Games by entering several
events, he was at his smoothest and best in the jump and hurdle
races. He had learned to flatten out his trailing leg in the low

hurdles and ran them with unusual economy and grace for his experience. In a triangular meet against Dickinson and Swarthmore he set the school record for the 220-yard hurdles at 26 seconds (later he would get his time down to 23.8). He was outreaching Exendine who had taught him how to high jump a year before, and although Ex was there to coach and encourage he let Thorpe go with his own style. "If Jim had a problem then it was one that stayed with him," Exendine said. "He didn't care about records as such. He badly wanted to win. That was enough. In races he sometimes took the last hurdle far in front and then just trotted across the finish line."

Thorpe was not at this point a one-man track team, as popular history persists; he was one of a very swift group of Indians who outpointed eight other Pennsylvania colleges in a state meet at Harrisburg on Memorial Day. A crowd of eight thousand cheered Thorpe's high jumping, the sprinting of Walter Hunt, Mt. Pleasant's great leaps in the broad jump and the tireless laps run by tiny Louis Tewanima, his shirt and running shorts bagging in the wind. Tewanima's track career at Carlisle really started that spring, blooming out of the southwestern desert where running was a pride of life, and because at first he had to rely on little but his stamina he ran his competition into the ground sooner than Thorpe did. When Tewanima was brought to Carlisle the previous year, after he and the other Hopi boys had been taken prisoner and placed at a government school at Keams Canyon, on the edge of the Painted Desert, he was so physically frail he seemed a doubtful bet to last through a wet Pennsylvania winter. The doctor's report referred to his "round shoulders, prominent clavicle . . . has emaciated look." Tewanima and his Hopi friends—Glenn Josytewa, Joshua Hermeysava, Tala Yamtewa, Washington Talyumptewa—took to hanging around the running track where Warner noticed them as "a wild-looking bunch with furtive eyes." But when he saw them circle the track again and again, running evenly and with little effort, he knew he had the core of a cross-country squad and in Tewanima, the fastest of the Hopi boys, a long-distance runner with infinite possibilities. By mid-spring 1908 Tewanima was running so far ahead of the crowd that Warner decided to enter him with Frank Mt. Pleasant in the Olympic Trials. That summer, in the games in

England, he finished ninth in the crowded, controversial marathon that began on the lawn of Windsor Castle and ended 26 miles and 385 yards later in the London stadium where Dorando Pietri, an Italian candy maker, led the field only to collapse four times on the track and be bodily supported across the finish line in front of the Royal Box by overconsiderate race officials. Tewanima's personal showing so soon after he had put on his first pair of running shoes was lost in the international clamor that followed when Pietri was disqualified and Johnny Hayes of the United States was awarded the gold medal.

When the '08 track season came to a close at Carlisle, Thorpe realized an ambition he had suppressed through April and May —he pitched a couple of ball games at the end of Carlisle's 27-game schedule, including a 1–0 shutout against Albright. In June Thorpe asked for and was given home leave, not a difficult arrangement for one of Warner's boys to make. Thorpe left with the understanding that he would return and finish his course at Carlisle, which obviously was going to take him more than the prescribed five years. Superintendent Friedman, who had less faith in Thorpe's return than Warner sent out this Indian Service bulletin after he had gone: "I beg leave to inform you that the following pupil should not be enrolled at any Indian School— on leave from the Carlisle School: James Thorpe."

VI   THE FOOT-LOOSE LEFT HALFBACK

Over the Winter Hill

On his first authorized leave from the Indian schools Thorpe "went home to do some fishing," as he put it, which suggests that he had already slipped comfortably into the argot of his new occupation. He was early in a long line of baseball and football players who would return to Oklahoma in the off-season "to go fishing," a term that did apply to the active pursuit of channel cat-fish, bass and crappie in those still waters but also covered a wide range of pleasure-seeking, from plain visiting to indoor and outdoor carousing. (Just before admission to the States the Territory had succumbed to the hellfire speeches of the anti-saloonists and voted in prohibition, which was death to the swinging-door establishments of Keokuk Falls and did drive the distilleries into the bush. For the Indians, who had been "protected from liquor traffic . . . as long as the grass grows and water flows," it merely meant a relocation of the source of supply.)

Jim was able for the first time in four years to share talk and whiskey with brother Frank and get caught up with the family that Hiram had left behind to struggle with the allotted soil or grow into school age in the custody of guardian and Agency. His young sister, Adaline, "bright, attractive but extremely wilful," according to her elders, was about to be enrolled in the government school at Chilocco, in northern Oklahoma (where she demonstrated her Thorpe independence by running off from an Outing home and returning to Sac and Fox country). Ed, now nine, was the last Thorpe to be sent to the Sac and Fox boarding

school. Older brother George had an allotment and a first wife,
a Shawnee named Ella Washington.

Frank, the half brother, and Jim's sister, Mary, seemed to be
carrying the heaviest ends of the burden as Hiram's children and
of the subjugated role of the Indian in the new Oklahoma.
(Within the last two years white men had taken nearly three
million barrels of crude oil out of a place they called the Glenn
Pool; in fast-growing Shawnee, half-breeds and full bloods now
found it more comfortable to keep to the far end of East Main
Street.) Mary was considered deaf and dumb, but she had
learned to read, write and do some lip reading. Frank, Jim and
other relatives could understand the broken, whispery sounds
that came from her damaged throat; outsiders found her strange
and vaguely threatening. At nineteen she was married to "a
worthless Mexican who does nothing and spends money fool-
ishly." They had one child, a son named Isreal. Mary divorced
her Mexican husband only to enter a disastrous one-year marriage
with a Potawatomi half-breed, "a man very averse to work" but
keen on whiskey.

In later years she took strength from her handicap, but it left
her humiliated and vulnerable as a young woman. She succumbed for a time to the charlatan promises of help at "Dr.
Keene's Private Sanitarium" ("We cure appendicitis, piles, fistula,
anal and rectal diseases without the knife. We also cure cancer
and rheumatism"). Dr. Keene did not cure Mary after $202 worth
of treatment. Jim's attachment to Mary may have developed from
an early concern for her miserable fortune (he later contributed
money to provide proper medical attention). He also admired
her fighting qualities, which were both spiritual and very real.
The latter came to the attention of local law enforcement
officers one day when two Kickapoo women, who had made the
mistake of antagonizing or ridiculing Mary, filed complaints because of the injuries they had sustained in a fight with her. Another time she sent a Shawnee policeman sprawling when he
tried to intervene in a little street discipline she was giving
her son Isreal. Her physical strength, the strange voice sound
and the respect she had from those who knew her well led to a
belief that she possessed supernatural powers. Mary couldn't lift
an understandable English or Indian word out of her damaged

throat, but she could tie a bunch of cornstalks together and spread the fear of voodoo through neighborhood women. In weekend Indian football games the Sac and Fox played on Red Hill near the North Canadian (men had to kick the ball as in soccer; women could run with it) Mary's appearance could change the tone of the competition. Women dropped out of the game to look after their children and some of the men, who had bumped into Mary in past games, suddenly found things to do on the sidelines. It was regard for a Thorpe that much amused her football brother.

Frank's unennobled role in the restricted Indian world of Oklahoma that summer of 1908 was a mirror of what Jim's life likely would have been without Carlisle as an outlet. Frank was working thirty acres of cotton and corn near Bellemont, supporting his Shawnee wife and four children and occasional boarders like Jim or young Ed. He was as ill-equipped to grapple with the soil as most Sac and Fox crop growers; his needs included a team of horses, a wagon, plow, cultivator, harrow and hoes. At the Agency, where he applied for funds to buy tools, Frank was considered a willing enough worker but one "who cannot stand temptation very well," the euphemism for drinking whiskey steadily or simply on occasion. He had "a hard name among people that have had some dealing with him"—an easily acquired distinction for a son of Hiram.

To the Indians of Oklahoma, football was no longer a strange game played at distant eastern universities. The local Indian school at Chilocco had fielded a team against the Oklahoma Aggies at Stillwater, and Haskell was traveling as far as Texas, Arkansas and Louisiana for games. More and more tribe members were writing letters or returning from Carlisle with word of the football feats of the Hausers and Balenti of the Cheyennes, Exendine of the Delaware, Hendricks of the Caddo and now, in the fall of 1908, Thorpe and Newashe of the Sac and Fox.

Both Jim and Bill Newashe had left Oklahoma in late summer to report for football practice, paying the rail fare of $31.95 from Oklahoma City. Newashe, a substitute lineman, had grown so fat over the summer that his sister Emma was embarrassed to stand next to him; Thorpe, filled out to about 175 pounds, was certain to start at left halfback and do much of the punting and place-kicking. (Newashe spent most of the games on the bench, as Thorpe had the previous year, but he became a faithful chronicler of his fellow tribesman's football rise, writing of his place-kicking that defeated Penn State and Syracuse and of his long run against Penn.)

Thorpe's kicking and his occasional breakaway runs were the surprise developments of Pop Warner's second season after his return to Carlisle. The team badly missed the leadership and play-calling of Mt. Pleasant. Balenti did well enough mechanically at quarter, but the offense lacked the passing finesse and quick-hitting capability of the '07 team. Games against Penn State, Syracuse and Navy were won by the field-goal kicking of Thorpe and Balenti; there were no impressive touchdown drives or pass-run plays for scores against Penn or Harvard.

Yet the Pennsylvania game was one of the most bitterly contested in the long series. Thorpe, years later, said it was the hardest game of football he had played. Both teams were unbeaten going into the game on October 24, and Penn with its "fastest team ever" seemed a match for the Indians' speed. The Quakers offered several weighty, Walter Camp All-America selections, including tackle Dexter Draper, end Hunter Scarlett and a towering halfback, Bill Hollenback, strong on offense and defense. The game was given a proper Carlisle-Penn build-up of press clichés which, at the time, still had some fresh flavor. Warner worried about the bruised and limping on his squad, and Penn responded with: "We place as much stock in the ambulance clang that comes from Carlisle as we would in the story of a woman telling how old she is."

"Penn fears the placement kick!" was the cry of a bulletin out of Philadelphia, which went on with a dramatic description of Carlisle's unstoppable weapon: "The Indian field general does not even wait for 3rd down in order to try for a field goal. Thorpe drops back, the little quarterback (Balenti) kneels on the ground, the Indian forwards dovetail themselves into a tight line of defense. The ball is shot back hard to the little quarter, quickly placed on the ground and bing! the cunning toe of Thorpe sends it spinning between the goal posts and four points go up on the scoreboard."

Perhaps Thorpe and Balenti saw too many such press clippings in the reading room at the football quarters in Carlisle because on game day they couldn't get together on a successful field-goal try. Thorpe's failures from placement in the first half left the Indians behind, 6-0, Penn having scored after punting and downing the ball (an onside kick then) at the Carlisle 5-yard line. Thorpe experienced the major frustrations and minor triumphs of a tightly drawn defensive battle, giving and taking in the collisions against Dexter, Hollenback and others. Penn's discovery of the afternoon was that Thorpe, in an open field, had too much speed to overcome. In the second half he jumped through an opening outside Penn's left tackle, made two quick cuts in the backfield to avoid Hollenback and safetyman Reagan and ran sixty yards for a touchdown, tumbling over the goal with the ball. His extra point tied the game, the only non-victory in twelve games for Penn that season.

Thorpe's long run proved costly to one Sac and Fox girl, Stella Ellis, who had come from Carlisle to cheer him on. In all the touchdown delirium she lost her voice and was left with a whisper for a few days. Shelah Guthrie had to be treated for hoarseness, as did several of the other girls. Emma Newashe came to cheer, too, but she found more than just football excitement in Philadelphia: "I didn't get to see enough of the city," she wrote. "We had to sing for our dinner before we got it. It did not cost us one cent. This was at 'Gimbles.' We had colored people to wait on us and we had everything we wanted. In going to the Auditorium we went up in elevators and my they made me dizzy. Our object in going to Philadelphia was to see the football game. It was between Pennsylvania University and the Indians of Carlisle. James Thorpe certainly did fine work. I cannot say anything about my brother because he did not play although he was ready to play in case someone got hurt."

The Indians lost only twice in thirteen games but the draw in Philadelphia was the peak of a season that saw the sons of Harvard—and burly products of Gunnery, Andover, St. Paul's, Middlesex and St. Mark's—shut out the Indians 17-0. Harvard controlled the game and Thorpe spent a long afternoon in kick formation (eight for 342 yards). Once on a kickoff—from the 55-yard line—he sent the ball over the goal posts. It was Thorpe's strong leg more than anything else that fall which drew the attention of Camp and earned him a listing on the third All-America team. Only once did Carlisle threaten Harvard with some of the Indian daring and enterprise that had won the game a year before. On a direct pass from center Thorpe faked an end run and pitched out to Hendricks. The right halfback then threw a long pass to Wauseka who was pulled down on the Harvard ten. Thorpe rushed to the four and then, to the mortification of Pop Warner, the Indians tried a pass that was intercepted.

Warner had scheduled late-November games with the University of Minnesota and St. Louis University, counting on the promised gate percentages of 33–50 per cent to make the trip well worth while. After losing to Minnesota and beating St. Louis (with receipts of $7,297) Pop put the boys back on the train and headed west for two hastily arranged games at a flat $2,500 guarantee. On December 2 Carlisle beat Nebraska, 37–6, leaving the Midwesterners dazed by cross-bucks, fake kicks and passes. The Nebraska papers referred to the visitors as the "Aborigines," the capital A apparently out of respect for the "wonderful interference that sometimes bowled over as many as five or six Cornhuskers." After convincing the natives at Lincoln the Indians boarded the Union Pacific for Denver and a game three days later. It was, expectedly, snowing in Denver and Carlisle had to rely on field goals by Hauser for its winning scores. Thorpe worked hard on the frozen, snow-swept ground but he fumbled occasionally and was shaken badly enough on a couple of occasions that time had to be called. It was with relief that the team climbed into its Pullman car and returned to Carlisle, even though the boys were greeted with the discouraging news that measles was rampant in the girls' quarters and more than thirty were quarantined two weeks before Christmas.

For the winter social season at Carlisle—the regimented one on campus and the more impromptu, unsanctioned occasions—the football boys had only to visit Mose Blumenthal's shop on Hanover Street and fill in their wardrobe needs. Before the team had gone west in November 1908 Warner had written Blumenthal one of his customary authorizations: "These are the boys to supply with clothes and other merchandise [and charge to the

9. Coach Warner with Indian stars, 1907–8: Emil Wauseka (Cheyenne), Jimmy Johnson (Stockbridge), Albert Exendine (Delaware). *(Photo courtesy of Cumberland County (Pa.) Historical Society)*

10. In the Carlisle backfield: Alex Arcasa (Colville) at left, Gus Welch (Chippewa), Possum Powell (Cherokee), Thorpe (Sac and Fox). *(Photo courtesy of Cumberland County (Pa.) Historical Society)*

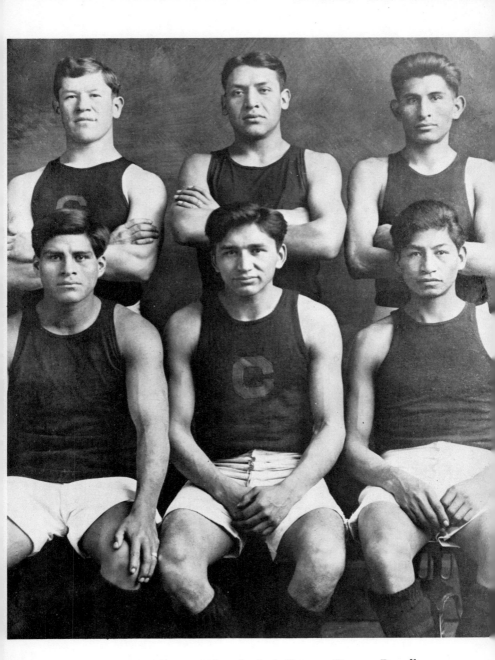

11. The 1911-12 Indian basketball team: Possum Powell, Joel Wheelock, Bruce Goesback (front row); Thorpe, Henry Roberts, Wounded Eye. *(Photo by Cumberland County (Pa.) Historical Society)*

12. The 1912 Carlisle varsity. *In back row, from left:* Williams, Welch, Thorpe, Warner, Hill, Garlow. *Middle row:* Calac, Bergie, Wheelock, Powell, Guyon, Bush. *In front:* Vetterneck, Large, Arcasa.

13. For the wedding photo, October 1913, at Carlisle, Thorpe stood behind his bride and former schoolmate, Eva Miller. Best man Gus Welch is on Thorpe's right.

14. Thorpe hurls the discus during preparations for the 1912 Olympic Games. (*Photo by Culver Pictures, Inc.*)

15. In a line-up of members of the 1912 U. S. Olympic squad Thorpe wore turtleneck warm-up sweater. *(Photo by Culver Pictures, Inc.)*

16. Before the 1912 Olympics, Indian competitors Sockalexis, Thorpe, Tewanima. *(Photo by Culver Pictures, Inc.)*

17. In the New York Giants offices Thorpe, in 1913, posed for signing of his contract. (*Photo by Culver Pictures, Inc.*)

18. On the Universal Studios set, movie bit player Thorpe
with Harry Stuhldreher (*left*) and Frank Carideo, during
filming of *The Spirit of Notre Dame*. (*Photo by Culver Pictures, Inc.*)

athletic association] . . ." He listed the first twenty-two football names. Thorpe's needs over a period of time, which did not exceed fifty dollars and were sometimes only ten or fifteen dollars, hardly approached those of several clotheshorses on the team.

There was more to visiting Blumenthal's than selecting suits off the rack. Mose was a rooter, patron and custodian of a legitimate hangout where the Indian athletes could stand under the glory of their team photographs and banners and talk shop among themselves or with local admirers. It was a place to discuss the basketball game in Philly with Pennsylvania in which Thorpe had contributed to the poor shooting but clean play of Carlisle in a 9–30 rout (no fouls against the Indians for an entire half!); or the indoor track meet at Trenton where Thorpe won the high jump; or the new baseball coach, Toby Bassford, who was taking over for the busy Pop Warner and faced a 1909 schedule of thirty games. A visit to Blumenthal's for merchandise also could mean an added $.75 or $1.00 for a little whiskey to cut through the midwinter boredom and help enliven the Saturday night dance in the gym.

Thorpe had not yet acquired the reputation of being one of the quicker football boys to a beer or bottle of whiskey, but he was making progress in a very competitive field. Drinking, like other simple pleasures, was made easier and the penalty for getting caught less severe if you were an Indian athlete and not just an anonymous student struggling for an industrial certificate in the tinsmith shop. Since Carlisle saloon keepers were prohibited from selling to Indians, the students either paid local blacks to get liquor for them or had a tribe member with a near-white appearance in civilian clothes buy for them. The sources for the football boys were more diverse—one of the assistant quartermasters became a reliable supplier; a school clerk received regular deliveries from the local beer wagon; bartenders were disposed to the idea of serving a player whose name made the Harrisburg and Philadelphia papers. The football boys stood a much better chance of getting drunk, disorderly, caught—and of surviving the school's most severe punishment, expulsion. (They were, however, often enough clapped in the guardhouse to sober up for a few days and it was the duty of Arthur Martin, Warner's secretary and public relations man, to go to the superintendent's office with a written request to release key personnel before a game.) The school's principal teacher, John Whitwell, admitted that the problem of drinking among the students was always just beyond disciplinary control. "If we sent them all home that have gotten drunk I am afraid we would not have many left," he said. Superintendent Friedman did mount an effort to shut off the liquor supply at its source by sending a group of volunteer students, each furnished with one dollar or more, into town to buy bottles. Co-operative police were then supposed to swoop down on the guilty saloon-keepers. But the police, not wishing to upset the local economy, had tipped off the saloon owners in advance and the young student-detectives came back to school empty handed.

Drinking by the Indian students, which would not appear excessive by modern boarding-school standards of consumption, ranked somewhat below "debauchery" and certain forms of theft among the serious offenses in the school's disciplinary code under Friedman. Stealing—specifically pie-stealing from the bakery— was a heinous crime, judging from the experience of a boy who had found a way to make off with pies in the middle of the night and bring them back to his room for a feast; he was caught, turned over to the local law and put in jail for thirty days. (In Captain Pratt's administration a student charged with stealing was required to march up and down wearing a sign, "I Am a Thief," over his uniform.)

Debauchery included just about any covert commingling of the sexes at the school—a boy or girl getting together in the back part of the school chapel or meeting at the edge of the fairgrounds, or a boy sneaking into a room at the large girls' quarters. If debauchery wasn't committed on these occasions, school authorities seemed to assume it was only because they moved in in the nick of time. The example of the two students who were discovered making love and were sentenced to the county jail for two months made normal relations between twenty-year-old boys and girls (many of whom would have been married at that age on the reservations) acts of considerable daring. Still "debauchery" plunged on, despite the puritan lines drawn tightly around the campus. Girls were "ruined" going to pageants and visiting cities with the football team; a girl "unfit to represent the school" was allowed to accompany the band to a concert series at the Jersey shore; a transfer student from Haskell, named Minnie Apache, stirred distress in the superintendent's office when it was learned she was receiving peyote in packages from home; during two school terms sixteen girls were expelled for "immoral behaviour," which covered a range of transgressions; the football boys, like all football boys in seasons to come, appeared to indulge more and get away with more. If it all hadn't happened at a government training school for Indians in the early 1900s, it would have seemed a most normal rite of passage in the American educational system.

Thorpe's name did not frequent this list of intemperate athletes, but by late winter of 1909 he was stretching the patience of Superintendent Friedman by his disregard for school attendance requirements. In a letter to Agent Kohlenberg, Friedman described Thorpe as "far from being a desireable student." In February and again in March he and teammate Sampson Burd disappeared from school together for a few days—long enough to be marked "ran," the Carlisle equivalent of AWOL, in their permanent records. Despite his breakout, Thorpe managed to receive "good" in deportment that sophomore term; his running mate Burd was "fair" in industrial conduct, "poor" in dormitory.

As typical football boys, Burd and Thorpe shared much in common in their backgrounds. Burd's father was white, his mother was a full-blood member of the combative Blackfeet (Piegan) tribe. While Thorpe was attending the Sac and Fox Agency School in the 1890s, Burd was at Willow Creek Boarding School beneath the Tobacco Root Mountains of southern Montana. Burd, who arrived at Carlisle two years after Thorpe, was similar in size, both about 5′ 11″ and a little under 180 pounds in 1909. Sampson was a good-looking boy with a near smile in his dark eyes most of the time, and his appeal to girls led to a small scandal and also to a tragic marriage. On girls' day in town Sampson was accused by a teacher of "victimizing" an Alaskan girl, "one of our very best girls." Sampson's real personal anguish came in a love affair with a Chippewa girl from Michigan named Margaret Blackwood, whom he married after her graduation from Carlisle in 1910. She and Sampson went to Montana to meet his parents after the July wedding. Soon after their arrival she became ill of acute meningitis and died. They had been married six weeks.

Sampson wired the news to Carlisle, attended to the burial in Michigan and returned to Carlisle and went on to record a few personal achievements. He was elected captain of the 1911 football team; became a spirited campus debater (he and Gus Welch argued "The Sherman Anti-Trust Act Is a Hindrance to Progress in the U.S."); and as soon as the 1911 season ended he entered Conway Hall for college-preparatory work.

If winter at Carlisle sent the football boys over the hill, it brought edgy complaints from the usually buoyant Emma Newashe, who wrote Agent Kohlenberg in late January 1909:

> I have not had a coat this winter. I do not prefer a short coat but the long warm coat. I am also in need of shirt waists and would be pleased if you would send me a few at least, a few corset covers, petticoats, a dress fit to be worn at a reception. The Mercers will have a reception this month and as I am the President of that society I certainly will have to look descent. If I am not dressed as if I was at a reception why what will they think of their President? Mr. Kohlenberg just you put yourself in my place, having no parents to look after you, to send you no clothing . . .

In a following letter she took up the cause of brother Willie, saying that he was anxious to leave Carlisle but that Superintendent Friedman wants him to remain through the baseball season: "It is not for his own benefit that he wants him to stay here but only to stay and uphold the reputation of Carlisle in athletics. Not that I mean he is so important in athletics but he is a baseball player and a dandy first baseman."

Willie was not only a dandy first baseman he was a .400 hitter and the team's best catcher and he agreed to come back for another year on the Carlisle nine. By the time Class Day arrived at the beginning of spring Emma was again infused with school spirit: "Last Wednesday we had a class contest and it was not much of a contest after my class got through the others. We had James Thorpe, George Thomas, Joel Wheelock and Albert Scott to represent our class. James alone made 33 points and my we were in our glory sure when we carried our banner off and out points numbered 62 in all."

Each first place in the all-class meet was worth a watch fob from Pop Warner, and Thorpe ended up with a supply of five— enough to serve his own time-keeping needs with an ornament or two left over for a reluctant bartender. The presentation of watch fobs by Warner was symbolic of a new policy he and the others on the executive committee of the athletic association adopted early in 1909. The decision was made to stop cash bonuses from the association fund to the athletes, while maintaining the other fringe benefits such as the open merchandise accounts and the gifts of suits and coats. Warner may have felt pressure from other schools that had learned of the practice; the payments may have promoted too much independence on the part of the athletes; or there may have been concern over the drop in total assets, down from $42,000 in 1907 to $26,000 at the end of 1908. The cutoff led to some resentment among Warner's boys and, later, to serious questioning of what was happening to the money accumulated by the organization. The change in policy could only have encouraged Thorpe to seek an income by playing professional baseball.

In track that spring Thorpe, Tewanima, George Thomas and five or six others provided enough talent for Carlisle to sweep through a succession of dual, triangular and invitational meets. Thorpe continued to reduce his time in the hurdle races, became more consistent in the high jump and set a personal mark with the 16-pound shot at 43 feet. He found more time to play baseball in May and in his first start as a pitcher stopped a team from Hagerstown, Maryland, without a hit. At season's end he pitched a shutout against Millersville State.

In mid-June came the seasonal flight of the Indian ballplayers to the professional and semi-pro leagues. Mike Balenti, captain of the nine, joined St. Paul in the American Association; Bill Newashe had several offers but chose to go to Atlantic City and play in a hotel league (he had been surprised the previous summer when he learned he had to play every day in pro ball); Joe Libby, Possum Powell and Jesse Young Deer, Carlisle outfielders, headed for North Carolina, and Thorpe said later that he had decided he would tag along for the adventure because he didn't wish to return to Oklahoma. Actually he went to Superintendent Friedman and requested a leave so he could play summer ball. Friedman reminded him that he had been allowed to go home the summer before because he promised to return and stay until he had completed his course. Thorpe said, well, he had changed his mind. The superintendent reluctantly let him go and marked him "on leave" again. Three days after he had scored 25 points in the large Middle Atlantic Association track and field meet in Philadelphia, Thorpe left, apparently with little intention of re-turning to Carlisle.

The familiar exodus of the baseball boys grew with the oppor-tunities in organized ball—there were thirty-five minor leagues to choose from in 1909, more than forty the next season—and it led to a decision by Warner and Friedman to drop baseball from the athletic program. Baseball enthusiasts at the school claimed that Warner wanted the sport dropped in 1910 because it took too much attention and money from the more important business of track and football, which then included formal spring practice. The school announced that "because of summer professionalism baseball was abolished as an authorized sport. This marked one of the most advanced steps taken in the country and the wisdom of the move is now being recognized by the best colleges and universities."

King of the Tobacco Towns

For his first experience with baseball as a daily occupation Thorpe chanced upon one of the game's early backwater breed-ing areas, the flourishing little tobacco towns of North Carolina's coastal plain. He and Jesse Young Deer, a promising outfielder, made agreements with the Rocky Mount team, then in its second year of organized ball in the East Carolina League. Rocky Mount had had semi-pro teams since the 1890s, and the production of bright-leaf tobacco and an enthusiasm for baseball expanded to-

gether on those languid afternoons of Carolina spring and summer. League towns were conveniently strung along the Atlantic
Coast Line Railway, the essential means of travel for teams, from
Rocky Mount south through Wilson and Goldsboro to Wil-
mington in the Great Swamp area to the southeast. Thorpe was
paid twenty-five to thirty dollars a week, hardly an impressive
wage by his standards. But it was payment enough to certify him
as a "professional" among "amateurs" four years later.

In the company of experienced ballplayers from the region
and other schoolboy and college stars anxious to make summer
money and a mark for themselves, Thorpe broke into the league
as a light-hitting infielder. He was soon called upon to pitch,
which he did tirelessly with his untrained arm, winning nine
games and losing ten. Thorpe batted around the .250 level, often
surprising infielders by beating out balls which they expected to
handle for outs. John Glancy, a Fayetteville shortstop from
South Boston, recalled that the Indian's speed made an impact
the first time he saw him. "He hit a grounder in the hole toward
third base. I came up with the ball allright but my second-
baseman hollered over: 'Hold it—don't throw! He's already
there.' That's how fast Thorpe was getting down to first base."

Thorpe lived with several players at the New Cambridge Hotel in Rocky Mount, close by the Atlantic Coast Line passenger
depot and about a half-dozen blocks from the ball park. As arenas
appeared in Thorpe's experience, it was a long way from Harvard Stadium or Penn's Franklin Field—a small covered stand
behind home plate and a set of open-plank bleachers down the
left-field line. But Thorpe discovered that the size of the park or
the town didn't necessarily limit the amount of hero worship a
man could sense just by being a ballplayer. A member of the
Rocky Mount Railroaders had all the attention he could possibly
want. Each day, a couple of hours before game time, a group of
boys gathered outside the New Cambridge, waiting for their
heroes to come down from their rooms, wearing their uniforms,
soiled with yesterday's great slides into second and dives after
elusive balls, for the walk to the park. The lucky boys were desig-
nated to carry a player's glove and bat, sometimes shoes—although the players often walked through the dirt streets in their
spikes. Along with the immeasurable honor in the assignment

was the chance to get into the game free. One of Thorpe's favorite caddies, Tom McMillan, remembered him as "so unmistakably Indian—the face a mahogany color compared with the white ballplayers, the high cheek bones and the alert dark eyes. He stood about ten feet tall in my eyes. It was more strength and speed than just size. To me he was always a gentleman, a very gentle person."

The image that Thorpe would leave elsewhere—Thorpe the All-America, the Olympian, the Canton pro—was taking shape in the streets and on the playing fields of the Carolina towns that summer: he was the considerate, thoughtful hero to children, capable of leaving them burning with happiness from the attention he gave—a joke, an arm across the shoulders, a glove or bat they could carry; in adult company he was either quiet and soberly polite or an unruly lug who had had too much to drink too fast. Playing on the ball team at Rocky Mount gave Thorpe his first real stretch of freedom of choice, and in his two seasons he built up a fair deposit of stories of his drinking evenings. The incidents vary, from town to town, mostly in the number of local police it supposedly took to subdue him. In Rocky Mount it was said that Thorpe was never mean but occasionally hard to manage, that, yes, he did once leave one of the town's deputies upside down in a trash barrel.

When the East Carolina League season ran out in early September Thorpe left for Oklahoma determined, he told Bill Newashe, not to return to Carlisle again. The separation which went on for two years was much like the one between a strong-willed husband and wife who missed each other's cantankerous company —it did not rest easily with either side. Whatever the personal strain between Thorpe and Warner, "the coaches miss Jim very much," Newashe commented at midseason. It showed on the scoreboard as Warner's light team lost decisively to Penn and Brown, was beaten by Pittsburgh for the first time and tied by Penn State. (Warner suffered with less offense and one fresh disciplinary problem that made Thorpe's conduct exemplary by comparison. A hard-bodied Sioux named Asa Sweetcorn—at home in South Dakota he was Esau Fastbear—made the team. He was a good lean athlete, the kind Warner appreciated, with a huge scar across his chest that suggested he had survived tougher battles than football. But Sweetcorn had the deplorable habit of getting drunk before instead of after a game, and Warner had to ban him from taking the train just before one trip. Sweetcorn was so infuriated he tried to raze the Cumberland Depot in Carlisle all by himself. He was hauled off to jail—and thus contributed to a popular student joke that fall: "Where's Sweetcorn?" "Sweetcorn's where he belongs." "Where's that?" "Sweetcorn's in the can . . .")

In mid-October Thorpe asked Kohlenberg to have his funds from Carlisle transferred to the Agency, saying that he wanted to buy a horse and buggy he could use on his sister's farm. Superintendent Friedman was less than sympathetic to the idea. He replied that Thorpe was considered a deserter at Carlisle: "It is customary at this school, when students desert, that all funds to their credit are held until they return or until the matter is given special consideration after their original term of enrolment has expired. For the sake of discipline and in order that no precedent may be established it is necessary that James's money also should be withheld from him. I am enclosing you herewith two checks that were forwarded me during James's absence and which had not been placed to his credit."

With or without his annuity checks, Jim went out and bought a team and buggy for two hundred dollars and $88 worth of corn and hay to get through the winter feeding period. At Thanksgiving time he took a train to St. Louis to see Carlisle play the University, coached that fall by Bill ("Young Pop") Warner. Thorpe watched his teammates whip St. Louis, 39–0, and had a Thanksgiving with them, saying he would return to Carlisle after the beginning of the year. Then he and Warner headed for Oklahoma where Pop had the pleasure of hunting bird, turkey and deer in the eastern part of the state. When Christmas came to Carlisle so did Thorpe, bringing with him several new Sac and Fox students he had chaperoned from Stroud. His presence added a welcome stir to the familiar Christmas routine at the school—a party in the gym, the passing of presents and the gift boxes of candy from the school to each pupil, the feast of turkey in the dining hall. Thorpe, who seemed to have missed his friends, said he would go home for a month or so and

return in time for the new term and the beginning of track and
Warner's April football training program, which would be conducted by Pop, Wauseka and Bill Garlow. But track and football
began without him and Thorpe, a loner again, checked into the
New Cambridge in Rocky Mount for another season of pitching
in the tobacco towns.

VII   RETURN OF THE PRODIGAL

In the Backfield with Possum, Alex and Gus

By the spring of 1911 Pop Warner was aggressively close to bringing the Carlisle football—and with it Indian ascendancy in American sports—to the crest. He no longer had to depend upon a peripatetic schedule to sell the team, booking long-distance Pullman rides to games before curious crowds in Minnesota, Nebraska and farther west. Carlisle had established its reputation in the East and could play and beat the strongest, which was as strong as there was in football at the time. Warner held the kind of autonomous control at the school that coaches and athletic directors often reach for but seldom acquire; it made it possible for him to fill the athletic quarters with "appointments" of his own choosing, some of whom hardly fitted the admission guidelines set by the Bureau of Indian Affairs. By dropping baseball from the program he had eliminated a drain on the budget, interference with spring football and had reduced the threat of his best athletes leaving Carlisle prematurely for serious careers in the pro leagues. Lacrosse, which had replaced baseball, was becoming popular with the Indian students, many of whom had had little chance to play their native game, and it was catching enough public interest to turn a small profit. The major concern with the new enthusiasm over lacrosse was the ease with which the Indians inflicted—and acquired—lacerations, bruises, cracked bones when they met Johns Hopkins, Lehigh, Harvard and other experienced lacrosse teams.

The football squad was one that only Warner could assemble in the unique environment of Carlisle: lean young Indians who had come from isolated boarding schools and adapted swiftly to the game in the shop leagues; veterans he had persuaded to stay on at Carlisle or had placed in Conway Hall prep; a twenty-five-year-old student-teacher with a flair for art and a background as a tackle in semi-pro football in the West; a quarterback with instinct and intelligence enough to call the game on the field and cope with the assorted ages and egos of the Indians. Warner lacked one strong, crashing end to balance the defense, and he was also missing the best athlete—and potentially the best football player—he had had at Carlisle. He took care of the end problem by recruiting a recent Haskell team captain. Getting Thorpe to return didn't require much persuasion at all.

In late spring that year Albert Exendine, who had become football coach at Otterbein College in Ohio after finishing at Carlisle and Dickinson Law, made a visit to his home country in Oklahoma, looking up relatives and checking on family holdings. Walking the main street of Anadarko, where he had first taken his schooling, Ex saw the unmistakable figure and gait of Thorpe coming toward him. Thorpe's face expanded into a grin of welcome and as they shook hands Ex noticed that Jim had been drinking just enough to put him at ease. They talked about baseball and Thorpe's decision not to go on with minor-league ball (he had been acquired by the Fayetteville, North Carolina, team as a pitcher-outfielder just before the league quietly disbanded at the end of the previous season).

"Why don't you go back and finish at Carlisle?" Ex said.

"They wouldn't want me there now," Thorpe said.

"You bet they would," Ex said. Ex suggested they send a wire, indicating that Jim would be interested in readmission. His friend and teammate, Sampson Burd, was also working on Jim and Carlisle to get together. For Warner, who had written Thorpe a letter encouraging him to come back and train for the 1912 U. S. Olympic team, the signal from his wandering prodigy in Oklahoma couldn't have been more brightly timed. He had the key to turning on his football attack in September and a promising chance to escort both Thorpe and Tewanima to the Games in Stockholm the next summer.

Although Superintendent Friedman had let it be known that he didn't care to see Thorpe at Carlisle again and had taken care

of the last formality in closing his record at the school (the previous Christmas he had sent Thorpe a check covering the remains
of his savings account, $197.34) Jim re-entered as easily as he had
slipped away. By the first week in September he returned to
greet Warner and moved back into the familiar circle of football
boys in the athletic quarters. Then he sent off notice of his return
to Agent Kohlenberg at the Sac and Fox Agency:

> I would like you to send me or transfer some money
> here at Carlisle. I have decided to stay for two years
> longer. Mr Kohlenberg have you seen about my lease
> and what have you decided on doing. let me hear from
> you in concerning it for I have some offers William
> Newashe will be here soon and play the football season
> with us. our prospects for a good [season] is great, and
> I think we will have a winning team this fall. We have
> our first game today with Lebon Valley but they want
> be any trouble. Well I must close.
>
> Respectfulley Yours
James Thorpe

As Thorpe predicted, Lebanon Valley submitted without any
trouble that afternoon, 53–0.

As was his custom, Warner sharpened the team's reflexes and
quickened the Indians' urge for combat by playing a midweek
game at Carlisle four days later. He persuaded Muhlenberg College to serve as sacrificial skirmishers by offering a guarantee and
promising a regular, properly promoted game later on. The small
Lutheran school sent only sixteen players to the game. One of
them, Walter Reisner, recalled the apprehension he felt as the
team rode silently in a horse-drawn hack from the railroad station to the Carlisle campus where the school gates closed behind
them "with a clang that gave me a shudder." Before the game
some of the Muhlenberg players were brought face to face with
their doom during a tour of the gym where they gazed at the ar-
ray of trophies won by Indian athletes and at the photographs
of the discouragingly mature and confident-looking football
squad—Sam Burd, Bill Newashe, Stansil Powell, Hugh Wheelock,
Thorpe and others. Reisner, a 140-pound safety, spent an after-

noon of increasing misery as Warner gave Thorpe and fullback Powell a workout. "Time and again I hurled myself into Thorpe," he said. "But I couldn't get both my arms around his legs. The best I could do was to hang onto one leg and slow him down. The score went to 32–0 and it began to rain in the second half. I took Thorpe head-on in one play and when I hit the ground I thought my shoulder was broken [later he learned he had fractured his collarbone]. It was the first time I was glad to be taken out of a game."

Another warm-up opponent, Dickinson College, was not easily intimidated by the Indians. The Dickinson players were led by a gritty 165-pound quarterback, Hyman Goldstein, who was determined to prove to the local people that they could also football at the other end of town. Carlisle won, 17–0, but the game was scoreless at the half and it was a much more physical afternoon than the Indians had expected. Goldstein was able to stop Thorpe each time they met, one-on-one, a point of pride with the little quarterback. Out of these personal collisions developed a mutual respect between the pair that was tested frequently in meetings between the two teams. After that September game Warner invited Dickinson to be his regular guests at Wednesday scrimmages so that he could try out his plays under game conditions. "Those scrimmages at Indian Field were *battles*," Goldstein said. "They helped Warner but they also helped us."

Goldstein, at safety, was a fearless, puzzling returner of kicks (Thorpe called him "the trickiest I ever saw") and he gave the Indians a workout in bringing him down. There was no free catch then, no blockers to follow; Goldstein's was a lonely assignment. From his deep position he gained a familiarity with the Carlisle attack, watching the pattern of the relatively few delayed and quick-hitting running plays the Indians rehearsed. Warner worked the Indians hard for the precision shown in the diagramed plays of the book he was preparing (*A Course in Football for Players and Coaches,* Endorsed by Walter Camp and Hundreds of Satisfied Customers). "Thorpe always stood at tailback in a short punt formation. Powell would come straight through on bucks, but not Thorpe. When his signal was called the interference developed—the guards pulled, the strong tackle blocked momentarily and then went through and blocked in the secondary. The Indians were sharp blockers. I can remember moving up for a tackle and having two of them hit me at once. Carlisle had some big fellows in the line in 1911—Burd, Lone Star, Bushe, Bergie, Jordan, Newashe, Roberts. As quarterback I usually blocked the end and Carlisle had two tough ones."

Right end Sam Burd was back as team captain and Thorpe's old acquaintance and schoolmate from Haskell, Henry Roberts, was at left end. Roberts' arrival at Carlisle at the peak of need was typical Warner enterprise. Pop had acquired a proper line on Roberts at Haskell as a physically powerful and highly motivated Indian athlete. He had actually finished his courses at the Kansas school in 1910 and entered the Indian Service (as an assistant clerk in the Sisseton Agency in South Dakota) when Warner sought him out, offered him a salaried job at Carlisle, a chance to enroll in a few business courses and a chance at a starting position on the football team.

Roberts had an unusual Indian school background, even for the well-traveled football boys, and he had drawn as much profit from the experience as he could. Born in 1888 in a tepee in a clan settlement of the Pawnees in northern Oklahoma, he had been placed in the Agency boarding school when he was so young and frail that the teachers dressed him in girls' clothing and housed him in the girls' quarters because they were afraid the bigger boys might harm him. At age eight he was considered strong enough to be entered as a small boy at Haskell. The superintendent of the Pawnee Agency took a close interest in Henry's development as a student at Haskell and later encouraged him to enroll at Hampton Normal Institute in Virginia, a privately funded school for blacks and a minority of Indians. "I hardly knew where Hampton was except that it was a long way off," Roberts said. "I'm glad I agreed to go. It was higher education than the Indian schools and it put me to test." There were segregated quarters for Indians and blacks, and the Indians ate at separate tables in the dining room. The Hampton football team was limited to blacks and played a segregated schedule in the south, but because Roberts knew the game and was aggressively eager to play he was the one Indian who scrimmaged with the team during the week. After he received his diploma from Hampton at age nineteen, he returned to Haskell because he couldn't afford to follow his ambition to take business administration courses in a regular college. Roberts developed so rapidly as a football player at Haskell in 1908 that the superintendent asked him to stay on as an employee during the summer. "I realized he was holding me for football, that he must have seen some possibilities!"

Roberts received the kind of recognition in 1909 as a hard-nosed lineman and team captain that was certain to catch Warner's attentive ear. He and Louis Island, the former Carlisle reserve, led Haskell to a momentous victory over Nebraska. In Dallas, on a dusty wind-blown field at the state fairgrounds, Roberts' conversion beat Texas, 12–11, a tie-breaking, late-game kick that became famous at Haskell because Henry anxiously booted it before the holder had a chance to remove his left hand and place the ball on the ground. The kick may have been illegal and painful for the holder—but it beat Texas.

At Carlisle, Roberts was paired off as a team roommate with William Lone Star Dietz, the dean of the football boys at the age of twenty-seven. Warner had found Lone Star Dietz working his way through Friends University in Kansas by playing semi-pro baseball and football. Lone Star's arrangement at Carlisle enabled him to take a job as an assistant in art at $540 a year. Warner later gave him five hundred dollars out of the athletic fund as an assistant football coach. He was a competent illustrator, a persuasive football teacher, and in 1911 a very well-seasoned tackle in the Carlisle line. Dietz had been born in the Rosebud Reservation at Pine Ridge, South Dakota, in 1886, the son of a German civil engineer and a full-blood Indian mother, Julia One-star. His father had been on a surveying assignment in the West when he came under attack by Red Cloud and took refuge among the Oglala Sioux where he remained and took a wife. Lone Star (Wicarphi Ismala, his mother called him) showed an early en-thusiasm for American games and realistic drawing at boarding school in Rice Lake, Wisconsin. At Carlisle, Lone Star contrib-uted many of the cover illustrations for *The Red Man*, the school's professional-looking magazine, and later studied at the Pennsylvania Museum of Industrial Arts. His wife, Angel De-Cora, a talented Winnebago girl, attended Hampton and went on to study art at Smith College. Lone Star's reputation as an artist ran out long before his usefulness as a Warner-trained football man. He coached at several schools, including Washington State which he took to the first Rose Bowl in 1914. He retired as a coach at the age of sixty-six at Albright College, once the early doormat on Carlisle's schedule.

Along with the experience and maturity of Lone Star and Roberts, Warner had one of his own exceptional Indian field products coming into season. Gus Welch, twenty, had finished his training with the shop league and hotshots and was ready to quarterback the team. When Warner first told the Chippewa boy to move out of the dorm and into the athletic quarters he was so disbelieving of the fact that he had made the team that he had to be told again the next day. The early self-doubts gave way to an assertiveness on the football field. Welch had sprinter's speed and he was a quick, imaginative thinker, which filled Warner's chief requirements at the position. (Warner knew he could always make a blocker out of his quarterback, even one with such a light frame as Welch, who was 5 feet 9 and about 155 pounds in 1911.) With Warner's prodding, Welch steadily took over the full burden of the position. (Years later Welch said of Warner: "He let us use our own initiative, and the more I see of sports the more I realize that was the greatest thing about him.")

Welch's arrival as quarterback and Thorpe's return to the team resulted in a pair of well-matched roommates and a long-running friendship. For Welch the relationship began as a case of hero worship toward the older, athletically established Thorpe. It grew into something stronger than that when Jim made the unassuming effort to help Gus on the football field and in track. Welch's gratitude for Thorpe's easy-handed friendship stretched through the years and revealed itself in his one-man crusade to get Jim's Olympic medals and records restored and, later on, during some of the financial crises that Thorpe periodically stumbled into. Thorpe and Welch had enough in common—the independence of their early lives, their appreciation of aggressive football, their enjoyment of a carousing drink afterward—to sustain a good school friendship. Thorpe may have found reassurance in knowing that the intellectually superior Welch, who was ahead of his classmates in forensics and honor-roll grades, could be a happy boozer, too.

Welch grew into the habit of telling humorous, self-deprecating stories about his early game experiences with Thorpe which muddled reality of the 1911 season. He described how he nervously questioned Thorpe before the Lebanon Valley game, "What do I do if I miss the end on 48?" Thorpe told him to keep going down field. "When I called 48," Welch recounted, "I went after the end but he side-stepped me, and so I went on and tried to take out the halfback. But I missed him. So I took a shot at the safety who was coming up fast, and he avoided me. Then I realized that Thorpe was still behind me and we were going for a touchdown." Welch's anecdotal recital always failed to mention that he became a creditable blocker, adept at slicing down the end, and that two of the longest, most spectacular touchdown runs of the season were his own.

Thorpe's age and experience among the backs was well matched by that of a familiar running mate, Stansil Powell (with the football boys he was always Possum Powell), the Cherokee full blood who had headed south with him for summer ball two years earlier. Powell had a dark face and a mat of black hair which he kept in place with a small skullcap. He wore it during practice, and it became part of his hard, straight-ahead rushes into the line—flying into the air upon impact and requiring a quick ground search by Possum after every play. The right half or wing back, Alex Arcasa, had been trained at Indian Field since his arrival in 1908 as a trim, 160-pound Colville from the Northwest. The early report on Arcasa made Warner glow with optimism: "splendid development . . . a young man of excellent character and disposition."

Warner had cornered a stocky, full-blood Pomo boy from Potter Valley, California, Elmer Busch, to play in the middle of the line. Busch weighed over 200 (although Warner listed him as something less than that) and he held up the middle with two durable Chippewa (or Ojibway) boys, Joe Bergie at center and Peter Jordan at the other guard. Bergie was a 180-pounder, a "pea soup" Chippewa from the Devil's Lake Band in Dakota. Jordan, about fifteen pounds lighter, enrolled at Carlisle in 1907 from Red Lake, Minnesota, and followed Thorpe into the tailor shop. Jordan was also a good baseball player and he later attended the sports-minded Keewatin Academy in Prairie du Chien, Wisconsin. Keewatin had a winter campus in Florida where it played a heavy baseball schedule, and Jordan, who had come from the northernmost of Indian nations, developed an acute aversion to cold weather.

Thorpe was not the only vagabond athlete who returned for the 1911 Carlisle football season. William Garlow, a Tuscarora from New York State, had enrolled at Carlisle a year after Thorpe entered and almost immediately obtained a series of authorized summer leaves to play baseball. In 1910 he dropped out of school temporarily and later played ball in Ontario. Garlow was a short, solidly packed athlete whom Warner used as a guard or center. He was something of a favorite with Indian school officials because he was very studious and received high marks in English and history courses at Conway Hall. He later attended West Virginia Wesleyan.

Warner, now forty, was even more the commanding figure than he was when Thorpe left school. Many of the team members had been persuaded by him to remain at Carlisle just to play ball (the good-natured Bill Newashe had long since finished his normal enrollment obligations); their travel expenses from home and their miscellaneous costs around school had been taken care of by the athletic fund. And every afternoon at practice they were reminded of the sharp-tongued hold that Pop had over them.

Warner's control of many aspects of the life of the Indian students at Carlisle, his coaching and athletic director duties, his side-line enterprises filled a congested week-long schedule. It began each Monday morning after breakfast when he sat down at his bungalow on campus with his two scouts, F. E. ("Cap") Craver and D. D. Harris. Craver had coached off and on at Dickinson and was a keen student of football but had trouble projecting that knowledge to young players. Organized scouting was hardly an accepted practice at the time, and some of the Indians thought their coach was being devious and unsportsmanlike when he revealed to them the opponents' favorite plays, their strengths and weaknesses. In his briefing with the scouts, Warner would light up his first Turkish Trophy cigarette of the day (he was a chain smoker) and say, "What do they do and what kind of defense shall we work out?" Craver was not only a scout but he served a role that would be called "defense co-ordinator" to-day. When Warner had a defense for Saturday's game drawn out he would leave word with his secretary and public relations aide, Arthur Martin, that he was off to the bucket shop, the local stocks and bonds office, to attend to business. (Martin was instructed to tell inquirers that the coach had gone to town for a Coke.) Warner also had to devote time to his football teaching series, which he sold in installments to coaches around the country. He had gathered his subscribers from a New York mailing house that provided a list of addresses for every high school and college in the United States. Then there were the credit letters to be sent out to Mose Blumenthal's store, such as this handwritten one in 1911:

> Blumenthal,
>   Please credit for clothing:
>   Sampson Burd, to the amount of $50.00
>   William Dietz, "   "   "   " $15.00
>   James Thorpe, "   "   "   " $50.00
>   and charge to the Athletic Association.
>   G. S. Warner

Warner treated the 1911 group of veterans as he had previous Carlisle teams: He fed their stomachs well at the training table and their egos with the clippings and out-of-town papers which he made available in the reading room of the athletic quarters. At practice he worked them hard with a caustic tongue, sending them through monotonous signal drills to perfect their timing essential to the Warner reverses, the crisscross, the end runs of Thorpe behind the swarm of blockers. He was a great believer in the blocking and tackling aides that he had helped design, including the heavy blocking sled that the Indian linemen, their noses to the ground, pushed all over the field behind the urging of line coach Wauseka. Pop still could be physically persuasive when he put his huge bulk into a demonstration of a blocking technique against an Indian lineman. His use of such coaching expletives as "You godamn bonehead" or "You sonofabitch" had a stinging effect on many of the Indian players. Although they had come to recognize that profanity was part of the func-

tional language they had learned to use, it had an edge of humiliation to it. They weren't just being sharply disciplined or
prodded, they were being put in their place by a superior.
Swearing and cursing remained for the Indians the mark of a
bad influence. Warner's temper broke on a few occasions and
once he made the mistake of kicking a scrub, Louis DuPuis, and
on another occasion struck a player named John Wallette in front
of the team. The incidents weren't accepted as pieces of harsh
discipline by a tough coach; they became part of a backlog of
resentment against Warner's methods which, in time, were used
by some members of the team in affidavits of complaint against
him before a Congressional investigating committee.

But Warner's success since 1899 in handling an assortment of
Indian personalities—the eager learners to the recalcitrant—from
a variety of tribal backgrounds was not dependent on the big
stick. Warner respected the skill and experience of some of his
older athletes, such as Thorpe, and knew when to give them their
lead and let them work things out on their own. He knew that
Thorpe would not get heated up in practice sessions, although he
occasionally played him with the scrubs to give him a running
challenge. He let him work out his own pace in kicking and field
goals, knowing that Thorpe now had the strength and his own
style to reach his maximum. He sometimes leaned on Thorpe
for his lack of judgment or efficiency in a game. In the Penn game
in 1912 he criticized him for allowing a Penn pass completion for
a long gain simply because Thorpe didn't think the receiver could
get under the ball. When he did, Thorpe had to give chase and
bring him down from behind. He pulled him out of a Syracuse
game for his stubborn attempts in trying to run around a tough
line. And he and Thorpe had one major blowup after Carlisle's
shoddy performance against Washington and Jefferson. But the
coach and his workhorse halfback recognized a mutual need—
and there was respect on both sides for the way the other did his
job.

Carlisle ran through the first five games on its 1911 schedule
without pressure. At Forbes Field, against Pittsburgh on October
21, Thorpe responded to the first major challenge with one of his
dominating performances, which people began to expect of him
wherever Carlisle played. He piled up gains on the crisscross

and the fake pass from short-punt formation, but it was his long kicks and his ability to get down "under his own bootings," as the papers described it, that startled the crowd at Forbes Field. Carlisle used the kick frequently in the 17–0 victory as an offensive weapon; only twice was Pittsburgh able to make returns of Thorpe punts. The Pittsburgh *Dispatch* reported, "Once Thorpe kicked a beautiful long spiral almost into the midst of five Pitt players and got down the field in time to grab the pigskin, shake off three would-be tacklers and dart 20 yards across the line for a touchdown." In those days of rugbylike punting duels, the kicker was expected to turn up the field under the ball and he was sometimes faster in pursuit than his ends who had to check block at the line of scrimmage. Thorpe's quickness and the ball's lengthy airborne time turned his punts into a personal duel between himself and the safety for the free ball.

The *Dispatch* reporter continued with a clutch of superlatives for the Carlisle halfback: "This person Thorpe was a host in himself. Tall and sinewy, as quick as a flash and as powerful as a turbine engine he appeared impervious to injury . . . this Sac and Fox shone resplendent and then some."

Thorpe was not entirely impervious to injury. Early in the game against Lafayette the following Saturday he was sent limping off the field and contributed little to the Carlisle win. There was a week of speculation in Carlisle and Philadelphia about the readiness of Thorpe to play on his tender ankle against Penn, the focal point of the season for the Indians. When Warner grouped the players together on Friday afternoon for the train ride to Philadelphia and the traditional overnight stay at the Normandie Hotel neither the coach nor his star kicker and ball carrier knew whether he could take the field.

The team was followed to Philadelphia early Saturday morning by the Penn game crowd from the Indian school. The Penn game was the off-campus party which the students who had saved enough money for train fare had looked forward to for weeks. There was the usually large, chaperoned group of girls, wearing their wide dark blue hats, their long coats and carrying their Carlisle flags; the band led by musical director Claude Stauffer had the chance to demonstrate its new formations that had been in rehearsal since September; the scrub football players were given their morale-boosting trip escorted from Carlisle early Saturday morning by Warner's aide, Arthur Martin. He took them to the complimentary lunch provided by Gimbel Bros. at the store's dining room, where the Carlisle girls entertained with their school songs. After lunch he herded the two dozen players toward the subway for the ride to the Normandie Hotel where they would join the regular football boys before the game. Martin gave them each a nickel for the subway turnstile but couldn't get them to follow. When he asked what the problem was one of them said they were confused. "If we put a nickel in the machine," he said, "we will have nothing to give the conductor when we get on the train." Martin explained to them that the machine was the same as the conductor. They followed him to the underground platform and onto the train, sitting in nervous silence as it rattled through the tunnel. When it surfaced and broke into the daylight at Thirtieth Street the boys flashed startled grins.

At the Normandie the scrubs and the Carlisle students gave the crowd gathered in the lobby a few songs and cheers and then headed for Franklin Field for what developed into the most one-sided Indian victory in the series between the two schools. Thorpe warmed up on the sidelines but punted so gingerly that Warner knew he could not count on him. He moved Alex Arcasa, who was the best lacrosse player at the school, to left halfback and started Joel Wheelock, the youngest of two Oneida Wheelocks from Wisconsin, at right halfback. Joel was a quiet, unassuming twenty-three-year-old who would have been playing clarinet in the band if he hadn't the size (175 pounds) and sure instinct for football.

Carlisle scored the first time it had the ball and the efficient running of Arcasa and Possum Powell behind the Indian forwards proved early that without Thorpe, Carlisle was still much too experienced and fast for Penn. At the 15-yard line Lone Star dropped back from the line to become a ball carrier, took a hand-off from Welch and ran straight up the middle for the first touchdown. After he crossed the goal he touched the ball to the grass in the prevailing gesture of a score. The Indian band was still playing when Newashe kicked the extra point, boosting the score to 6–0. A pass interception by Powell moments after the kickoff set up another quick touchdown. Welch called his own signal on a double pass, an old Carlisle standby in which he handed off to the right halfback and then took a short lateral. Welch was hit quickly by Penn's left end, Wilson, but regained his balance, shook off fullback Keogh who grabbed at his jersey and then sprinted eighty-five yards for a touchdown. Once he broke free, the Carlisle quarterback seemed to have all of the speed of a Thorpe, something he would later prove as a middle-distance runner in track.

Arcasa later added a third touchdown, prompting the correspondent for the Philadelphia *North American* to comment, "The fleet Arcasa and the rapid-moving Welch skirted the Penn ends as though the gentlemen set to guard these points were stakes driven into the skirts of tepees to foil the wind." Carlisle ran for 421 yards, throwing only a couple of ineffectual passes; Penn gained only 41 yards rushing and might not even have achieved that if Roberts hadn't been sent out of the game for slugging a Penn ball carrier and Sampson Burd had not twisted his knee late in the game.

Penn played without its injured fullback and captain, LeRoy Mercer, who was considered as essential to the team's offense as was Thorpe to Carlisle. While Thorpe calmly watched the game from the sidelines with an occasional grin on his face, the Penn captain spent an afternoon of high emotion on the bench. Finally, with the score at 16–0, he made one of those dramatic, I'd-die-for-dear-old-Penn gestures expected of captains. He tossed off his red-and-blue blanket and ran up to coach Andy Smith and his assistant, Charles Wharton, appealing to be sent into the game. The crowd picked up the chant, "Mercer, Mercer, Mercer," but the coaches refused to risk further injury for wasted cause. He slumped back to the bench to the rising cheers from the Penn stands. A teammate placed the blanket over his shoulders and the captain put his face in his hands and wept.

After the game as the Penn rooters were moving toward the exit at Franklin Field one of them quipped to his companion: "Do you really think it pays to educate the Indian?"

For the Carlisle team members and the girls they had invited to Philadelphia for the game there was the opportunity to celebrate with the unusual elegance of a dinner out in the city. Thorpe's date was Iva Miller, a Carlisle girl he had danced with at Saturday socials. She had just turned eighteen and was one of the brightest girls in the class of seniors who were due to graduate the following spring. Another football date, Rose DeNomie, sat in the hotel dining room that evening and watched in astonishment as her escort, Henry Roberts, ordered and consumed a huge plate of oysters, just as if they were a familiar part of a Pawnee feast. "Henry eating oysters—I could hardly believe it!" she exclaimed. She and the big end, whom Warner imported from the West, were well into a romance that resulted in a marriage two months later. Rose, a Chippewa, was a student nurse at the Indian school and the newspaper reports of their wedding insisted, romantically but inaccurately, that the relationship bloomed in an infirmary ward. ("Football Star Weds Girl Who Nursed Him/ Carlisle Indian End Wins Maiden in the School Hospital" was the head over one story of the wedding.) Rose did briefly attend Roberts after a game injury, and she helped treat Thorpe when he was hospitalized with granulated eyes. "As a patient Jim was either mischievous or just ornery," she said.

Roberts' injury at midseason, a dislocation to a bone in the back of the hand, tested the amateur orthopaedic skills of Pop Warner, who was inspired to construct protective devices for injured players which sometimes combined the best elements of a shield and a handy weapon. He came up with a bandage for Roberts that included a leather handle fitted across the back of his hand. After the Penn game Pop turned his attention to Thorpe's ankle and the need to protect it so that he could operate with some reassurance and freedom of motion against Harvard the following Saturday.

A Beautiful Accomplishment at Cambridge

Thorpe had come out of the obscurity of his hibernation in Oklahoma less than two months earlier, but by the week of the Harvard game he had attracted attention across the country, through the outpour of releases from Warner's publicity hands in Carlisle and wire-service coverage of the Indians' games. In the syndicated hyperbole from the typewriters of E. L. Martin of the Carlisle *Evening Herald* and Hugh Miller, owner of the Letter Shop, Thorpe was described as not only the most exciting football player of the 1911 season but as an absolute wonder in any sport he chose to try. The Carlisle publicists had unfurled the "greatest all-around athlete in the world" slogan that would accompany Thorpe the rest of his active life.

In early November the Muskogee *Times-Democrat*, boasting "the best sports page in Oklahoma," carried a splashy Carlisle-originated feature, with a picture of Indian school girls cheering at a game and the following introduction to Thorpe:

> The 1911 season has brought into the public eye a young Indian student at the Carlisle School who promises to become the greatest athlete the world has ever seen. James Thorpe, a Sac and Fox from Oklahoma, came to Carlisle in 1908 with no knowledge whatever of athletics . . . The world of college trainers has been astonished by his achievements. He is not only a basketball player at which game he fills the center post with truly remarkable skill, but he is a baseball player of great talent and covers any of the sacks or outfields with as much credit as a professional. He can put the 16-pound shot 43 feet, broad jump 22 feet 10 inches, runs 100 in 10 seconds. The high hurdles are pie for him in 15⅘ seconds, while the 220 hurdles he negotiates in 26 seconds. The youthful redskin hunts, plays lacrosse, tennis, indoor baseball, handball, hockey all with equal skill and can fill almost any position on a football team with superlative credit. As a football halfback he is probably seen best, whirling, twisting, dashing and plunging, bewildering his opponents with little panther-like leaps. Thorpe, who is only 22 years old, is 6 feet tall and averages about 178 pounds in weight.

The bare particulars of this publicity release on Thorpe were later picked up by the Philadelphia *Inquirer* and, embellished by further exaggeration and error, were turned into a two-page feature which could only have amused Thorpe and other football boys who read it—or attempted to wade through the florid passages—in the reading room of the athletic quarters. "This Indian the Athletic Marvel of the Age" was the headline over an article by-lined "Jim Nasium." The author saw Thorpe refuting the belief that the Indians were a dying race. "The red blood of his fathers, who, years agone, buried the war hatchet and watched with dimming eyes the plow point of civilization desecrating his hunting grounds, while his people slowly vanished from the face of the earth, still courses through the veins of the scattered remnants of the race and occasionally so asserts itself in the most warlike of the peaceful pursuits of the paleface that it compels the descendant of the conqueror of his fathers to take the count . . ." The acknowledgment that the Indians were beating the stuffing out of the white schools on their schedule was followed by this assessment of Thorpe: "[His] whole ambition in life now is to gain a place on the Olympic team, which ambition will no doubt be gratified, and if any old nation in the wide universe can dig up anything that can smother this redskin marvel in the all-around events all past records will be kicked into the middle of the Mediterranean Sea, that's all. . . . Thorpe is probably the most indifferent athlete we have ever had. He makes no special preparations for his efforts, and simply meanders carelessly up to his tasks and does them in an unconscious way that paralyzes the spectators. There is nothing showy or suggestive of extreme effort in his work." Thus, the myth that Thorpe always brought such superior talent into competition that he never had to prepare for it was sent aloft. It was never really shot down.

Warner liked to get the Indians out of one game and into a mood to prepare for the next by sending them off on a Sunday afternoon walk. But he had the lame, including Thorpe and Captain Burd, to consider after the Penn game. There was the customary opportunity when the team was back on campus for the football boys to indulge in a Sunday ritual—making piles of pancakes in the athletic quarters kitchen for their own consumption and for a few privileged guests. The next day Warner put Thorpe on a schedule of light field-goal kicking, to test the strength of the ankle, and sent the healthy in the squad through a normal two-hour Monday drill. During the workout Warner, assisted by Pat O'Brien, devoted about ten minutes to falling on the ball, a standard exercise to sharpen reflexes. The backs practiced tackling, the linemen charging for fifteen minutes. While the linemen went through a tackling drill, the backs worked on their starts and timing—an obsession with Warner. There was a light passing drill with Welch, Arcasa, Powell and sub halfback Eloy Sousa, the only Pueblo on the varsity. Carlisle was using the pass much less often than it did four years before. No one on the team had the throwing arm of Frank Mt. Pleasant, but more important, the pass had been placed under severe rule restrictions in 1910, limiting the length of a legal pass to twenty yards. (The rule was dropped in 1912.) Warner's Monday blackboard talk usually touched briefly on the mistakes of the previous Saturday and then turned to a defense and new plays for the next game. The plan that evolved for Harvard—and was used with success—called for a straight running attack in the first half (with Possum Powell doing the heavy work) and varying it later with halfback delay plays and reverses or the tirelessly executed Carlisle crisscross. When the Indians moved close enough to the Harvard goal they could turn to Thorpe for the field goal. Toward the end of the Monday practice, as the last of the November daylight was leaving Indian Field, Warner sent the first team through a signal drill and held a fifteen-minute scrimmage for the scrubs who had played little or not at all against Penn.

When the team was ready to leave for Cambridge on Friday Warner had satisfied himself that Thorpe could run and kick with the protection of an elaborate weaving of bandage and plaster that stretched from his foot to just below the knee. There was a boisterous ceremonial connected with the team's departure for most away games—students cheering them out of the campus and townspeople watching the horse-drawn bus, for years driven by a black named Mr. Pope, heading for Gettysburg Junction, the station closest to the school, and one of the twelve trains a day to Harrisburg. The bus had seats along the side and the two dozen players who filled them always seemed inadequate in number to take on a Penn or Harvard. They were supported on this trip to Boston by an all-girl rooting section of eighteen students who had used their own savings to pay for the rail fare and hotel.

Neither Thorpe's date for the Penn game, Iva Miller, nor Roberts' girl, Rose DeNomie, made the trip. But Emma Newashe did go to watch her brother Bill start at tackle for the first time against Harvard. On Saturday morning, outside the United States Hotel in Boston where they stayed, the Indian girls created a traffic jam of curious pedestrians and vehicles when they grouped together, waving their Carlisle pennants, before jumping into automobiles for a tour of the city.

Although Thorpe and others on the squad had faced Harvard at the Stadium in 1908, there still was something awesome about the reinforced steel horseshoe and the game atmosphere at Cambridge. Facing the scene for the first time, Henry Roberts was startled by the richness of the grass ("No one could get hurt here," he thought) and the size of the Crimson squad limbering up on the other side of the field. Harvard's coach, the blunt, theatrical Percy Haughton, believed in numbers and dressed as many as forty players for a game. Haughton had not only beaten Warner the last time they had met but he had rubbed in a joke with the defeat. Haughton had learned that earlier in the 1908 season Carlisle had defeated Syracuse while wearing Pop's hand-tailored football pads sewn into the jerseys of the backs and ends. Haughton, a great believer in the value of straight football, asked Warner the night before the game if he had pulled such "whiff-whaff," as Percy termed it. Warner said why, yes, of course. The next day before the Harvard-Carlisle kickoff Warner took the customary visiting coach's look at the game balls and found them all dyed a deep Crimson.

This time the Groton- and Harvard-educated Haughton appeared to be showing a clear disdain for Warner and his Indians. He announced that because of the unusual number of injuries suffered by the first team in a two-point loss to Princeton the week before and the over-riding importance of the approaching games with Dartmouth and Yale, he would go to New Haven to scout and let his assistants coach a reserve eleven against Carlisle.

Haughton could hardly have anticipated that it would be Thorpe's football game, that neither the reserve nor the first eleven could overcome the kicking and running of this single Indian. When Thorpe took the field, a little stiff and unsteady at first from the heavy bandaging on his lower leg, he became, as teammate Roberts recalled, an inspiration. "Jim didn't say anything—Gus called the signals and Captain Burd was the team leader—but we all played better because of him." In the early going the straight rushes of Possum Powell, his unruly hair flying, split the Harvard line time and again. Then Welch began to mix his attack with a halfback reverse that repeatedly caught the Crimson seconds off balance. Welch handed off to Arcasa, running to the outside, who fed the ball to Thorpe heading in the other direction. With a guard and end in front of him Jim picked up great sweeps of ground (he gained 173 of Carlisle's 334 yards). The reverse played the big part in Carlisle's one touchdown drive, which covered seventy yards. Near the end of the third quarter Carlisle had a 15–9 lead, nine of the points coming on Thorpe field goals of thirteen, forty-three and thirty-seven yards—the last two against the wind. (Carlisle, which had some secondary defense lapses, gave up a touchdown on a long Harvard run.) In the small team shelter on the Harvard side of the field team captain Bob Fisher, a twenty-three-year-old 210-pound lineman, the All-America halfback Percy Wendell and the other regulars watched nervously as Thorpe threatened to put the game beyond reach. Fisher conferred with assistant coach Corbett and trainer "Pooch" Donovan, but they insisted they hold to the Haughton game plan and stay with the reserves. At the end of the period as the Indians took a needed two-minute rest—they had played with little relief, although Joel Wheelock did sub for the pneumonia-weakened Bill Newashe—Fisher used his rank and prerogative and led the varsity onto the field. A roar went up in the stadium and Henry Roberts, slumped in the grass, felt a wave of dismay as he saw the fresh Crimson uniforms swarming onto the field. He wondered if they could possibly hold on until the end of the game. The fresh Harvard varsity did change the tone of the game somewhat; they stopped the Welch to Arcasa to Thorpe reverse, although Thorpe did turn their ends behind good blocking a few times. When Thorpe went back to punt they broke through the weary Indian front line and blocked it. Tackle Bob Storer picked up the loose ball and ran for a Harvard touchdown. But they still could not overcome Thorpe. With the ball on the Crimson 48 and a fourth down coming up for Carlisle, Welch surprised the Indians by calling for a place kick, such was his belief in Thorpe's good leg. Thorpe complained, "Who in hell heard of a place kick from here. Let's punt the ball." Welch said a placement was as good as a punt and they might even score. Thorpe went back, this time a couple of yards deeper than normal behind the crouching holder, Alex Arcasa. Because Thorpe took longer getting to the ball and hit it on a low, driving trajectory, a Harvard guard managed to get his spread fingers on the ball. But neither a Harvard hand nor a capricious wind could ruin the force and accuracy of Thorpe's kick. The ball went through the posts and hit the ground a dozen yards beyond, points enough for an 18–15 Carlisle victory, the second since it had begun playing Harvard in the 1890s. The afternoon's drama called for an appropriate exit by this heroic Indian who had given his ultimate performance at Harvard Stadium. It came in the late moments of the game when Thorpe's ankle gave way under the tackling and pounding he had taken. He had to be carried off the field, as the crowd stood with its cheers. When the game ended Henry Roberts, his lungs and legs aching from the long trial at left end, headed joyously to the sidelines where Warner, assistant Pat O'Brien and the little group of Indian reserves had erupted in celebration. A tall Harvard lineman turned to offer Roberts congratulations with tears of humiliation streaking his face.

A proper Boston appreciation of Jimmy Thorpe, as the *American* called him, was offered the next day: "Even the most partisan Crimson supporter will gladly admit, through their admiration for his wonderful work against Harvard, that he not only upheld an already great reputation, but that he has placed his name in the Hall of Fame, not only of Carlisle but also of the entire football world. It was indeed a pleasure to see a man not only live up to a great reputation but add to it through work beautifully accomplished."

Thorpe's magnificent goal kicking would be exceeded by Harvard's Charley Brickley (who beat Yale with five field goals in 1913), but the stadium probably had never held a finer all-around performance of place kicking, punting (all of his kicks, except the one blocked, carried forty-five yards or more) and ball carrying. Although he was restricted by the bad leg in the Harvard game, Thorpe played a tough role during the season in Carlisle's seven-diamond defense. He was particularly menacing when he moved up behind the line to rush the kicker or to add force on a third-down defense (the rule was changed in 1912 allowing four instead of three downs to gain ten yards and a first down).

The first era of the dominance of the field goal in college football was about to end with the flourish of Thorpe and Brickley. After Brickley kicked twenty-four field goals in 1912 and '13 the art began to lose its practitioners and there was a drop in the emphasis on this three-point play until the needs of the professionals inspired kickers in the 1950s and '60s. The ball that Thorpe and Brickley kicked for such distance—Brickley was very effective with the drop kick—offered a better target than the modern ball. It was the same size in long circumference (28 inches) and weighed approximately the same 14–15 ounces, but it was 23 inches, instead of 21, at the short axis. The kickers of the day, however, worked under conditions that would appall the modern pro placement specialist. There were no helpful hash marks to which the ball was moved to assure a head-on swing at the goal posts; the ball was kicked from wherever the previous play ended, which could mean a sharply angled kick from the near sidelines. There was no steady rotation of fresh, clean footballs into the game. The kicker often had to cope with a slippery, water-soaked ball.

There was more satisfaction for Carlisle from the Harvard game than Thorpe's ascendancy and the team victory. Warner received $10,400 in gate receipts, the largest one-day profit to the athletic association in four years. As Pop led the team into Syracuse five days later for a familiar appearance in western New York State the Indians had gone nine games without a loss and ranked with Princeton and Penn State as the best of the unbeaten teams in the East. With only light-scoring Syracuse, Johns Hopkins and Brown ahead, Warner could have buoyantly anticipated his first unbeaten season and, perhaps, recognition as national champion. But when the Indians took the field at Syracuse Stadium they found it covered with mud and slush, a gift from a November storm off Lake Ontario. Thorpe's leg was strong enough for the heavy going, but Gus Welch had been in bed with a lame back and didn't put on a uniform before the game.

Thorpe, who carried a cloth onto the field to keep his kicking shoe clean, had trouble with his punts. He let one slip off his foot from the Carlisle 15 and Syracuse ran it in for a touchdown. Welch did dress at half time as a piece of inspiration; Thorpe scored from a short distance late in the game. It wasn't enough. By a 12–11 margin the game and an undefeated season fell out of reach.

The Indians' failure on the unstable ground of the Onondagas fed the belief that neither their game nor their temperaments were much suited for rain, snow or mud. Their attack did depend upon timing and quickness; Thorpe's punting and place kicking both suffered if he couldn't find a reasonably solid patch of turf to work on. But there was nothing excessively demoralizing to the Indians about playing in sloppy weather—Warner often had them wallowing in it during practice sessions at Indian Field.

The Brown game, the last of the long 1911 season, was set in the mire left by rain and snow at Providence, R.I. Warner and his traveling squad of twenty-four had been on the road for seven weekends, and the experience of checking into hotel rooms and strolling around strange streets in their military uniforms (while gathering smiles and stares) had become almost as routine as attending class or shop. The game was scheduled for mid-morning on Thanksgiving Day. On Wednesday Warner led the Indians into Keiths Theater, arrayed in Brown and Carlisle colors, for a party and show that included vaudeville jokes and skits about Indians, bears (Brown's mascot) and football. By this end point of the season the Carlisle players were becoming worldly theatergoers and dinner guests, accustomed to being entertained by the spectacle of New York's Hippodrome (after the Harvard game) or by a special performance from a world famous mystic (before the Syracuse game). In Washington to play Georgetown they had been surrounded by Congressmen and Indian Affairs bureaucrats. It was, in a sense, an advanced Outing course, restricted to the football boys at Carlisle. It was also strong public relations for the school and for Pop Warner's football program.

A long season of popular culture and travel did not interfere with the Indians' ability to rise above the mud of Andrews Field and defeat Brown, 12–0, on Thanksgiving Day morning with a performance that at least flashed some of the brighter character-

istics of the Carlisle game: Fullback Possum Powell bored straight
up the middle for short gains; Lone Star Dietz took the ball from
Powell on the tackle-around-end play often enough to catch the
defense going the wrong way; Thorpe made large inroads by
faking a kick and then running from punt formation. The Carlisle
touchdown came on a sixty-two-yard run by Welch who took the
ball without a signal count and sprinted around right end before
the Brown players knew what had happened. Thorpe carefully
wiped the mud off his kicking shoe and made field goals of
twenty-seven and thirty-three yards. He once sailed a kick from
his own 12-yard line over the head of safetyman Bill Sprackling
which rolled dead on the Brown 15—eighty-three yards on the
field that was then 110 yards long. Carlisle made two substitutions
in the line but the backfield of Welch, Arcasa, Powell and Thorpe
played nonstop on defense and offense, working up an appropriate appetite for the Thanksgiving meal of that afternoon.

Winter was about to close in on the Carlisle campus when the
football team returned to resume their assigned places in the
Indian education process that had been grinding on without them
during most of the fall. The football boys gathered to elect
Thorpe captain for the next season. Jim and Henry Roberts spoke
at the Sunday evening meeting of the Catholic students and
talked of the Brown game and of the trip to Providence. Possum
Powell volunteered to go into the woods and chop down enough
Christmas trees to decorate the gym for the annual school party.
Thorpe, Roberts, Powell, Joel Wheelock and Bruce Goesback
changed into the school basketball uniforms—maroon shirts,
white shorts, striped knee socks—for the new season. Thorpe kept
up with basketball until it interfered with the indoor track season.

A girl student who attended Carlisle in 1911 and '12 recalled
that Jim seemed more outgoing than ever that winter. "He could
be very jolly," she said. "He liked to have fun. He enjoyed dancing, although he certainly didn't seem to be a ladies' man. He
was a little tacky in his dress and didn't seem to care that much
about his appearance." But Thorpe was gradually beginning to
care about how he appeared in the eyes of Iva Miller. Their
friendship, which began with the Penn weekend, developed into
a campus romance—the school's star athlete and finest physical
specimen and the witty young belle of the senior class—and led

to marriage two years later. They had been introduced by Jim's buddy, Sam Burd, and the relationship survived an awkward start and later some forceful opposition by Warner, friends and family of Iva Miller. When they met Jim greeted Iva with a nonchivalrous, "You're a cute little thing," and she had doubts of enduring their first date.

Iva Miller had been caught up in the Indian education system in Oklahoma where she entered the training school at Chilocco at the age of eight. She was one of the small minority of whites with a tenuous claim to Indian ancestry who gained admission to boarding school without severe scrutiny by authorities. (The minimum degree of Indian blood required for admission to Carlisle was one-fourth.) Her mother, who died when she was five, had a trace of Cherokee; her father was a white hotel owner and stage operator in Okmulgee. In 1904 the fair-skinned Iva was selected as one of 150 outstanding Indian students to appear as part of the Ethnology Exhibit at the St. Louis World's Fair. As a ten-year-old performer in the Indian musical-literary program, Iva entertained Fair visitors with recitation ("Pa He Stole the Parson's Sheep") and song ("The Little Game Called Kissing"). During her several months at the Fair, Iva became acquainted with the star Indian attraction, Geronimo, whose ethnological offerings included Apache dances. Iva supplied him with cards on which he signed his autograph and sold to the public for ten cents. The operation turned into such a business success that it kept Geronimo supplied with whiskey and Iva with an occasional $5 for her assistance. By the time she reached Carlisle, Iva's education had grown considerably outside the bounds of Indian boarding school. She was eighteen in the fall of 1911 when she became friends with Jim, who was twenty-four.

The major athletic social of the winter, which usually took place with the annual awarding of the C's, was upstaged in mid-January by a celebration of the football boys to mark the wedding of teammate Henry Roberts and Rose DeNomie. The couple had received permission to hold the Catholic ceremony in the superintendent's mansion. The wedding party in the athletic quarters was the players' idea, and they invited dates and arranged for a large banquet to be prepared in the football kitchen.

When Roberts looked around at the group of friends he had recently acquired and would soon be leaving—his roommate Lone Star, his best man Sampson Burd, the taciturn Alex Arcasa, the smiling Thorpe, talkative Gus Welch, the rugged Powell—he realized they had gone through the season without a suggestion of jealousy or personal tension among the group. They had accepted Thorpe's predominance, they had counted on the vocal leadership from Burd and Welch, they had endured Warner's hard line in training. They shared a pride in being Indians who had made national success in sports. They got along because they accepted each other's personal and tribal differences with the racial similarities that bound them together. "I know Jim had the reputation for drinking," Roberts said. "But I remember him as being as sober as the rest of us. He knew I didn't drink, and he never offered me one. The fact that we never shared a drink together didn't matter at all."

Following the wedding celebration Superintendent Friedman provided a cutter to take the newlyweds through the snowbanked streets of Carlisle to the railroad depot where they caught a train for the West and Henry's new government job at the Shoshoni Indian Agency in Wind River, Wyoming. After they left, Friedman allowed the school to celebrate the event with a special dance in the gym.

VIII   MASTERY AT STOCKHOLM

A Very Chivalrous Nonscholar

A winter issue of the school publication, *The Red Man by Red Men*, reported on the annual athletic celebration at which the new president of Dickinson College, Dr. Eugene A. Noble, assured the Carlisle athletes and their guests that "the young men in the colleges today are clearer-minded, more law-abiding, and more respectful, and this improvement in academic life is chiefly due to the growing interest in school athletics." Superintendent Friedman announced that it was almost certain that Louis Tewanima would go to Europe to represent the United States in the Olympic marathon. The 1912 athletic captains—Welch in track, Arcasa in lacrosse, Thorpe in football—gave optimistic speeches on prospects for the coming season.

The Red Man was normally filled with boosterism, reassurance that the Carlisle way would lead the Indian into a better life in the civilized world, and occasional protest against injustice to the Indian. The December 1911 issue offered criticism of the "untrue and libelous brand of moving pictures of Indian life and romance which are shown throughout the country, and are supposed by the uninitiated public to be true to life . . . The majority of these pictures are not only without foundation in fact, but do not even have Indians to pose for them . . . White men or Mexicans usually pose as Indians, with blackened faces, wigs and Indian costume; their actions and gestures are absurdly grotesque, and exaggerated. These make-believes do not run, talk or walk like Indians, and their whole make-up brands them as 'fakirs.'" *The Red Man* suggested that Indians and the government make an effort to censure these pictures which "tend to create hostility against the Indian among many of his friends, and to alienate many white people."

The Red Man was something less than a precursory voice of the Indian Movement. It devoted columns of "alumni notes," extolling the progress of ex-students in the white world ("Egbert Big Hail owns a fine place, located near a creek at Pryor, Montana. He owns a nice frame house and several head of work horses . . . James Horner, an Onondago Indian, is working at his trade of carpentry in Syracuse, N.Y., and is doing good work") but gave little attention to the re-entry problems of those graduates who went back to the reservation. A short commentary by J. P. Dunn on "The Preservation of Indian Names and Languages" served to remind students and graduates that Carlisle had from the beginning been as much committed to the removal of their identity as Indians as safeguarding it. Dunn wrote: "It would be a disgrace to the people of the U.S. to permit the language of Pontiac and The Little Turtle, and Tecumthe, and Black Hawk to perish from the face of the earth . . . In a letter to me General Pratt said, 'The subject has not especially concerned me for the reason that, in my experience, not one in 20 of the Indian names in use could be recognized by any member of the tribe from which the name was derived. The attempts to perpetuate such names are therefore only sentimental abortion.'

"Because we have butchered the names," Dunn concluded, "is no reason why we should also lose their true form and meaning. And there is no question of perpetuating them. They will perpetuate themselves.

Their name is on your waters,
Ye may not wash it out."

Both *The Red Man* and *The Arrow*, the weekly paper, did carry Indian legends and stories prepared or simply copied by students with help from the history department and published with by-line and tribe identity ("'The Raccoon and the Opossum,' Estella Ellis, Sac & Fox"). They were well circulated by the administration and were often reprinted in the large daily papers and magazines in the East and Midwest. While they served to perpetuate Indian folklore, they were used as a showcase of student achievement for the public and Indian education authorities, a boost for the academic corner of the training at Carlisle. Some of the pieces came out so professionally polished that the student-authors must have had trouble recognizing their work. *The Arrow* ran a story titled, "Co Fa Che Qui" by James Thorpe that suggested Jim had absorbed considerable folklore of Spanish exploration and had a gift for description of the magnolia and cypress forests along the Savannah River. Co fa che qui was the name of an Indian queen who was forced to serve as a guide for DeSoto and his followers. The ending, at least, does sound like an economy-worded conclusion by Jim: "The soldiers met with many hostile Indians on their way and some friendly Indians. They treated the Indians cruelly. They captured them and made slaves of them; they were compelled to carry their burdens. The Spaniards had a great battle at Mobile, where many Indians and Spaniards were killed. DeSoto discovered the Mississippi River. DeSoto was the first white man to see this river. DeSoto became warm and feeble and died. He was buried in the Mississippi River. DeSoto was a selfish man. He wanted riches."

Whatever Thorpe's deficiencies in the classrooms at Carlisle— and there were many that were rooted in disinterest or lack of preparation—he became fluent enough with a pen and later a typewriter to express himself reasonably well. He kept his brother Frank in Oklahoma informed with occasional notes, typed his own requests to the Sac and Fox Agency, and while he was in Sweden for the 1912 Olympics he sent a steady flow of romantic letters to Iva Miller. If he couldn't stand up and debate on a platform with Gus Welch or Sam Burd, he had had enough experience before audiences (particularly at the Catholic students' meetings) to give with plain-spoken sincerity talks on "Athletics in General at Carlisle."

During his final academic terms Jim was enrolled in the Business Department which, along with telegraphy, was one of the few high-school senior-level courses offered at Carlisle. The teacher, the late poet Marianne Moore, found him poorly prepared for the challenge and inclined toward absenteeism. (When the disciplinarian was told that Jim was not bothering to show up for classes, word was finally sent down from Superintendent Friedman that he *should* attend every day. Thorpe had reached the status, as Pop Warner's leading protégé, where it was hoped he would stay out of loud trouble even if he didn't adhere to all the work whistles, recall bells and assembly calls.) Miss Moore, who taught arithmetic, typing and a course in commercial law that was intended to acquaint students with basic legal documents they would have to handle much sooner than most whites, developed a personal fondness for Jim and some of the other football boys, including Gus Welch, Joel Wheelock and Alex Arcasa. The athletes apparently felt protective toward Miss Moore, a delicately small young lady who rode a bicycle that seemed unsuitably large to classes each day. Miss Moore later said she found that her Indian students had "great behavior and ceremony, and were exceedingly chivalrous and decent and cooperative." She recalled that in the spring of 1912 when she chaperoned a group of older students on a trip to the circus in town it was Thorpe who stepped up and said, "Miss Moore, may I carry your parasol?"

A music teacher at Carlisle, Miss Verna Donegan, was struck with another quality of the Indian students she knew—their deep sense of loyalty to one they respected. "They could appear so stoical and unmoved," she said, "but if they came to like you they gave 100 per cent and you had their loyalty always." She found them most eager to learn, even though the music and style of singing she taught was so alien to them. "When I first asked one of my pupils to sing me songs he had learned in childhood, he said he was sorry but he couldn't. I asked him why and he said, reluctantly, 'You make us open our mouths when we sing.'" Miss Donegan, who later became a long-time Carlisle resident as Mrs. Verna Whistler, felt that the Warner-fashioned emphasis on athletic success cost many young Indian achievers the recognition they deserved in music, crafts and scholarship. There was, she believed, too much made of the athletic boys who went on to play professional ball and not enough of the Carlisle students who joined John Philip Sousa's band.

Gold Medals, a Hat and a Shoe

In February of 1912, eight years after Thorpe had entered Carlisle, student concerns were spread over such familiar distractions as the skating ice on the pond—would it hold hard and clear through the weekend?—and the winter congestion of school shows and musical programs. ("There were programs and programs, programs going on all the time," said teacher Donegan. "One could hardly keep up with them.") At the gym the students watched the accelerated training of Carlisle's two Olympic prospects, Thorpe and Tewanima. Warner had Tewanima pounding methodically around the board track and Thorpe working to maintain a consistency of six feet and more in the high jump. When weather permitted they took to the outdoor track, recently resurfaced with fresh cinders, or Tewanima ran for long stretches on Carlisle walks and roads. Warner took them to as much winter competition as he could—the Boston relays, the Georgetown Invitational in Washington, the annual indoor meet at Trenton where Thorpe scored four firsts and a second. Tewanima and Thorpe seemed certain to qualify for the Olympics, and Gus Welch had to be rated as a strong possibility with his excellent times in the quarter and half mile.

When winter gave up in the Cumberland Valley and the lacrosse and track squads turned to the outdoors, Thorpe's training picked up and so did the opportunities to break out of the routine of the classroom and Indian Field. Thorpe had an attractive reason to buy a flower for the weekend dance from the town boys who came to the dorms and athletic quarters on Saturdays. (The red rose and the fragrant tubular rose were the best sellers among the Indians; they were usually priced at about ten cents each and the Indians were so partial to their fragrance and bright color they bought them up as eagerly as they might candy sticks.) Thorpe's outlets ranged from the well-chaperoned Saturday night dances (during the winter he and a partner had won a prize for the two-step during the intermission of a Penn-Carlisle basketball game) to hanging around Halbert's Pool Hall on West High Street where he showed an enthusiasm for the sport but hardly yet rated as a pool shark. With the privilege that went with athletic prominence, Thorpe could stray from school duty long enough to join Mac Pittinger and other local boys down at the Pest House below the school's No. 1 farm, a small building that had been erected as an isolation ward for smallpox victims but had never been used for that purpose. The Pest House offered a convenient sanctuary—there was a swimming hole nearby and under the house the boys caught fish in a seine; it was also an agreeable location for a little beer drinking.

Graduation came the third week in April and although Thorpe was a member of the Class of 1912 he had not qualified for a general or academic certificate. But some of his closest friends were among the twenty-one who received academic certificates. Emma Newashe, who had turned twenty, wrote Sac and Fox Agent Kohlenberg: "At last the dawn of my graduation has appeared. It makes me feel sad . . . I wish you could be here to attend the exercises." In the quotes dedicated to seniors, the lines for Emma were: "Half hidden by the lifting veil of modest maidenhood, God's rarest gift to all mankind, a noble woman, stood."

The class historian, Ernestine Venne, a Chippewa, gave tribute to the boys of 1912 who won the championship banner in athletics: James Thorpe, Joel Wheelock, Gus Welch, Cliff Taylor and Albert Scott. She listed the most interesting trips the class had taken as "a walk to The Cave, a trip to town one evening, a visit to Carlisle High School. New Year's Eve was our best remembered social event . . . we stayed up to watch the New Year. We wouldn't dance because it was Sunday but we had music, games, refreshments."

Iva Miller wrote of Room No. 14 in the Academic Building, "a haunted room full of sweet memories of classes that have gone forth ready to begin their life battle . . . Looking south the beholder has a birdseye view of the eastern half of the city with its numerous spires and steeples and the battlements of the county jail looming large in the foreground, a counterpart of the historic French Chateau d'If. From the opposite window, a well-kept road winding through trees and cutting our beautiful campus, laid out in lawns, artistic flower beds, walks . . . On the wall our banner of tan and blue with 'Loyalty 1912' embroidered on it."

Class president Gus Welch was honored with this limerick by Emma Newashe in the graduation book:

> There is a young man, Welch by name,
> For whom we predict immense fame;
> He was class president,
> Which means he is meant
> O'er this our great country to reign.

Gus and Louis Tewanima, with certificates as expert tailors, went from the commencement exercises back to the business of running for Carlisle through the remainder of the track season. Tewanima became the hero of a feat a few weeks later which, at the local level, became as legendary as any of Thorpe's performances with the Carlisle track team. For the annual state collegiate meet held on the island in the Susquehanna River at Harrisburg, the little Hopi agreed to run all the way from Carlisle, a distance of eighteen miles then, as a useful and dramatic way of preparing for the Olympic marathon. (The meet was held without the dominating figure of Thorpe, who was involved in pre-Olympic pentathlon competition in New York.) Tewanima covered the road between Carlisle and Harrisburg in one hour and fifty minutes and when he entered the stadium the two-mile run was in progress. Tewanima never broke stride; to the rising cheers of the crowd he joined the field of two-milers and pulled far ahead of them as he circled the track twice before calling it a day's run. Even the succession of personal and school records Thorpe posted that spring—among them a high jump of six-five, a shot put of 47 feet 9 inches, 23.8 in the 220-yard hurdles, 15 seconds in the 120-high hurdles—were less of a conversation piece around Carlisle and the nearby state capital than Tewanima's great run.

Carlisle closed the regular track season in late May against Lafayette in Easton, Pennsylvania, an event that later found a prominent place in Carlisle folklore. The attractive story was that when the Indians suited up at Easton there were only four of them, including Thorpe, much to the astonishment of their Lafayette hosts with a squad of thirty or more. Actually Warner took eight Indians with him, which he considered a reasonable selection for a dual meet. Thorpe won six firsts, Welch took the quarter and half miles, Tewanima the mile and two mile, and Sam Burd won the hammer throw. With second-place points by other Indians, Carlisle won, 71–41, a typical if less than legend-making exhibition.

Thorpe and Tewanima were given leave from Carlisle in the middle of June to prepare for the Olympics. Illness had prevented Gus Welch from the chance to become the third member of the Indian track squad to represent the United States in the Games at Stockholm, a disappointment to Gus and Jim who had hoped to share the adventure together. Two weeks before his departure Thorpe sent a message with covering note from Moses Friedman to the new superintendent of the Sac and Fox Agency, Horace Johnson, in Stroud: "Please send me $100 from my account. Will need same this summer in taking trip to Sweden with Olympic team."

But Superintendent Johnson was neither impressed with Thorpe's Olympic honor nor of the belief that he should be spending his energies running around the world in a track suit. Johnson answered Friedman: "I have to advise that I cannot conscientiously recommend to the Indian Office that this be done, for the reason that he has had $300 since last August, which appears to me to be an excessive sum for him to have expended during the period mentioned . . . and when it is also understood that he is 25 years of age and should be perfectly content to make his own living without depending on trust and lease funds which have cost him no effort to obtain.

"I understand that a trip to Sweden might be of considerable benefit to the young man but I am strongly convinced that instead of being a benefit it will be a deterent. He has now reached the age, when, instead of gallivanting around the country, he should be at work on his allotment, or in some other location, where, instead of being a tax on his resources, he would be adding something thereto."

On June 11 Friedman wired Johnson: "Thorpe is to leave today. Can you wire part or all of $100 recommended for him? Please reply."

Johnson's answer came by government night rate collect: "Have no authority to wire Thorp money."

Thorpe left for a pre-Olympic exhibition at Celtic Park in New York and a sailing on the ocean liner *Finland* with whatever monies Friedman and Warner gave him. He had been picked to represent the United States in both the pentathlon and decathlon events, but he had been reminded again that for all of his athletic stature he was still very much a ward of the government whose privileges had their limit.

Nothing that Thorpe was to experience at the Games in Stockholm was to prove more awesome than his discovery of the size and accommodations of the *Finland*. His traveling companions, Louis Tewanima and Pop Warner, acting as trainer and appointed chaperone for the two Indian wards, had encountered the wonders of ocean voyaging before. Thorpe was overwhelmed. Years later he said that boarding and touring the boat remained with him as the largest thrill of the Olympic trip. "I'd never seen a boat as big as that before. I've seen a lot since. But nothing was like that—walking on the boat, and all those cabins and the decks and eating and sleeping on it."

Thorpe also trained on it, despite the common stories that he took the Olympic challenge so casually that he drank and slept his way across the Atlantic. The five-event pentathlon was one of the first on the Olympic program and Thorpe worked out regularly with other Olympic team members, as did Tewanima whose Hopi endurance would be tested in the 10,000-meter run and the marathon. For a few hours each day the ship's long decks and recreation areas were filled with men jogging, stretching, jumping, wrestling, practicing starts and sprints. If Thorpe's preparation seemed less feverish than that of some of the other U. S. Olympians, it was not as indifferent as Johnny Hayes, the U. S. marathoner, reported after the Games: "One day I looked out from our quarters in Stockholm and saw Jim get out of a hammock and walk to the sidewalk. I saw him mark off about 23 feet. I thought he was going to do some jumping and was shocked at the idea he would try it on the pavement. He walked back to the hammock and climbed in, eyeing the two marks. For all I could see, that was the training he did for the broad jump." The Hayes' anecdote provided the accepted picture over the years of

Thorpe's Olympic preparations. It was at least slightly removed from reality—Thorpe and other team members were quartered aboard the *Finland* during the Games and he did his relaxing in bunk or deck chair and his measuring along the wooden decks.

Somehow Thorpe managed to get into magnificent condition for the Olympic pentathlon held on July 7, the second day of competition. He was, by calculation of physicians at Carlisle, at the peak of his physical development that summer. He stood just over 5-11 and weighed 181. His reach was 72.5 inches. He was 15.9 inches at the neck, 39.7 around the chest, and 32.3 at the waist. Thorpe's shoulders were narrow, about 18 inches, but he was deep-chested, 11.8 inches. Thorpe's physical mannerisms just before he was to go into action were slightly lumbering, similar in a way to the indifferent gait of professional football's Jimmy Brown as he returned to the huddle of the Cleveland Browns after one of his matchless runs. He was slightly bowlegged, which may have accentuated the attitude of casualness. Thorpe's height and weight would compare favorably with that of a defensive safety man in modern pro football, but his chest, biceps and thighs were those of a man of great physical power in 1912. Olympic spectators, watching him dominate the pentathlon and decathlon competition used the exclamation, "Isn't he a horse!" to show their admiration for his versatility. After a little celebrating of his Olympic position one evening in the spas of Stockholm, Thorpe took to galloping around the decks of the *Finland,* yelling, "I'm a horse! I'm a horse!"

While American sprinters were finishing one, two, three in the Olympic 100 meters—a sweep that occupied most of the headlines in the U. S. papers the following day—Thorpe was methodically winning four of the five pentathlon events. He was first in the 200 meters (22.9), the 1,500-meter run (4:44.8), the broad jump (23 feet, 2$\frac{7}{10}$ inches), discus (116 feet, 8$\frac{4}{10}$ inches). He was third in the javelin with an effort of just over 153 feet. Thorpe's low score of seven points was well ahead of Norway's F. R. Bie with 21. If his performance drew less than headline attention at home, it greatly impressed the crowd of twenty thousand that followed him through each track and field event at the Olympic stadium, and it swelled the breast of national pride in the AAU's James Sullivan. "His all around work was certainly sensational," said the commissioner. "It answers the charge that Americans specialize in athletics. It also answers the allegation that most of our runners are of foreign parentage for Thorpe is a real American if there ever was one."

There were six days between the pentathlon and the start of the decathlon competition, and during that time the Swedish people, with their great fascination for long-distance runners, were captivated by the other half of Carlisle's Olympic representation, Louis Tewanima. In the 10,000 meters Tewanima ran second to Finland's renowned Hannes Kolehmainen with the most impressive showing at that Olympic distance until Billy Mills, another American Indian, finished first at Tokyo in 1964.

The decathlon test was spread over three days instead of the two which Bob Mathias, Rafer Johnson and later decathlon champions had to endure. It began with a field of twenty-nine competing early in the morning in the 100-meter heats. Although Thorpe had run the 100-yard dash in 10 seconds flat and Pop Warner had clocked him at 9.8 in a practice sprint, he finished third in the 100 meters with a time of 11.2. Thorpe was fourth in the 400-meter race and in the javelin throw, one of his weakest events. (Technique in hurling the javelin improved so much over the years that Rafer Johnson, in his record-breaking decathlon effort in Moscow in 1958, reached a distance of 238 feet, 2 inches —some 88 feet farther than Thorpe did in 1912.) But Thorpe's co-ordination and strength of arm and leg began to tell in other events. He finished first in the 1,500 meters in 4:40.1, a good ten seconds faster than decathlon winner Bob Mathias covered the long distance in 1952. He scored firsts in the 110-meter hurdles in 15.6, in the shot-put with 42 feet, 5½ inches, and the high jump at 6 feet, 1⁶⁄₁₀ inches. The leap was something less than Thorpe's best. He had cleared 6 feet, 5 inches while preparing for the Games.

Thorpe's point total in the ten events, 8,142.96, was strong enough to stand as an Olympic record for sixteen years. Viewed with his domination of the pentathlon, it gave the crowds watching from the covered stands in Stockholm and the readers of newspapers around the world a portrait of a super-athlete of the times. The decathlon was spread over so many days and events that his demonstration of skills had a cumulative effect on the crowds following this ultimate test; wherever they focused their attention there was the light-skinned Indian in white shorts and white top with the American shield breaking across the finish line first or hurtling his body high over the crossbar. Thorpe's performance and a string of gold medal finishers by U. S. runners and weight men gave a heavy American presence to the Games that was both admired and deplored by foreign observers. *The Times* of London offered this compliment to the U. S. team: "A finer lot of men was probably never got together. The average height is nearly six feet and not even the Swedish gymnasts are more symetrically built." But the London correspondent found the loud cheering for Thorpe and other American winners *by* Americans as a threat to the very character of the Games: "A body of English athletes has taken here to using an imitation of the American 'college cries' and a number of Swedes also endeavour, quite ineffectually, to answer the American claque, bark for bark . . . if the Games are to continue in any amicableness, it will be necessary for the authorities hereafter to adopt rules which will prevent the seating of a number of representatives of a particular nation *en bloc,* while prohibiting the waving of foreign flags or prescribing the form in which applause may find utterance."

It was appropriate for chauvinistic representatives and neutrals alike that the final decathlon events were held on the last day of the Fifth Olympiad so that Thorpe's triumphs could be instantly acclaimed by King Gustav and the crowd that filled the stadium. There were sixteen gold medals for Americans and Thorpe's two appearances before King Gustav at the victory stand drew the greatest ovations. (Louis Tewanima received his silver medal from the Crown Prince, who handed out the second-place awards.) In addition to the gold medal for the pentathlon Thorpe received a bronze bust of the King of Sweden which was placed on the awards platform and stood about half as high as the austere-looking, top-hatted King Gustav himself. The king, who had seemed mildly amused at the discomfort some of the gold medalists showed when they were crowned with the traditional laurel wreath, spoke solemnly to the Sac and Fox Indian, who stood holding his familiar felt hat in hand, "Sir, you are the greatest athlete in the world." Thorpe's reply was supposedly a straight-forward, "Thanks, King." The words of King Gustav were to follow Thorpe literally to his grave, carved into the stone marker of his final resting place. Six months after the Games when the two gold medals, the bronze bust of the King of Sweden and the jeweled chalice in the form of a Viking ship offered by the Czar of Russia to the decathlon winner and his records were expunged, the superlative from King Gustav became trophy enough.

The acclamation at the carpeted victory platform at the Stadium soon gave way to less ritualistic celebration in which Thorpe was able to take a little thirst-quenching comfort; it spread from Stockholm to other European cities where he competed in post-Olympic track meets and to the United States where citizens and public officials eagerly awaited his return. The welcomes in New York and Philadelphia were of enormous scale, enough to leave the two teammates from Carlisle tight-lipped and solemn. In New York the entire U. S. team rode in a car caravan down Fifth Avenue. Thorpe was alone in an open car, behind one bearing his trophies from the King of Sweden and Czar of Russia, and he shared the biggest responses from the crowd estimated at one million with local hero, Pat McDonald, the traffic cop who was a surprise winner in the Olympic shot-put. As the cars reached the reviewing stand Thorpe finally broke from his unsmiling reserve, jumped out of the car and happily shook hands with Commissioner James Sullivan. In Philadelphia, where Thorpe and Tewanima were honored with a half-dozen other Pennsylvania athletes who had competed in the Games, the pentathlon and decathlon trophies went on display at Wanamaker's store, and Thorpe sat down at a banquet with the world's most famous ballplayer, Ty Cobb, joined in the tribute to the Olympians.

The warmest welcome for the two Indians came at Carlisle where townspeople raised $1,059.20 for a celebration as lavish as any held in the Cumberland Valley. Thorpe, Tewanima and Warner—Jim in his soft felt and Pop and Louis in straw skimmers —were hauled through the streets in a horse-drawn victoria with uniformed driver. Behind came the platoons of Indian cadets from school, the Steelton band, the Mount Holly Fire Department, the Improved Order of Red Men, the Empire Hook and Ladder Company—hardly an organization within miles was unrepresented. In bright mid-August sunlight at Dickinson's Biddle Field, where five thousand people—with many of the ladies under parasols—crowded the stands and playing area, Superintendent Friedman spoke of the wondrous advancement of Louis Tewanima, one of twelve Hopis who had come to Carlisle as "pagans" with long hair and earrings. Tewanima, his skinny neck surrounded by the white man's hard starched collar, listened impassively. As did Thorpe when the letter sent to him at Carlisle from President Taft was read by Friedman. The message noted, "You have set a high standard of physical development which is only attained by right living and right thinking, and your victory will serve as an incentive to all to improve those qualities which characterize the best type of American citizen."

Pop Warner addressed the crowd, saying he had been delegated by Thorpe and Tewanima to make a thank-you speech for both of them. Thorpe did get on his feet long enough to say, "You have shown us a splendid time and we are grateful for it." Tewanima bobbed up, grinned and said, "Thanks for this honor," and sat down to great cheers. It was for Tewanima a speech of near record length. There was a baseball game between Carlisle and Chambersburg that went into extra innings and wore on the patience of spectator Thorpe. At some point before the dinner at the Elks Club, where there were more speeches, Thorpe managed to wander away from the group. Pop sent Arthur Martin off to find him and get him back on the program. Martin's instinct led him to a saloon on East Louther Street where he found the Olympic hero pleasantly unwinding at the bar. At the Elks Club, Thorpe and Tewanima were relieved to be rescued by a turnout of their schoolmates, wearing night shirts and carrying torches for a parade down Hanover Street to the campus and a dance at the gym. The party began at 9 to the strains of *La Boheme* and stretched until 1:45. Thorpe was seldom off the dance floor.

In the following days of reunion with Carlisle friends Thorpe and Tewanima happily passed out a few souvenirs from Europe. Jim gave his pal Gus Welch, who had missed the chance to qualify for the Olympic squad, the hat worn by team members and one of the track shoes he used in winning the decathlon. The other had gone to some quick-handed souvenir hunter. For Tewanima the homecoming events of that August were also a protracted farewell to Carlisle, the Indian school and the forced five-year exposure to the white world. He had his tailor's certificate and his silver Olympic medal among so many awards and ribbons—and a desire to return to the mesa of northeastern Arizona where he could wear his red hairband and turquoise earrings again. Before leaving, Tewanima scattered tokens of his great running achievements around the school. Several of the Carlisle girls took to wearing buckles on their shoes made from the track medals he had given them.

IX   TALL TOUCHDOWNS

Dropping Out at W & J

When the salutes to the Olympians had scaled down from the civic demonstrations to the saloons of Carlisle—and even a rare beer pour at Pop Warner's cottage—Thorpe could look at some of the opportunities that had suddenly become available to him and which seemed to stretch as wide as the Oklahoma horizon he knew as a child. Gus Welch had strongly advised him to accept the offer of some ten thousand dollars to go on tour for the indefatigable promoter, C. C. ("Cash & Carry") Pyle before turning to a more stable career in baseball. But Warner, as friend, advisor, agent and coach, wanted him to return to the Carlisle backfield for a fourth year, bowling over opponents and boosting the gate in a 1912 schedule which had grown to fourteen games. Another season of football, Warner argued, could only increase his market value when it came time to negotiate with the ball clubs.

Thorpe finally agreed that he would return to Carlisle and finish his requirements for a certificate—and play again for Pop. In a letter to "Dear Brother Frank," Jim explained:

> Well, Bud, I'm right in the game again, playing football. We have our first game next Saturday . . . Frank, I have the chance to make a bunch of dough after leaving this school. Just started going today (September 17). God it's hard to go back again but it is for my good, so I will make the best of things. Well, I saw about getting the "kids" to Carlisle when I was in Washington and

think that it will be all right. Well, Pal, you will be back home this year and you will say there is no place like home sweet home. Frank, it is getting late and I must close hoping to hear from you real soon. Your brother James Thorpe

The "kids" were sister Adaline (or Adeline, as she commonly spelled it) and brother Ed, both attending Chilocco in Oklahoma. Ed was admitted to Carlisle the following January, at age fourteen, as a Sac and Fox orphan with "no fixed home." Ed became a member of the Carlisle band and dreamed of buying his own cornet "gold plated, engraved all over, jeweled with wreath of emeralds and in a plush-lined case." But Adaline, age seventeen, was not easily removed from Chilocco. The superintendent, Edgar Allen, objected to the transfer, saying: "I am absolutely certain that it will work harm to this girl to go to Carlisle particularly since they have such a loose conception of what constitutes proper conduct these days—I have in my possession a number of letters written by girls from there to girls at this school telling of their glorious times and freedom from restraint. To a girl such as Adaline freedom will work seriously against her. Taken also in connection with this the drunken episode of her brother at the school it appears to me as a very serious error to have her go to Carlisle." Adaline solved the debate by running off and getting married.

Thorpe's ability to handle himself in the international arena apparently impressed Sac and Fox Agent Horace Johnson; in mid-September he recommended that the balance of his account in Stroud—$295.23—be turned over to him for "use without restriction." Johnson noted that Thorpe also received $250 annual rent on his allotment, that he had visited the agency and "is not a bad appearing fellow though somewhat inclined to indulge his appetite in intoxicating liquors." With $295 in ready spending money and a bottomless supply of free drinks assured by his celebrity status, Jim went back to the football wars for Carlisle.

Major changes in the rules and two exceptional additions to Warner's varsity enlivened the Indians' training for their home opener on September 21. The new regulations helped liberate the offense and brought the game in closer proximity to modern football: four downs, instead of three, were allowed to gain ten yards and a first down; the field was shortened to 100 yards, with an extra ten yards behind each goal (pass zones) for receiving forward passes; the twenty-yard restriction on the pass was removed; there were more disqualification and stiff yardage penalties for roughness; a coach could draw a fifteen-yard penalty for coaching from the sidelines and it was just as costly for a player who failed to report to the referee as a substitute. The rules prohibiting tripping, the flying tackle, any tackling below the knees except on the line of scrimmage were certain to stimulate Carlisle's wondrous running game.

Warner had managed to preserve his set backfield of Welch, Thorpe, Arcasa and Powell (Gus, the graduate of 1911, was getting most of his education at Conway Hall). He had two excellent ball carriers from the scrubs—good enough to make most backfields in the country—whom he decided to use at tackle. Both of them, Pete Calac and Joe Guyon, were to have illustrious years in college competition and to play with Thorpe later on as professionals.

Calac was a nineteen-year-old Mission Indian from California —a full blood who was called Pedro by his mother Felicida Molido. Enrolled at the government boarding school at Riverside, California, in 1901, Calac soon began to show exceptional physical development, which may or may not have come to the attention of Pop Warner nearly three thousand miles east. After Calac was enrolled at Carlisle by his mother, entry papers noted "this young man is very strong and better fitted to do heavy manual labor. He is to be trusted." When he was ready to start at right tackle he was five-ten and weighed about 185. Calac combined leadership qualities and a lively mind with his muscular strength; he was elected captain of the 1915 Indian team and with Warner no longer on the scene had a prominent voice in everything from the selection of new uniforms to the revising of schedules in football and lacrosse. During his last year at Carlisle, Calac was one of a half-dozen Indians selected for a special training program by the Ford Motor Company in Detroit.

The other halfback turned temporary tackle was Joe Guyon, who at nineteen was also fast and strong enough (nearly 190 pounds) to play in the line. Guyon—his French father's name was

Gagnon and his mother was a full-blood Chippewa—was enrolled from the White Earth Agency in Minnesota. Guyon's athletic promise in the West made it inevitable that he would find his way into the football quarters at Carlisle, where doctors who examined him at admission time described him as "a picture of health . . . splendidly developed." Guyon was to play only two years at Carlisle before he was persuaded to develop his fine football talent elsewhere, first at Keewatin Academy and then at Georgia Tech where he became an All-America halfback with the sports-page sobriquet, Indian Joe Guyon. (When Guyon enrolled at Georgia Tech in September 1916 the president asked the superintendent's office at Carlisle if the institute qualified as a college or only a prep school; if it was basically a prep, he explained, Joe could play varsity football at Georgia Tech immediately. The new superintendent, O. H. Lipps, wired back that Carlisle was "a vocational school giving academic work equivalent to ordinary high school . . . but in athletics Carlisle has had collegiate rank.")

As Warner prepared his Indians for the usual September warm-up games—Albright, Lebanon Valley and Dickinson were to be met within eight days—he had reason to believe that Carlisle might indeed have a collegiate rank of No. 1 in the country by the end of the 1912 season. Thorpe was as strong and as fast as he ever would be, the ultimate ball carrier, and it was a matter of keeping him motivated for the succession of Saturday opponents. Without Henry Roberts and Sam Burd, Warner did have uncertainties at end. He favored two small scrappy blockers, George ("Cotton") Vetternack, a Chippewa who weighed only 140 pounds, and Roy Large, a Shoshone who despite his name was around 150. Large suffered from a debilitating trachoma condition which left him nearly sightless two years later.

To the entertainment of the students and townspeople, Carlisle ran through Albright and Lebanon Valley without much need of Thorpe and other regulars. The Dickinson game, played at Biddle Field across town, might have proved a more spirited test but Thorpe demoralized their underdog rivals by picking off a bad pass from center on a kicking down and running sixty-five yards for a second touchdown. The final score was 34–0.

Before the Villanova game at Harrisburg the following Saturday Warner and Thorpe were invited to attend a football clinic at the capital. Thorpe begged off with a cold and so Warner drove alone to the clinic where he explained to the audience the mysteries of the crisscross, the double pass from which Arcasa and Thorpe made such quick gains, the advantage of having the ball snapped directly to the tailback (for years the quarterback was required to handle the ball before another player could run with it). Warner undoubtedly did not discuss a new formation he was experimenting with for use at an appropriate time later in the year. He placed two backs outside the defensive tackles, instead of the one in the single wing. The double-wing formation offered the quick release of a wing back and an end from each side of the line on passes, which would get more emphasis under the new rules, and it was ideal for reverses which the Indians ran with such swiftness and precision. Warner's formation eventually became basic with advocates of wide-open football.

There was no need for innovation against Villanova. Thorpe played for little more than twenty minutes and scored three touchdowns. He also kicked seven extra points in the 65–0 rout. When Warner gave Thorpe permission to leave the field and join waiting friends, hundreds of children and many adults poured out of the stands and followed him to the line of cars parked near the clubhouse, a burst of hero worship and curiosity that Thorpe would encounter whenever he stepped into the public arena from then on.

The Indians had been averaging nearly fifty points a game against their early opponents and Thorpe and Arcasa had shown that they needed but one down, not four, to move the ball ten yards. But their next opponent, Washington and Jefferson, was made of much sterner material and had football ambitions as presumptuous as that of any small college (W&J represented the East in the 1922 Rose Bowl game). The match between the two state powers drew 10,000 people to the western Pennsylvania campus and left nearly everyone in a state of frustration. The game ended in a scoreless tie, a condition that Thorpe might have corrected had he been physically and emotionally keyed for the game. On three field goal attempts he was wide from the 27, short from the 45 and an attempt from the 40 was partially blocked. The Indians had not been shut out in eighteen games and the experience was an agonizing one for Pop Warner, his team captain and great running back and the other twenty-odd players who had made the trip. A famous result of the day's frustrations was that Thorpe got drunk, Warner reacted angrily and there was an explosion between coach and momentarily collapsed hero that was to acquire a variety of colorations over the years.

After the game the team stopped in Pittsburgh for a meal and a change of trains. Thorpe and Welch took not unusual advantage of the opportunity and found their way to a nearby bar. Gus stopped drowning his regrets over the game in time to make the team dinner, but Thorpe, who had more cause for regret over his near misses during the afternoon, stayed on. When the train departure neared Warner went after his star. Pop insisted that he did not—as the story went—have to slam Thorpe's head against the wall to persuade him to leave. (Later, after a game at the University of Pittsburgh, Warner did lose his temper in front of the team over the performance of his left end, Roy Large, and threatened the little Shoshone, "I'll knock your damn block off." The public humiliation of Large angered Gus Welch and others.) Getting Thorpe separated from the saloon stirred up a noisy scene, and Warner, despite his bull strength, had to get help from a couple of players to move Jim onto the train en route to Carlisle.

Warner waited until the following day to give Thorpe a tongue lashing. It was a hell of a note for an Olympic champion to make a public disgrace of himself, the coach said; it was not only bad for his image but it hurt the rest of the team. Warner ordered him to apologize. At the athletic quarters Jim stood up among his friends and mumbled that he was sorry.

The Indians were sent through a hard scrimmage against Dickinson at midweek, Warner's way of getting them fit for Syracuse, the team that had knocked them out of a national title the year before. Again a hard rain fell at Syracuse stadium, reducing the effectiveness of the popular sweeps, reverses and laterals which Welch tried to make work with Thorpe, Arcasa and Powell. At half time, with the Indians holding a slight lead, Warner told them he had had enough of the fancy ball handling and end runs —it was time to go straight at the heavy Syracuse line. Thorpe and Arcasa took to the inglorious role of line plunger, which had long been fullback Possum Powell's job, and the score soared to 33–0.

Some views of the victory, well removed from the precise mechanics of the game, were offered by Carlisle rooter Anna Bancroft in the *Arrow:*

"Yes, it was a great game. In the first half—I'm sure it was called a half—a nice boy from Syracuse was thrown with such force that one leg was broken and his shoulder dislocated. He struggled to his feet, only to fall over again in the arms of the man in back of him. Then he was carried to the side of the field and the physician began his examination. Ten minutes later his broken leg was bound up and in reply to eager questioning of the injured one the physician handed him a cigar and a match. There didn't seem to be anything in that except a little act of courtesy and thoughtfulness (to us) but the expression on the face of the injured one when the cigar was accepted was one of deepest disappointment and discouragement . . . it was that permission to smoke that meant he was 'down and out' for this year, so far as football is concerned, as football players in training are not permitted to indulge in smoking, etc. . . . Poor boy; months of training and hard work, all for what—a broken leg and dislocated shoulder— and that even before the game had begun in earnest.

"Towards the end of the second half a big fine looking Indian was marching unceremoniously from the field because he had grabbed a Syracusan by the collar and tossed him lightly over the wild struggling mass that was fighting for the ball. It seems that the United States Government don't permit the Government school boys to do anything in the way of "slugging" and consequently the stalwart visitor was 'out of the game.' At its best, football is brutal and broken arms, broken legs, broken heads—all the same—it's a part of the game, and the last to complain are those who are injured, especially if their side wins . . .

"I'm glad anyhow that the Carlisle boys won, because of a great many things: first of all, because they played a fine all 'round square game, and secondly, because in the beginning everything seemed to be in favor of Syracuse. Syracuse, or rather Sarahcuse, as the rooters shouted, had the band; Syracuse had the rooters, several hundred of them; Syracuse had the heavy men; well, Syracuse seemed to have the best of it all 'round—and perhaps I'm a little prejudiced because of that 'no slugging' clause. Anyhow Carlisle won and I'm glad, glad of it."

Warner was glad of it, too, because he had the Indians booked for four games on the road in the next three weeks—first at Pittsburgh, where they scored a 45–0 rout, and then at Georgetown in Washington, D.C., where they won with moderate ease before the traditional gathering of Congressmen, government bureaucrats and members of the Department of Interior anxious for visible signs of progress in the Indian education program. One of the most avid of the Carlisle supporters in the capital was Congressman Charles Carter, a first representative from the new state of Oklahoma in 1907 and a former member of the Chickasaw council. Carter tried to see the Indians play whenever they were within range of Washington and he often took his young daughter, Julia. After the Georgetown-Carlisle game she had a date with handsome Joe Guyon and they took a trolley ride through the streets of Georgetown to the Capitol. As part Indian, Julia fully expected a certain amount of reserve from Guyon during the early stages of their acquaintance. But she was not prepared for total silence from the young athlete. Guyon finally shattered the wordless evening as the trolley swayed around a curve at the bottom of a Georgetown hill: "Now I see why they put the boys on the outside seat," he said. It was the only complete sentence he uttered on their date. (Julia, who attended Johns Hopkins in Baltimore, later became friends with the most loquacious member of the team, Gus Welch. The friendship resulted in a marriage in 1923, after Gus had served as a captain in the U. S. Cavalry during World War I and had been head coach for a few seasons at Washington State.)

On Sunday Warner led the team from Washington into Canada for a hastily arranged game with the Toronto rugby club, champions of the Dominion. There was much talk of the game being an expression of friendship and understanding between the two nations, of the honor being paid by original Americans to the visiting Duke and Duchess of Connaught, who were to attend the game. Warner said he was determined to prove the superiority of the American sport to rugby. But the game had been arranged by Warner around the sure smell of heavy gate receipts. It was played mostly under U. S. football rules and with the running and kicking of Thorpe, Carlisle won the international, intersport competition easily, 49–1. The side trip to Canada turned a three thousand dollar profit for the athletic association.

The Army game, played on November 9 at West Point, was one of the events of that autumn that gave rise to much myth-making. The result is firm: Carlisle beat the Cadets, 27–6, and the score did not reflect the all-around superiority of the Indians or the ease with which Thorpe moved the ball on most carries. Warner wanted so badly to win the game by a convincing score to knock down the criticism of Carlisle's soft schedule that he resorted to a pep talk before the game. Pop's message was a worn piece of inspiration the Indians really didn't need; he reminded them that the Army had been responsible for some of the government's worst inflictions on their forefathers. Carlisle scored only four touchdowns—and none by Thorpe despite histories to the contrary—but the backs ran freely over most of the field, being stopped frequently by fumbles or the desperate goal-line defense of Army's All-America tackle Devore. In an early series of downs Thorpe made runs of twenty and twenty-five yards, carrying the ball to the Army 15 where he fumbled it away. The next time the Indians were on the attack Thorpe broke free for forty-five yards but fumbled when he was tackled and the ball was picked up by Elmer Busch.

Popular legend says that Thorpe ran back an Army punt for a touchdown that was nullified by a holding penalty and then angrily returned the next kick one hundred yards for a score. The story fitted so suitably with Thorpe folklore that Jim later accepted it himself. He did make a spectacular run back of an Army kick for forty-five yards and an apparent score, with help from good blocks from Welch and Arcasa. After Thorpe learned that his touchdown didn't count because a teammate had been caught holding, he asked the referee to identify the guilty player, a request permitted by the rules. The official spent a confused moment trying to sort out the impassive Indian faces before settling on Cotton Vetternack. Yes, the small end admitted he had hooked one of the Cadets. Thorpe, exercising his captain's authority, made Vetternack stand on the side lines for a play or two.

Army's next kick was taken by Welch, not Thorpe, and in the drive that followed it was Arcasa who scored the touchdown. The hard-running Colville Indian scored three times and Bergie once.

The play was rough but never riotous. Possum Powell was expelled and Devore was sent off—and Army penalized half the distance to the goal—after the Cadets' field leader had jumped on Joe Guyon on the second-half kickoff. The future generals, including starting halfback Dwight Eisenhower, experienced increasing humiliation as the game was played out under heavy dark clouds. At one point Thorpe hurt his tender left shoulder and play was delayed for three minutes while Pop Warner removed the shoulder pads and tended to the injury. When Thorpe finally got back on his feet and trotted to his position in the Indians' line-up, the small West Point crowd of less than five thousand gave him the loudest cheer of the day.

The famous football authority, coach and All-America selector, Walter Camp, rode back on the train to New York with the Carlisle team. There was admiration shown for the crisscross plays worked by Arcasa and Thorpe and for the double-flanker formation that Warner threw in as a surprise. But Camp thought Welch was a little foolhardy for ignoring Thorpe's foot and letting him run from punt formation—a bit of fakery that produced big gains against Army. He also thought that Welch was too hasty in running off plays instead of taking more time to study the Army defense. The comment amused Thorpe. He said to Camp, "How can Gus study the defense when there isn't any defense?"

The easy conquest of Army, which had ranked as one of the best in the East, was followed by a dismaying letdown against Pennsylvania. Overconfidence and a sub-performance cost the Indians an unbeaten season. A crowd of 25,000 turned out for the opportunity to see Thorpe play at Franklin Field for the first time in four years. The Philadelphia *Inquirer* described the momentous occasion: "It was 2:25 P.M. when the Indians, looking the part of the best football team in America, with the world's greatest athlete, their captain, Jim Thorpe, at their head, came running on the field. Four minutes later Penn came into the arena. Captain Mercer and Captain Thorpe met before the goal post and Penn prepared to kick off."

Penn kicked off and within two minutes had scored on the first of a series of Carlisle mistakes. Bergie's pass from center slipped through the reliable Arcasa's hands and the ball was recovered in the end zone for a Penn touchdown. Later, a fumble by Possum Powell cost another score, Thorpe missed what seemed to be an easy field goal, and the Indians fell for a fake and let a Penn pass receiver get free for a touchdown. Just before the end of the half, with the joyous home team in a 20–6 lead, Thorpe suddenly broke up the game's pattern with one of his great runs. At the Carlisle 20 he broke around end behind clean blocking and raced away from everyone except Penn's Tubby Green who grabbed onto his jersey at midfield. Thorpe shook Green off and ran straight between the goal posts. "Thorpe tore off many other runs during the game," reported the *Inquirer*, "but nothing near so sensational or thrilling as this eighty-yard sprint for a score. During the second half the Carlisle eleven used Thorpe continually to carry the ball, but as his interference wilted under Penn's sharp and battering attack, the great Indian was invariably smothered by Quaker tacklers in the closing minutes. Penn played and waited for Thorpe and he came to them tired but pluckily in the fading minutes of the battle." Carlisle took the lead, 26–21, in the second half but lost it, and Thorpe's fumble of a short forward pass led to Penn's final touchdown and a score of 34–26. Pop Warner was enormously frustrated watching his usually precise, sure-handed Indians turn the ball over to Penn. Carlisle had gained nearly four hundred yards (eighty of them by Thorpe on one run and forty-three on another) to Penn's 177. Thorpe could barely live with the blunders he and his teammates made during the afternoon. Once he took a swing at a cluster of Penn tacklers who piled into him—and was roundly booed. After the game as he made his way to the gymnasium some of the Penn students forming a victory snake dance broke from formation and approached him to shake his hand. Thorpe quickly brushed them aside. He was little accustomed to boos and defeats.

There were other pressures on Thorpe, in addition to the hero role through a long season (Penn was the twelfth team the Indians had played since September 21). His girl, Iva, had gone to California to be with relatives after his graduation and was being heavily advised to drop all thoughts of marrying Jim. The ring he sent was taken away from her and even letter writing became difficult. Jim had that problem on his mind, as well as the decision of how and when to start cashing in on the best of the professional offers.

Encounter in the Leicester Hills

In a bizarre way Thorpe's immediate future was shaped—and his life much influenced—by an episode that followed Carlisle's next game, against little Springfield Training School (the YMCA college) in Massachusetts. Warner had booked the physical education school to fill in the Saturday before the popular Thanksgiving Day game with Brown at Providence. He had been guaranteed two thousand dollars plus a percentage of the gate profits (it came to $33). The Indians were given an unexpectedly bruising workout by the physical education students before winning, 30–24. They needed another big effort by Thorpe who scored four touchdowns, three conversions and a field goal.

After the game Warner and his twenty-one players retreated to the Leicester Inn outside Worcester for a few days of recuperation, light drills and hikes before Thanksgiving Day. Thorpe and Bill Garlow were given a day's rest while Warner and his boys walked over the hills around the Inn. Thorpe began to take part in the signal drills which Warner held on an open field and which attracted curious locals and newspapermen in the area. The Indians at practice were a show—Thorpe's long punts and placements, the speed and slickness of the ball handling of Welch, Arcasa and the others. One seldom watched tackles as quick and co-ordinated as Guyon and Calac. At one of the drills, a baseball man from nearby Southbridge, Charley Glancy, was talking to a reporter he knew from the Worcester *Telegram*, Roy Johnson. When Thorpe circled by them on the side lines, Glancy suddenly exclaimed, "Why, I know that guy. He played for me a couple of years ago." Glancy had been at Fayetteville while Thorpe was pitching for Rocky Mount in 1910 and toward the end of the season he acquired him in a trade. In 1912 Glancy managed the Winston-Salem club in the revived East Carolina League and was spending the off-season in Southbridge. Glancy's revelation was not startling news to Johnson. College athletes in the area, notably at baseball-minded Holy Cross in Worcester, were in the habit of making summer money in resort or twilight leagues, or playing under assumed names in the professional minors. But because of Thorpe's prominence as an Olympic hero Johnson knew he had a story for his paper, one that was so sensitive he sat on it for nearly two months.

The Indians' last game of the long season, Thorpe's last for Pop Warner, was played against a familiar background—on the road far from Carlisle, as most of their games had been, and as a piece of family entertainment on one of the most traditional of American holidays. If any of the Indians had once resented their role in this white ritual they surely had overcome it by the habit of following Pop into a strange city for another game on Thanksgiving Day. It was as much a part of playing for Pop as receiving a free suit of clothes from Blumenthal's.

Heavy snow was falling on the campus hill in Providence when Thorpe led the dark red caped Indians onto the field against Brown. Warner had predicted they would win, despite the conditions and the absence of Welch and Powell from the starting line-up. He moved Arcasa to quarterback and paired Bruce Goesback, who had been one of the small boys along with Thorpe who had enrolled at Carlisle eight years before, at the other halfback. Joe Bergie moved from center to fullback. As they lined up to receive the Brown kickoff the Indians showed that impassive air of confidence befitting a team about to win its twelfth game of the season. A long kick sent Goesback to the 5-yard line where he was downed. Arcasa immediately turned to Thorpe to set the offensive pattern in the swirling snow and against a heavier Brown line. Thorpe made two quick plunges for a first down and then on the third play of the game he cut outside right tackle behind blocking from Large and Guyon and raced thirty yards to midfield. It was a tempo that had worn down so many previous opponents—a rush at the center of the line and then Thorpe on a reverse or sweep to the outside for long yardage. In addition to his short gains he made runs across the slippery ground of 14, 18,

27, 50, 15, 45 and 18 yards. The Providence *Journal* commented: "The redskins had a finely developed interference for their big star, but time and again Thorpe broke away from it, doubled back on his trail and was off through open territory on a lope that looked slow, but which in reality was fast running and baffled the tacklers. He eluded the outstretched arms of the tacklers with ridiculous ease, giving the finest exhibition of dodging ever shown on the field." There were superlatives for his passing and receiving (Carlisle passed five times and completed three, one for a touchdown by Joe Guyon) and his defensive work: "His great strength on defense was strikingly evident in the second period in particular when Brown, making her greatest bid for a touchdown, had the ball inside Carlisle's five-yard line. Twice Tenney, a 192-pound back, hurled himself into the line and each time Thorpe caught him in mid-air, and without giving ground an inch, literally hurled him back four yards." Thorpe's only recognizable deficiency was in his kicking—he missed two field goal attempts and did not get his usual distance punting the wet ball.

Warner let his starting Indians, young and old, famous and obscure, play the entire game—although he did substitute briefly for Goesback and sent Possum Powell in to hold up the line during the fourth quarter. With the score at 26–0 and the snow blotting visibility, some in the crowd of 8,000 began to leave Andrews Field and missed Thorpe's third touchdown of the game. It came at the end of a typical Carlisle attack that began on the Brown 47-yard line. Bergie plunged for two yards and then Arcasa tried to throw Brown off balance by sending Thorpe into the line without calling a signal. Then Thorpe faked a run and threw a pass to substitute halfback Hugh Wheelock for a twenty-yard gain to the 26. Thorpe tried to pass for the touchdown but the ball was knocked away from the receiver by Brown's safety over the goal line. (By the rules of the day, if the ball had fallen untouched behind the goal it would have been a touchback and Brown's ball on the 20.) Thorpe and Bergie made short gains. On third down Thorpe took a direct pass, split the line between Guyon and Powell and raced eighteen yards for a touchdown. He touched the ball to the snowy ground, circled back through the goal posts and took his position for the kick off.

There was no commemoration of the achievement by Thorpe, no recognition by anyone that he had scored his twenty-fifth touch-down of the year for an all-time college record for a season of 198 points.

It is doubtful that Thorpe knew of his record-breaking totals until he returned to the athletic quarters at Carlisle and looked at the clippings that had accumulated on the game. The conservative Providence *Journal* referred to "the magnificent work of Capt. Jim Thorpe, the world's champion athlete, and the greatest half-back that ever ranged the gridiron." The boxed headline on Thorpe's last game offered the most satisfaction of all:

The Real Score
Thorpe . . . 32, Brown . . . 0

Simply an Indian Schoolboy

The week after the Brown game Thorpe, who was Walter Camp's choice as an All-America halfback for a second succes-sive year, was given permission to spend a few weeks in Okla-homa. Thorpe said good-by to his close friends Sam Burd, who had been taking courses at Conway Hall, and Gus Welch, captain elect of the 1913 team, and Possum Powell, anxious to return to his Cherokee relatives in North Carolina. Powell had quit Car-lisle the previous winter only to be persuaded by Warner to come back and line up alongside Thorpe for one more season. Thorpe was also leaving behind, now for the last time, the December sounds of Christmas preparation that came from the school's music and club rooms, and those reminders of the regimen that had ruled his life before he became the most privileged of the football boys—the 6 A.M. rising bell, the 7:25 work whistle, the 11:45 assembly, the roll call and prayers for the small boys at 8:45 each night, and all the other punctuations in the day that had changed little since he first entered Carlisle.

Thorpe's return to the Sac and Fox reservation was as a recognizable hero this time, whose triumphs in the Olympics had been recorded in headlines and photographs in the papers tribe members could see in Stroud, Shawnee, Prague or Oklahoma City. Jim had a holiday reunion with Frank, Mary and other members of the family and did a little checking at the Agency on the lease of his 160-acre allotment. The farming and grazing rental brought only $250 a year (the lease was later raised to $400) although about one hundred acres of the land was producing a fair yield in cotton and kafir corn. When it came time for Thorpe to return to Carlisle in mid-January he went to Agency superintendent Horace Johnson and asked for an advance of $125. Jim's balance at the bank used by the Sac and Fox in Stroud was $0.00. Johnson authorized the advance.

Thorpe was readmitted at Carlisle on January 18 and the following weekend he attended the annual reception and dance of the Mercer Society in the school gym. The light-footed All-America halfback won first prize—a chocolate cake—as the best waltzer on the floor. The dance cake was the last award Thorpe received as a student at Carlisle—and the last recognition he would get for anything as a pure amateur. Two days later the papers were carrying the story of the "discovery" that he had once played professional baseball, a charge that if true would invalidate his record in the Olympics of 1912. James Sullivan, chairman of the National Registration Committee of the Amateur Athletic Union, promised that Thorpe would be given a proper hearing. The AAU's sudden awakening to the fact that Thorpe played pro ball, as did so many amateur college athletes of the day, was quickened by a story Roy Johnson wrote for the Worcester *Telegram* which appeared on January 22. (Johnson's story had Thorpe playing in the wrong town but in the right league.) Pop Warner blamed a Pittsburgh Pirates scout, anxious to sign Thorpe to a baseball contract, for calling the AAU's attention to the record of his two seasons with the Rocky Mount club of the Eastern Carolina League.

For public consumption there came a sanctimonious reaction to the news that must have left several of Thorpe's official custodians and superiors ill at ease. Thorpe was said to have "confessed" to Pop Warner and Superintendent Friedman that he had indeed gone off to play ball for pay, a revelation they had encountered four years earlier when Jim decided to quit Carlisle and was granted "a summer leave to play baseball in the south." Thorpe's use of his own name instead of a pseudonym while playing for Rocky Mount and Fayetteville—the hard evidence in the case—was simply indication that at the time he had no intention of returning to Carlisle. But the popularly accepted interpretation was that Thorpe had become a victim of his own honesty and innocence, that it had not occurred to him to change his name.

Warner and Friedman suggested Thorpe appeal to whatever compassion might be lodged in the AAU organization with a humble confession. They drafted a letter for him to copy which, in part, read: "I hope I will be partly excused by the fact that I was simply an Indian schoolboy and I did not know all about such things. In fact I did not know I was doing wrong because I was doing what I knew several other college men had done . . . I have always liked sport and only played or ran races for the fun of the thing and never to earn money."

The AAU selection committee for the Olympics, which had been so eager to have a full-blooded American athlete represent the United States against foreign competition in the pentathlon and decathlon, reacted as eagerly to this heavily publicized threat to the sanctity of amateur athletics. It quickly absolved itself of having "the least suspicion as there having been any act of professionalism on Thorpe's part," and announced the decision to remove Thorpe's name from the Olympic records just as if he had missed the boat to Stockholm, return the pentathlon and decathlon trophies to the Swedish Olympic Committee, and award the gold medals to the second-place finishers in the two events. The AAU statement said that "while Mr. Thorpe is deserving of the severest condemnation for concealing the fact that he had professionalized himself . . . those who knew of his professional acts are deserving of still greater censure for their silence." Superintendent Friedman assured the AAU "that the faculty and athletic director, Mr. Glen Warner, were without any knowledge of this fact until today. It is a most unpleasant affair and has brought gloom on the entire institution."

The AAU's James Sullivan did allow that Indian athletes such as Thorpe might be excused for not being completely aware of the amateur code: "Here we have the Indian youth taken from environments that to say the least for them are peculiar, put in an institution controlled by the United States Government, and from reports emanating from these institutions from time to time we are prone to feel proud of the way we are bringing up the heretofore benighted red man. It had been the custom to make pets of the crack Indian athletes, and because of their strange origin nothing back of their government school careers has ever been delved into. It probably came naturally before these lads came into contact with the registration feature of the AAU to go out in their free times like summer vacations and play baseball."

Somehow it escaped the attention of the AAU, according to the official statements, that amateur lads of all colors and from most colleges were in the habit of spending their free time playing baseball for pay. Or if they were healthy, enterprising college football players they often found an opportunity to play as anonymous professionals on Sunday afternoons. The AAU promised that after the regrettable discovery about Thorpe it would indeed investigate summer baseball.

The AAU decision, which was to stand fast despite the scorn and criticism of public and press for the next sixty years, drew more compassion to Thorpe at Carlisle than he needed that January. Whatever his immediate reaction—and friends variously interpreted his quiet acceptance of the blow as either indicating a deep hurt or his comfort with the knowledge that he had proved he was the best all-around athlete and the whole world knew it—he turned immediately to the business of negotiating a major-league baseball contract. (Ironically, he still belonged to Fayetteville where his name had last appeared on an organized baseball roster.) Among the several major-league teams bidding for his services—and his name—Cincinnati seemed to have the strongest appeal to Thorpe and Warner, acting as his advisor. But the persuasive manager of the New York Giants, John Mc-Graw, an acquaintance of Warner's, made an offer of a one-year contract of close to five thousand dollars, unusual money for a rookie and a sum that Thorpe could hardly expect to match.

The agreement was announced on Saturday, February 1, at the Giants' offices in New York. Thorpe spoke of his long ambition to be a big-league ballplayer and said he enjoyed pitching as much as anything else. McGraw encouraged speculation that Thorpe and the Giants' catcher, Chief Meyers, might form the first all-Indian battery when the team began its training later in the month at Marlin, Texas. But one realistic observer at the news conference said, "Everyone believes Thorpe was corraled chiefly for advertising purposes."

While the press was meeting the Giants' new rookie the trophies Thorpe had won but six months earlier went aboard the SS *New York* on their way to the return to Sweden. Back at Carlisle on that day local citizens began taking up a collection to purchase a trophy in Thorpe's honor. As people were dropping their coins off at Brady's Cigar Store, the Mansion House, the Hotel Wellington, the Elks—where Jim and Gus Welch and other of the football boys could never seem to pay for their own beer—Thorpe was officially dropped from the school rolls. The date was a few days less than nine years after he had enrolled at Carlisle for the usual five-year term. The final entry went down on his record:

"2 - 1 - '13   discharged to play ball"

X   THE LONG GOOD-BY IN OHIO

A Bulldog Born

Although baseball was to give Thorpe a seasonal occupation for the next several years, neither his personal enthusiasms nor his public image benefited much from the job. It took a return to football and a reunion with former teammates at Carlisle to keep Thorpe and his reputation fully engaged. The Indians' professional football experience was a logical and, for the character of the sport, most felicitous extension of the flare and skills they had displayed at Carlisle over the years. Collectively they had an important impact on this early phase of pro football, and Thorpe, of course, added the individual star quality which was sorely needed at the box office.

Football among the pros came to Thorpe as a great relief in 1915 after three summers of baseball which were mostly spent sitting stolidly on the bench and squinting into the sun where manager John McGraw's more talented hired hands performed before National League crowds. In that time he appeared in sixty-six games and had twenty-three hits, hardly enough to provide the Giants with even any advertising value. "I felt like a sitting hen not a ballplayer," Thorpe said of the experience. He had had little training as a hitter, at sorting out the curve, change-up and fast ball, and it showed early at the Giants' training base in Texas. He could run and throw hard enough but there was no polish on his basic skills, which he might have acquired with more experience in the minor leagues. McGraw's impatience with college athletes and the established quality of the Giants' regulars combined to limit Thorpe's future with the New York club.

He did, however, develop a reputation as the best one-against-three (or four) wrestler in the league. The rugged competition, which Thorpe had been schooled in throughout his Indian education, started as friendly diversion at the Giants' camp in Marlin with such muscular players as Fred Merkle, Eddie Roush and the big pitcher, Jeff Tesreau, vs Thorpe. When McGraw learned of the sporting chances some of his best players were taking with their arms and legs, he threatened Thorpe with a $100 fine if he caught him in a match. The rough-housing became more discreet and it left Thorpe in the uncomfortable public position of accepting a lot of elbow jabs, tweaks of the nose and ears, playful slaps and shoulder shoves from veteran Giants without striking back. (It was the sort of physical provocation that Thorpe would be subjected to for years to come, some of it sporting and friendly and some of it of the drunken, I-can-flatten-you variety which frayed his temper.)

The rookie season in the big league held long stretches between times at bat for Thorpe; he went to bat thirty-five times and played in the outfield in only a half-dozen games. But there were post-season rewards to ease the frustration of inactivity. He and Iva Miller were married in mid-October, 1913, and left immediately on an unusual, expenses-paid honeymoon—a goodwill tour around the world with members (and wives) of the Giants and Chicago White Sox. Iva's determination to break through the opposition of family and friends and marry Thorpe sharpened after he told her of the opportunity to visit Hawaii, New Zealand, Australia, Egypt and the countries of Europe. The marriage ceremony, at St. Patrick's Catholic Church in Carlisle, was conducted by their old friend and teacher, Father Mark Stock. (Iva, an Episcopalian by family background, had been converted to Catholicism.) Gus Welch was Jim's best man and Iva walked down the aisle on the arm of Superintendent Moses Friedman. The Carlisle *Evening Herald* of October 14 described the bride as "a laughing dark-eyed princess of the Cherokee tribe, resembling in her dusky beauty the poet's conception of the storied Minnehaha." The choir, "especially augmented for the occasion with a number of the best singers of this and neighboring towns," sang Ganss' "Second Mass." The ushers included familiar faces from the football team—Pete Calac, Bill Hodge, Joe Guyon,

Gus Lookaround—and Jim's younger brother Ed, who had entered Carlisle earlier in the year. After the ceremony Mr. and Mrs. Friedman opened the superintendent's home to students and Carlisle friends of the Thorpes and band leader Claude Stauffer led the school band in a surprise serenade on the campus walk outside the residence. That evening there was a dance in the gym for the bride and groom, giving the football boys a chance to break Pop Warner's midweek training regimen. The team was into another excellent season, Warner's last at Carlisle, and the quarterbacking of Welch, the running of Guyon and Calac all but compensated for the absence of Thorpe. (Later in the fall, at New York's Polo Grounds, Carlisle met Dartmouth, which claimed a share of the eastern leadership with Harvard; the real Indians whipped the pale-faced Indians of New Hampshire, 34–10.) But the conversation at the social in the gym was not familiarly of football or campus events or of Thorpe's waltzing skills, but of the wedding, the sparkling appearance of Mrs. Thorpe and of the itinerary for the around-the-world tour the newlyweds were to begin the following weekend.

The Thorpes were experiencing the nomadic life of professional baseball families—they had a summer apartment not far from the Polo Grounds on West 157th Street in New York—when a first child was born on May 8, 1915. He was named James Francis Thorpe, Jr. The father's enormous pride in the boy, as well as pragmatic considerations, encouraged Thorpe to request that his son be added immediately to the rolls of the Sac and Fox. But Thorpe's birth notice to the Agency, the routine followed by his forefathers to assure an additional annuity on Sac and Fox reserves in Kansas and Oklahoma, drew a bureaucratic rebuff. The tribe's most famous member was told, in effect, that his own status now appeared to be that of a fellow citizen among whites and they could not enroll James, Jr., who "was born away from the reservation and has never lived among or affiliated with the Indians thereof." (Thorpe was, of course, free of government boarding school bondage, but he did not officially give up his status as an Indian ward for several years. Had James, Jr., lived long enough, he would have been placed on the Sac and Fox rolls with the degree of blood indicated as $\frac{1}{16}$, as were all of the Thorpe children who were born later.) The arrival of James, Jr.—the start of a family—contributed to Thorpe's decision within a few months to bolster his income by accepting an attractive offer to play pro football. There were more than commercial motives involved. Thorpe's Indian-Irish pride needed shoring.

Thorpe had not been far removed from football since leaving Carlisle. He had followed the course of other Warner-trained Indians—Mt. Pleasant, Bemus Pierce, Lone Star Dietz, Exendine, among others—and gone into coaching. Thorpe took a part-time job as an assistant at the University of Indiana, where he taught student athletes the art of kicking. In 1915 the October-November assignment on the campus at Bloomington put Thorpe a short train ride away from the center of pro football enthusiasm in Indiana which had grown as a small offshoot of the game's popular activity in the industrial towns of Ohio—Canton, Massillon, Shelby, Lorain, Toledo, Columbus and Youngstown. Sunday games for small stakes were played by the recently organized Wabash Athletic Association and the Pine Village Athletic Club in the Wabash River area. Assistant coach Thorpe appeared, quite unceremoniously, as a Sunday halfback for Pine Village, whose games were held at Lafayette, home of Purdue University. Pine Village drew some of its better talent from Notre Dame, bona fide collegians—or as bona fide as necessary—who played under assumed names.

That October, Thorpe had a visit from ex-Carlisle Indian Bill Gardner, who had been a starting left end for Warner when Jim was breaking in as a sub. Gardner played regularly for the Canton Bulldogs and he came to Thorpe with a proposal from the team manager, Jack Cusack. If Thorpe would agree to play for Canton in its big November games against Massillon, Cusack would pay him $250 a game, a princely figure in the hazardous, cash-and-carry business that was then pro football. Thorpe accepted, and it was agreed with Cusack that the announcement of Thorpe's joining the Bulldogs would be timed for maximum reaction at the gate and as a stunning strategem in the last-hour competition for talent between the two rivals.

Pro football was in the midst of a comeback in the adjoining Stark County towns when Thorpe agreed to play for Canton.

Just after the turn of the century the game flourished, in a very local fashion, in the Pittsburgh area, in the mill centers of Jeanette, McKeesport, Latrobe; it also developed a following through the athletic clubs in the upstate New York towns of Ogdensburg, Auburn, Watertown and Corinth. But nowhere was it a more feverish expression of civic pride than in Canton and its smaller neighbor, Massillon, eight miles away across the Tuscarawas River. Football events in the two towns came to a thunderous climax in 1906, and the aftermath of the scandal wiped out much of the enthusiasm for the pro game, leaving Canton without a team for a half-dozen years; Massillon stayed out of the game even longer.

In November 1906, while Carlisle cadet Thorpe was suffering through an Outing experience on a New Jersey farm, the citizens of Canton and Massillon were consumed with anticipation of the rivalry between their professional teams. Football in general served as an intense interest point among the workers in the local industries, many of whom were recent immigrants. (There were two travel agencies in Canton then whose sole business concerned the transportation of immigrants from Ellis Island to jobs at the local factory making farm machinery, the iron bridge works or the drop forging mill.) Football—high school, college, the pro Bulldogs—filled the pages of the Canton *Repository*. On November 4 the paper ran a pictorial feature on Carlisle under the heading, "These Indians Beat Pensy Last Saturday." There were pictures of Libby, Little Boy, Dillon, Gardner, Mt. Pleasant, Wauseka, Exendine—the best of what Pop Warner called his best team in 1907. The sports columns were surrounded with ads aimed at the big game: "We Close Friday Noon on Account of the Canton-Massillon Football Game—Noakes Ice Cream Co."; "The boys of our store are anxious to see tomorrow's game. They have been faithful and worked hard. We have decided to close from 1:30 to 4:30 and take in the game—W. E. Homer Co." Canton schools, faced with mass truancy, stopped classes at noon. There were rumors and denials that the game had been fixed, which caused quarterback Ed Stewart of Massillon to comment: "It would be impossible to fix the coming game. It would mean the management is rotten to the core . . . that 40 or more players must be dishonest and minus all sense of honor." The Canton team was apparently untouched by the pre-game frenzy; player-coach Blondy Wallace, a former Penn tackle, had taken the players to Pennsylvania State College for secret practices. The fix rumors did not halt the flow of betting money at the Courtland Hotel in downtown Canton where an estimated $8,000 was wagered just before the game.

Canton had scored 287 points to none for its opponents during the season; Massillon had averaged 55 points a game. The great battle of the unconquered ended with a 10–5 victory for Canton before 5,500, the only Massillon score coming on a run with a fumbled ball by 260-pound guard Tiny Maxwell. Canton players stopped chasing Maxwell when the referee blew his whistle—an untimely accident, he claimed. The rematch at Massillon the next weekend resulted in a surprising 13–6 loss for Canton. Two days later it brought headlines in the Massillon *Independent* and *Evening Gleaner* of a gambling plot involving Blondy Wallace of Canton and Walter East, an end for Massillon. "Their Honor Inviolate—the Famous Massillon Tigers of 1906 Could Not Be Bought Off With a Price" ran the head in the *Evening Gleaner*. East, who later confessed he was involved in the scheme, was accused of conspiring with Wallace to see to it that Canton won the first game and Massillon the second. A third "clean" game was to be played in Cleveland. The stakes included a pay-off of $4,000 for the Massillon players willing to get into the fix—plus the chance to get into a $50,000 betting pool. The *Gleaner* insisted that most of the Tigers would have nothing of the "treacherous negotiations." The paper commented, "Many who saw the game Saturday were surprised to see the hitherto daring Hayden [Jack Hayden, Canton's quarterback from Penn] apparently deliberately shirk several scrimmages with Massillon. Whether the former Tiger quarterback had cold feet, rheumatic joints or avoided the contact with Tiger beef from pure politeness is not known. In Canton Saturday night it was rumored Hayden had sold out."

East suddenly disappeared from the Canton-Massillon area, but Blondy Wallace, a popular sports figure in Ohio, immediately filed a libel suit against the Massillon *Independent*—an action that was later withdrawn by his attorneys. The revelation of the plots on and off the field came as a severe blow to the hard-betting, hard-believing people of Canton and Massillon. Jack Cusack, then a sixteen-year-old schoolboy in Canton, recalled accompanying a neighbor, Victor Kaufman, who had bet heavily on the game, to the Courtland Hotel Bar after Canton lost to Massillon. Kaufman was angry—and suspicious of the inept performance of the Bulldogs. "If you want to know what I think," he said to a fellow drinker, "I think that game was crooked." Someone answered Kaufman's remark with a swinging fist and suddenly the bar was the scene of a free-for-all among the edgy Canton fans, which sprawled onto the street outside the hotel and had to be stopped by the police. The brawl signaled the beginning of the end of pro football in the two cities for a period of time. The fans satisfied their hunger for the sport by watching the school and sand-lot teams. But the scandal did not wipe out the belief of young Jack Cusack that professional football could be conducted honestly and profitably in Canton. When a team was organized again in 1912—they were called the Canton Professionals at first because Bulldogs was still considered a dirty word in town—he became the manager, intent on recruiting top college talent and winning back the confidence of the public.

When Thorpe joined Cusack in Canton schoolboys were still singing the refrain, "And we'll hang Blondy Wallace from a sour apple tree," but the public and press had forgotten enough about the fix of nine years before so that the Bulldogs were called Bulldogs again. The persuasive recruiting of Cusack had added several name college players to the pay roll and a few good ones who did not feel it wise to use their own names. Hube Wagner, a former All-America player at Pitt, and Carp Julian of the Michigan Aggies were the regular running backs; the captain and quarterback was Don Hamilton of Notre Dame. Greasy Neale, head coach at West Virginia Wesleyan, played under the name of Fisher in Cusack's backfield. Gardner had been coaching football in North Dakota when Cusack hired him to play end and sent him off to recruit Thorpe. The Bulldogs had stirred considerable local hope by overwhelming Wheeling, West Virginia, in their home opener, 75–0. Carp Julian was described as a ball carrier who "gallops, hops, fox trots, paces, slips and glides."

The city of Canton, which was to become Thorpe's part-time residence for a few years, had a population of just over 59,000 in the fall of 1915, with many of its citizens involved in the production of safes, axles, metal roofing, steel, heavy machinery and the new home appliance known as suction sweepers. There were more than fifty auto agencies in the city (it was estimated that one of every twenty-nine people in the state had an automobile) and the arrival and departure of dozens of B&O, Wheeling and Lake Erie, and Pennsylvania Railroad trains each day kept the depots and freight yards busy. Both evangelist Billy Sunday and William Jennings Bryan had made recent attempts to swing local sentiment toward prohibition, but the hard-working, God-fearing workers weren't yet ready for it—in November the "drys" lost a state-wide referendum to bring prohibition to Ohio by 51,000 votes—and the owners of the 116 saloons licensed in Canton breathed a sigh of relief. The vigorous young city was obviously in a proper mood for a rugged-and-ready hero of the dimensions of Thorpe.

The Bulldogs warmed up for the renewal of their rivalry with Massillon by defeating the Altoona Indians, with a half-dozen former Carlisle football boys in the line-up, including Joel Wheelock and Alex Arcasa, employed by a local boiler shop. In the easy 38–0 victory "an eastern college chap traveling as Fisher" made a big impression with his end sweeps.

The week before the game, which was scheduled for Massillon's Driving Park, there was limited betting action because fans wanted to wait and see who Massillon would slip into their line-up besides the two Notre Dame stars, Knute Rockne and Gus Dorais, playing under their own names. Cusack let it be known that his Bulldogs would go with a familiar line-up, with the possible addition of Bugs Raymond, a tackle from Ohio State. But on Friday the news leaked through a paper in Cleveland that Canton had signed "the noted Jim Thorpe" and the surprise that Cusack had hoped to hold until just before game time on Sunday had been lifted. The disclosure did allow the Bulldogs' manager to explain to the public that Thorpe was the big reason for the boost in ticket price from $.50 to $.75.

A crowd of six thousand paid the price to see the resumption of the professional competition between the two cities—and watch Thorpe go through his first contact with the game he would dominate intermittently for a few years. But this game was dominated by Massillon and the Notre Dame quarterback Gus Dorais. When Thorpe entered the game, to hard cheers from fans on both sides of the field, Dorais had already kicked a field goal and was driving the Tigers toward a second-quarter touchdown with a passing attack that Canton couldn't control. Thorpe, who took over for Hube Wagner at left halfback, provided just enough individual exploit to give Canton fans hope that the rematch at the end of November would be more joyful. He got off the longest run of the day, forty yards, slipping and falling out of bounds on the 9-yard line while trying to avoid safetyman Dorais. He broke open around end on another carry but slipped on the rain-soaked field. "Grace and power are written in every move made by him," commented the *Repository* reporter after the game. "Canton had but two plays that were worth the breath used to call them—Thorpe around end, the short pass by Julian." Thorpe's lack of preparation with the team did show in erratic kicking, with one of his punts blocked. The game was called with five minutes left to play because of darkness. Massillon was state champion, at least temporarily, with a 16–0 victory.

Jack Cusack promised that Thorpe would be back for the second game and that the team would gather on Thanksgiving Day for more drilling under high school coach Harry Hazlett. Actually Hazlett couldn't get his eleven together until the Friday before the game, but even two days of practice was more than the Bull-dogs—or any other pro team of the day—could usually afford. Both Cusack and the Massillon management made bids for the services of the great field-goal kicker, Charley Brickley, but the price was not high enough for the former Harvard hero then coaching at Johns Hopkins. Cusack did add some line strength to help open the defense for Thorpe, Greasy Neale and Carp Julian. His most important recruit was tackle Charlie Smith, a black from Michigan Aggies. With Smith, Gardner and Thorpe and eight whites in the starting line-up Cusack had what may have been the first such racially mixed team in pro football. Thorpe was named team captain, which gave him the responsibility of making all substitutions along with other field decisions —more authority than he cared to exercise with his unfamiliar teammates. The day before the game Thorpe's prediction that Canton was prepared to win by as much as eighteen points led

to bolder wagering by Bulldog fans who had been kept in confusion about the identity of several of Cusack's new men. (Massillon started four college "unknowns" called Cole, Jones, Hayes
and Day.)

In some hope and considerable ignorance 8,000 people showed
up at Canton's League Park to see if the locals could prevent Massillon from gaining "the professional championship of the world,"
as the match was being billed. The overflow crowd became part
of the most controversial finish to a Massillon-Canton game that
the two towns had experienced in all of their passionate competition.

For three periods the heavily loaded line-ups were locked in
a defensive tug-of-war. Two Massillon fumbles led to field-goal
opportunities for Thorpe; he drop-kicked the first from the 18-
yard line and kicked another from placement at the 38. Except
for a twenty-eight-yard run around end, Thorpe was kept in
check by Massillon and Canton managed only two first downs.
With Canton holding a 6–0 lead at the start of the fourth period,
Dorais began moving Massillon with passes to Rockne and to his
halfbacks Briggs and Kelleher. In the gathering late November
darkness the crowd sensed an inevitability about the Massillon
drive. From midfield Dorais passed for a twelve-yard gain, then
completed another to the Canton 18-yard line. As the crowd
edged closer to the goal, shouting their hostility or encouragement, Dorais appealed to referee Ed Conners, suggesting that
the ball be moved back and the 10-yard line be ruled as the goal.
But Conners told him to speed up play before conditions turned
worse. Dorais passed again and Briggs grabbed the ball near
the 10-yard line and raced for the goal and the tying touchdown
—and disappeared into the crowd. At some point he became separated from the football and it bounced free in the end zone
where Canton's Charlie Smith recovered it. Referee Conners
ruled a touchback and the ball be given to Canton at the 20-yard
line. Briggs came out of the melee beyond the goal line screaming. He claimed the ball had been kicked out of his hands by a
uniformed policeman after he was on the ground and had made
a Massillon touchdown. The argument surged between players,
managers, officials and the crowd which had trampled down the
fences along the side lines. Efforts by officials to clear the field

before twilight turned to darkness were futile, and the game was called, with three minutes remaining, and Canton a 6–0 winner. But the Massillon team, its backers and betting supporters refused to accept the decision until all three officials—referee, umpire and head linesman—render a joint verdict on the "fumble" by Briggs. It was agreed that the officials' statement would be available to the Massillon management and the public at the Courtland Hotel at 12:30 that night, allowing plenty of time for deliberation and for the officials to depart the Canton-Massillon area.

Doubt had been cast on Briggs's argument of how he lost the ball in the crowd because there were no uniformed police on duty around the field. (A local rule prohibited their working in uniform when off duty; so Cusack had hired plainclothes police who proved ineffectual.) The officials' decision, read to the crowd in the Courtland lobby, backed the referee's original judgment. Canton and Massillon shared the 1915 professional football championship of the world. It wasn't until years later that Cusack, in a conversation with a Canton streetcar conductor, met the "uniformed policeman" Briggs had accused. The conductor, an avid Bulldogs fan, had gone in uniform from his trolley to the standing-room-only crowd near the goal posts at the Canton park. The conductor said that when Briggs tumbled over the goal at his feet his first thought was of the thirty dollar bet he had made on the Bulldogs. So he instinctively made the most decisive Canton kick of the season.

High Stakes Against Massillon

Thorpe's brief, frenzied acquaintance with pro football as played by Canton and Massillon and the appreciation shown him by Jack Cusack were enough to convince him that here, for a short period in the fall, was an agreeable place to earn a living while playing the game he most enjoyed. He and the New York Giants appeared to be of no more use to one another, and after the 1915 baseball season he found himself employed with Milwaukee of the American Association. Pro football was still very minor league compared to the high-powered game the eastern colleges played but, largely because of Thorpe and the pioneering efforts of Cusack, it was soon generating a world of weekend excitement in the middle of Ohio.

Now nearly at the end of his 20s, Thorpe's appetite for football and the vigorous environment that stretched outside the game was at a peak. A teammate who spent time on the road with him recalled his capacity for a meal before a game: "Jim would blow into the dining room about 10 and immediately be surrounded by waiters. He would always begin by saying he wasn't very hungry. This is what usually followed: grapefruit, cereal, half a dozen eggs with ham, sirloin steak with onions, fried potatoes, sausages, rolls, a pot of coffee. When displeased with waiter service he promptly warned them to go away and not return. At one hotel he was served by a darky who stuck his fingers in the butter dishes while serving. Jim picked up a fork, rapped the waiter's hands and told him to 'Git.' Nearby guests looked on astounded as the waiter, with a great fear on his face, fled from the dining room."

The limited obligations in playing pro—the Bulldogs seldom practiced more than two days a week in the early years—allowed time for both other business and pleasure. Thorpe took a job coaching the backs at nearby Akron University and later helped Pop Warner instruct his kickers at the University of Pittsburgh. The Stark County countryside offered accessible bird and small-game hunting. With the arrival in Canton in 1916 of Pete Calac and Bill Garlow, Thorpe had two more familiar teammates in the Bulldogs' starting line-up and a pair of easy hunting and social companions. He and Garlow took to the fields on the opening day of the rabbit season and came back with a hoot owl which they offered to Massillon as a substitute mascot for the nonexistent tiger. Thorpe had struck up a friendship with a non-Indian on the team, Norman ("Dutch") Speck. A local boy who had never played in high school or college, Speck had learned enough in the rough scrimmage of sand lot to play for Canton for several seasons. He was playing guard when Thorpe arrived in town, and he was still playing guard when Thorpe left. Speck, a mill hand, epitomized the rough perennial pro who gave the team local flavor. When the Bulldogs line-up listed both name and college, it was "Speck, Sandlot" or, occasionally, "Speck, Canton University."

If the Bulldog players favored a little drinking, there was a wide choice of sources in town. The bar at the Courtland Hotel was football headquarters, but the players could raise their consumption more discreetly by gathering at the home of Bill Melbourne, a general contractor, who maintained a cellar full of whiskey. Cusack, who was close enough to Thorpe to be called "Buddy" most of the time, said he never remembered him taking a drink before a game, which some of the players found useful preparation. "Thorpe certainly didn't need the courage. He didn't drink all that heavily—four or five drinks and he'd be out of it. And he would get sick and want to die."

Thorpe's fondness for food, drink, the most familiar pleasures, was exceeded only by his devotion to his hunting dogs. Ohio or Oklahoma—wherever he stayed for long after he left Carlisle—he was seldom far removed from his dogs. The pro football experience in Ohio led him to the Oorang kennels in LaRue, Ohio, where he acquired the unusually large and scrappy airedales, ideally bred for hunting and guard dogs. Thorpe's favorite Oorang airedale, Tip, developed into an excellent companion for him and a source of pride because of his extreme combativeness. Pete Calac was with Thorpe when they encountered a dog-owner from Marion, Ohio, who took to bragging about his fighting pit bulldog. "I have a dog whose legs your dog can't touch," Thorpe told him. "Want to test him for a few bucks?" The challenge and terms were arranged and Thorpe brought Tip to a farm outside Marion. It was the airedale's first fight, but he grabbed the bulldog, shook him, tossed him—and sent him howling. Thorpe was as pleased as if he had just won the Olympic decathlon.

Canton had struggled to early-season victories over Altoona and the Pitcairn (Pennsylvania) Friars before Thorpe arrived in the second week of October 1916 from Oklahoma. Both Altoona and Pitcairn had so many Carlisle Indians, past and current, in their line-ups that the games would have seemed like old Wednesday scrimmages at Indian Field. Cusack had decided he could afford Thorpe for the season if he would play in the backfield and serve as head coach. His first effort in the dual role turned into smashing success—a 77–0 win over the "highly touted" Buffalo All-Stars. Thorpe had three touchdowns and so did a sensational new end from the East, playing under the name of Drake. He was Ernie Soucy, an All-America from Harvard. Frank Mt. Pleasant, slower and eight years older than his best games at Carlisle, was a Buffalo All-Star. When Thorpe led the Bulldogs against the Columbus Panhandles (named for the railroad yards) he faced one of the most unusual family operations in the early days of pro football. The Panhandles were captained by Fred Nesser, one of seven football-playing brothers in a Columbus family. Five Nessers—Fred, Frank, Phil, Ted and John—played the entire game for the Panhandles and gave Canton a testing afternoon. Thorpe's kicks—one for eighty-five yards—made the difference. Peggy Parratt, a former Massillon Tiger and then the owner-manager-quarterback of the Cleveland Indians, gave Thorpe a painful afternoon at American League park after Canton had easily won the first game. Jim scored the decisive touchdown in a 14–7 win but he twisted his ankle and sat out part of the game, a first injury with the pros that forced him to take himself out of the following week's contest against Youngstown. It also left him lame and uncertain for the Massillon game on November 27.

Few of the wagering fans doubted that Thorpe would not be ready, and since only Cleveland had scored against the Bulldogs all season they were a 5–3 choice at game time. High winds and a muddy field at Massillon's home park restricted the play on both sides. Thorpe could make only twenty-eight yards in eight carries, and the nearest either team came to scoring were two drop kicks by Gus Dorais which were blown away from the goal posts by the wind. The Canton *Repository* admitted local "confidence suffered a body blow which is likely to have a strong influence on the wagering in the second game."

The scoreless tie with Massillon may have reduced the self-assurance of Canton bettors, but it only heightened the anticipation of the deciding game—set for the first weekend in December at Canton's ball park next to the amusement center at Meyers Lake. The wagering was even money most of the week. On street corners, in engine houses, pool halls and bowling alleys fans asked about line-up changes and how the betting was going. One Canton supporter said, "I'm keeping my money out of it, but I wouldn't miss the game for a farm."

The rumor spread through the city that a Massillon booster had appeared at the Courtland on Saturday at lunch time, pushing for a high-stakes bet, and that Thorpe had taken up the challenge and written out a $2,500 check and told the Massillon man to cover it. The reported incident was given a pregame box in the Canton papers. Manager Jack Cusack denied that Thorpe had bet on the Bulldogs or that he had sufficient funds in the bank to make such a wager. "I kept all of his earnings until the end of the season," he said, "and then gave him a check for the full amount which he deposited in an Oklahoma bank. He wasn't the type to do a foolish thing like that." (The Canton-Massillon scandal of 1905 had hardly separated the gambling element from the pro game. Betting among the fans was part of the atmosphere, and opportunities for players to make money with gamblers were always just across the hotel lobby. Joe Guyon, who later played for Thorpe at Canton, said, "There were guys who took their money—I guess. We had one guy. Oh, he was a high traveler. A halfback. We saw his contacts at the hotel. Then we saw his play. He was detailed to cover a man, and when he didn't, why, we said it was an accident. But the second time it was too obvious. I said, 'What the hell is going on?' I went over to the bench and said, 'He didn't cover his man, Jim. This guy is not covering his man.' Jim braced him right there. He fired him.")

If Thorpe did no betting on Canton, he did some boasting at the Courtland on the night before the game, saying that Massillon couldn't stop him or the Bulldogs. Thorpe's conviction was strengthened by the knowledge that Pete Calac would be with him in the backfield for the first time. Canton also had two formidable Dartmouth stars, All-America quarterback Milton Ghee and Doc Spears at guard. Fats Waldsmith, a center from Akron, was a large discouragement to any opponent's running game. Thorpe had had the group together for more practice than usual, although quarterback Ghee would depend on the basic end sweeps by Thorpe, the plunging of Calac and his own passing. Soucy of Harvard was his favorite target.

Thousands rode the special trolleys from downtown Canton to the lakeside park dominated by the wooden skeleton of the roller coaster. Pickpockets had a busy day in the cars and around the entrance gates, and several fans found themselves without the $1.00 for general admission (the same price in town for one quart full measure of "The Old Corn Whisky"). By game time there were 10,000 people in the fourteen-row bleachers or standing behind the fences. They saw one of the most one-sided—gloriously so, for Canton supporters—games in the long series. Although the play was not dominated by Thorpe—he scored one of four Canton touchdowns while Massillon went scoreless—it was one of his finest afternoons as a professional. With the quarterbacking of Ghee and help from running mate Calac, Thorpe brought "the undisputed professional football championship of the world" to the city of Canton for the first time. The Bulldogs had twenty-one players dressed in their red-and-white home jerseys for the game, but Thorpe stayed with the same eleven throughout the game. No one was injured, no one made any horrendous mistakes—there was no reason for him to call in a sub. The team effort on defense kept Massillon outside the 30-yard line; six of the fourteen passes thrown by Massillon were intercepted by Canton's backs. Thorpe could give a slashing, fumble-making momentum to a defense. He tackled by driving his shoulder into the body or legs of the ball carrier or pass receiver, virtually assuring them of a punishing blow. He was no arm tackler: His style was that of a modern defensive back and it provoked many fumbles—and stories that persisted for years about the composition of his shoulder pads. It was said that they contained steel ribbing or iron plating, depending upon the eyewitness account one chose to believe. They were made, at least in his Canton days, of riveted hard leather, hard enough to protect his narrow, sloping shoulders and to inflict discomfort on both offense and defense. Later, when Thorpe was more kicker than runner, he wore a pair of flimsy shoulder pads, made of canvas, felt and leather and weighing less than a pound.

The day after the rout of Massillon Thorpe might have sat in any office in the city of Canton, but he announced plans to return to Oklahoma to do some hunting. He talked vaguely of retiring from football while he was still in sound shape and of playing baseball for the Giants again after his good performance in the American Association.

Because of the vast war mobilization in 1917 Thorpe did return to major league baseball for his most active season. Christy Mathewson, then manager of the Cincinnati Reds, was in need of an outfielder and used Thorpe, with consideration and with results, through much of the season. He batted around .250 in seventy-seven games—and, as he later said, some of the hits must have come off curve balls. When the Giants found themselves battling for a pennant without enough bench strength Thorpe went to New York briefly, long enough for a token appearance in the World Series against the White Sox. In mid-October Thorpe went back to Canton only to realize that football in the city had at last been upstaged. The concerns of the people were of Liberty Bonds (the industrial workers were patriotic buyers), with voluntary wheatless and meatless days of the week, and with the hundreds of draftees from the city undergoing training at Ohio's Camp Sherman. When the Bulldogs played the Patricians in Youngstown it was announced that for the first time in years there would be no special trains to the game "but auto parties will be much in style." Thorpe became overworked as a ball carrier and, occasionally, as quarterback. He finally appealed to Gus Welch, in officers' training at Camp Meade, Maryland, to commute for a few weekends. Jim offered him a hundred dollars a game plus expenses.

The season-end games against Massillon brought Thorpe, Calac and Welch together as teammates. Their old coach Pop Warner watched Canton win the first and commented, "They play a great defensive game but don't show the teamwork of a successful college team. Give Canton a few weeks practice under a good coach and it would be invincible. Jim is the same old Thorpe—the best."

But there were moments in the final meeting with Massillon (the last between the rivals for two years) when Thorpe looked second best to Stanley Cofall, a splendid kicker and running back from Notre Dame who played left half for the Tigers. Thorpe and Cofall engaged in an intense personal battle—running, kicking, tackling—which finally erupted into a near fist fight. In the first quarter Cofall blocked one of Jim's kicks and later when his field goal attempt was also blocked it was Cofall who recovered.

The two were the hardest working runners in the game—and Thorpe clearly outrushed Cofall. But it was Cofall's two field goals that gave Massillon its 6–0 victory. Once Cofall rammed into Thorpe after play had been ruled dead and the crowd watched in surprise as Thorpe, usually under cool restraint during games, jumped up and charged his opponent until he was held back by teammates. In his frustration at his failure to lead Canton to a touchdown, Thorpe may have suddenly sensed the inevitability of his diminishing role in games of the future. He would keep on playing, even turning marvelous feats with his punts and field goals, but his dominance of all sides of the action was over. He had been recently reminded of how long he had been part of the game. Two weeks before the Canton-Massillon series the local papers carried the report of the end of football at Carlisle, where it had all really started for Thorpe some ten years earlier. As the government prepared to close the school and convert it to military needs, the Indians were beaten by Georgia Tech in their last game, 98–0.

"He Was an Indian"

In 1917 Thorpe took a step that suggested he was ready to submit to the traditional responsibilities of husband, father, provider—he bought a home in the small northeast Oklahoma town of Yale, his first "permanent" residence. It was also his first and last real attempt to return close to his roots in Oklahoma. A second child, daughter Gail, was born that fall and Iva was anxious to have a house in which to raise the children; Yale was the town her sister had chosen to live in. Over a short span it became the home for two more daughters, Charlotte and Grace. It was the home that Thorpe left less than five years later when his marriage with Iva broke up and his careers in football and baseball became ever more peripatetic and minor league. But Yale was, for a time, made a livelier location in the Cimmaron River basin by the appearance of Thorpe.

Yale was in the midst of an oil boom when the Thorpes arrived. It grew officially into a city with a population of about four thousand and with Twin State Oil, Gypsy Oil, Carter Oil, Magnolia Oil and others drilling furiously on sections of what had been slumbering cotton, wheat, cattle, poultry and pecan farms. Barbershops without doors did business twenty-four hours a day, the dance hall above the Studebaker garage was filled with oil workers and so were the speakeasies and pool halls on Main Street. "The bootleggers around here had to wear badges so they wouldn't bother to sell to one another," said one boom-time resident. "Hell, bootlegging whiskey wasn't a trade in Yale it was a profession."

Thorpe was frequently seen on Main Street in late fall and winter, riding his horse to the pool hall or speakeasy where he kept it tied to a post while he perfected his hand at snooker or raised a glass with locals. His most admired pocket billiards talent was that of leaping over the table, with both feet neatly tucked beneath him, after he had made a shot that pleased him. Locals were either appalled or delighted by his presence, depending upon their tastes. One who enjoyed him was Doc Potts, who got his name because he went to dental school in Kansas City before he made a small fortune in nearby oil rights. Potts found Thorpe impossible to keep up with on coon hunts—"He loved those coon dogs of his and the dogs and Jim could run all night. I never knew him in those few winters when he seemed unhappy. If he got drunk and hungover, he would sober up until he came out pleasant. If he didn't know you or took a dislike, he wouldn't offer you liquid in your throat to put out a fire in your belly. But if you were his friend there wasn't anything he wouldn't try to do for you. He was an Indian."

The Thorpe home on Boston Avenue was atop a steeply pitched hill above Main Street. Thorpe occasionally challenged locals to horse races *up* the hill, a dangerous gamble for strangers because he knew the track and his horse so well. The house was a small, neat, two-bedroom clapboard, with property enough to keep his dogs and the horse. The parents and tiny children occupied a back bedroom, a baby-sitter used the other bedroom and Thorpe plopped down on a cot in the living room when he had come up the hill bearing too much of a whiskey load.

Iva found that Jim's drinking—which had at first come as a surprise to her because she had never really associated with people who drank—had become worse in Yale. "He and Pete Calac and others used to go out hunting and return in the morning with the most enormous appetites. I would have to fix them bacon and a half-dozen eggs each. I wondered why they needed so much food—until I discovered the whiskey bottles Jim used to toss into the back closet. They had been drinking and hunting for hours. We had friends who were priests and they would talk to him about how irresponsible he was. He would get to feeling guilty and ashamed and say, 'How can you put up with me?' I told him we had a family and friends and I would put up with him until he really fell by the wayside."

He sometimes carried his sorrow in maudlin fashion. Once he sat up with a dying coon dog all night, insisting that he wanted to have the animal stuffed and kept in the house. But he suffered a devastating blow quietly enough, for all the anguish it caused him. His son, Jim, Jr., died an influenza victim in the outbreak of 1918. He had lived less than four years. Iva considered this the great tragedy in his life, one that made the Olympic disbarment and the loss of medals and trophies seem inconsequential by comparison. As a child he had lost his closest brother; now as a father he had lost a first son. "He was heartbroken when that boy died," she said. "His drinking problem increased after that."

Those winters in Yale were quick interludes in the last seasons of his active life in sports. He could go on playing baseball, from the National League to a string of minor-league stops, without suffering great declines in acclaim and performances. But in football his experience had been as the very best. He lost that ground slowly, reluctantly.

In that first October after the war Thorpe was back familiarly as player-coach at Canton, "looking the same old Jim and with a spring in every stride." But in the first game of the 1919 season he sat and watched the Bulldogs play Pitcairn until the fourth quarter when he answered the calls from the crowd of 2,000, put on his headgear with the flopping ear covers and entered the game. When he first touched the ball, fielding a punt, he dropped it and recovered, but on a run around end he fumbled when hit and a Pitcairn Quaker scooped it up and ran seventy yards for a score.

Jim tried a field goal that went wide—and was relieved to get out of the game with a 13–7 win.

The Canton season and its player-coach improved after that. He had brought in Joe Guyon from Georgia Tech, where he had been named All-America, to play right half, and the Carlisle backfield of Thorpe, Guyon and Calac began to lay waste to opposing lines. Guyon was combative, peppery and goaded his linemen and interference in a loud voice. Thorpe enjoyed taunting opponents after he had run through them for long yardage, "What's the matter—can't you stop old Jim?" Calac, at fullback, was the tireless straight-ahead man, bearing an opponent or two on his back as he plunged for three or four yards. More and more it was Calac who did most of the ball carrying. Guyon, who was paid one hundred dollars a game, took over some of the punting and passing responsibilities for Thorpe. Against Massillon, Calac carried the ball thirty-three times, twice as frequently as Thorpe. The strategy led to touchdowns by Guyon and his player-coach and a 23–0 victory. In the rematch with Massillon Thorpe was injured so badly that he was taken to the hospital with a suspected vertebrae dislocation. Before he left the field he scored on one of three field-goal attempts (the final score was 3–0) and he lifted a kick into a strong carrying wind that Cantonians talked about and remeasured for seasons to come. He stood on the Bulldogs' 5-yard line and put his foot into a spiral that landed at or near the goal line and bounced into the fence at the east end of the field. The game statistics credited him with ninety-five yards and fans called it the most wondrous kick they had ever seen— even with the hard wind.

The great kicks and runs Thorpe had provided Canton for four years and the spread of popularity he had given the game in other cities led to honorary recognition in September 1920, when he was named president of the American Professional Football Association, the forebear of the National Football League. The formal organization of the league took place when representatives of a dozen teams met in the office of Canton auto dealer Ralph Hay, who had taken over management of the Bulldogs when Jack Cusack entered the oil business. Ralph Hay did much of the anonymous ground work in forming the league, but he was anxious that Thorpe, his friend and player-coach, carry the title of president. The teams which finally paid the hundred-dollar membership fee and agreed to the league bylaws were the Canton Bulldogs, Rock Island Independents, Rochester Jeffersons, Buffalo All-Americans, Muncie (did not field a team), Decatur Staleys, Chicago Cardinals, Chicago Tigers, Cleveland Panthers, Dayton Triangles, Hammond Pros and Akron Pros. Massillon did not have a franchise, which darkened the future of the sport in Canton.

Thorpe became president of pro football's first league just days after playing out the baseball season with the Akron Internationals (where he batted .365). He and Ralph Hay agreed to a contract that would give him $2,500 for the season and a small percentage of the gate receipts if the club made a profit. All players were guaranteed $150 a game and Wilbur ("Fats") Henry, a huge tackle from Washington and Jefferson, was paid as much as $250. The Bulldogs of Hay and Thorpe soon proved to be over-burdened with costs and underprepared for the long season in the American Professional Football Association. The customers still came out early to watch Thorpe's warm-up exhibition of field-goal kicking in which he placed balls at midfield and kicked them alternately through the goal posts at each end. But two losses to Akron and a tie with Dayton—and the lack of anticipation of a Massillon game—cooled support in Canton. The game payroll went over three thousand dollars and long overnight train trips drained the budget. At the end of the season Thorpe led the Bulldogs into New York's Polo Grounds for a game with the Buffalo All-Americans. Thorpe, Calac and Guyon showed some of the old Carlisle appeal in the city by drawing a crowd of around 10,000. Canton lost, 7–3, as one of Thorpe's kicks was blocked for a Buffalo touchdown.

In mid-December, after Hay and Thorpe agreed they could not continue the franchise for another season, the Canton *Repository* ran this obituary on the sports page:

Patched Up Bulldogs Close Disastrous Season, Losing 13–7 Game to Union A.A. Team of Phoenixville, Pa. / Thorpe was in charge of the team but it had no connection with Canton, as all relations between the

city and the Bulldogs were severed a week ago after
their return from a trip to New York and New Haven.
[It was] a patched up team that took the field wearing
the red and white which until this fall had been symbolic of the highest grade of football ever played in a
professional organization.

The prolonged exit from football took Thorpe through parts
of professional games and seasons in Cleveland, Toledo, Rock
Island, New York and Chicago, where he made an appearance
as late as 1928. He kept a respectable measure of his kicking ability to the very end, but his token efforts at running the ball were
sometimes painful to watch. His career in football reached full
circle in the town of Marion, Ohio, in 1922 and '23, when
he helped assemble the Oorang Indians and led them through
irregular road schedules in the American Professional Football Association. Like other early pro teams, the All-Indians
served a commercial cause—for the Oorang dog kennels of Walter Lingo of LaRue, Ohio. Lingo got together with Thorpe on a
plan to field a team of Indians and let the players serve a dual
role of promoting his kennel and working part-time as trainers
for the Oorang airedales he was breeding. To help stimulate traffic at the gate, Lingo would offer pregame dog tricks with his
airedales and the Indians would entertain with a little dancing
and drumming.

For Thorpe, who had started playing football as part of the
white man's celebration of its system of educating Indians, trading on his background and football fame was a most logical way
of earning a living. Thorpe turned to old contacts at Carlisle,
Haskell and Sherman Institute and hired Guyon, Calac, Elmer
Busch, Bemus Pierce, Nick Lassa and a dozen others. There was
neither enough vaudeville know-how nor adequate cohesiveness
on the football field to make much success for the Oorang Indians. They were losers as often as winners as they traveled from
city to city. But they did have some good times together, with
Thorpe, the coach, setting a relaxed training pace. Individually
they brought some sophisticated techniques into their Sunday
games. They had long ago mastered the civilized methods of
hook blocking, of locking legs, of using their arms and elbows

across the scrimmage line, and they were exceedingly quick
with their cleated shoes. Joe Guyon said that despite their ages
and condition they still found exhilaration in giving and taking
the knocks of the game.

In mid-October 1922, Thorpe and his All-Indians—the papers
were inclined to refer to them as aborigines—came to Canton to
play the Bulldogs, who had been successfully revived by Guy
Chamberlin, an All-America end from Nebraska. Canton was into
a championship-winning season and the homecoming game with
Thorpe drew a large crowd to the park by Meyers Lake. The
All-Indians started seven players from Carlisle in a line-up commonly decorated with such names as Long Time Sleep, Xavier
Downwind, Little Twig, Lone Wolf, Laughing Gas, Red Fox and
Eagle Feather. Plain Joe Guyon, at left halfback, did the heavy
running, passing and kicking that had once been Thorpe's burden at Canton. The game settled into a hard defensive struggle,
with the much-favored Bulldogs holding a touchdown lead. After
a Canton running play Duke Osborne, a Bulldog guard, took exception to a late hit by Long Time Sleep and slammed an elbow
at his head. The game suddenly became something else. Indian
faces flashed with hatred as Long Time Sleep got up and shook
off the effects of the blow. For most of them a long Indian school
history of games against whites that were periled by racial bitterness was repeating itself. Thorpe and others at the side lines
could no longer check their anger and frustration. They let out
a yell and charged after Osborne, who fled toward the safety of
police and friends across the field. The crowd wedged into the
wooden bleachers roared and whooped with laughter at what
they thought was a delightful, well-rehearsed piece of Indian
pantomime.

EPILOGUE

The conspicuous role of the Indian in American football, from the early successes of the Carlisle teams against major universities to the pregame sideshows of the All-Indian professionals, had spanned barely two decades. The decline in prominence fits closely with that of Thorpe, as he went from active play to the exhibitions and personal appearances which occupied him, with little reward, for the rest of his life. But Thorpe, Guyon, Calac, Welch, Arcasa—all the brilliant rest of the football boys—were products of a time and a system that came to an end as government disenchantment set in with the way of educating and extolling the Indians at Carlisle. By the time the school closed in 1918 the bureaucratic surge toward removing the young Indian from the reservation and civilizing him into the white world had waned. The Indian problem was no longer a popular social theme in the land. Perhaps with the diminishing size of the tribes and their reserves it might quietly fade away.

The disappearance of Carlisle as the focal point of Indian athletic incentive and achievement was, ironically, hurried by its best-known athletes. When a Congressional investigating committee began hearings in 1914 on the school—inquiring heavily into discipline, lack of morals, finances, the domination of athletics—critical testimony was supplied by members of the football team. Gus Welch was a leader of a quiet student rebellion which drew up a petition signed by more than two hundred students calling for an investigation into the school. The uses made of the athletic funds were among the major student concerns. Pop Warner's success—and what were considered his excesses—were criticized. Welch and other team members apparently didn't mind being exploited as athletes, but they objected to the way that Warner overtly sold fifty to seventy-five game tickets in hotel lobbies on Friday nights and then presumably pocketed the money. Elmer Busch, the heavy-set Pomo from California, was one of the players who signed an affidavit detailing Warner's use of profanity in practices and on the side lines during games. There was testimony that Warner bet heavily on the 1913 game with Dartmouth and told the team at half time that if they won he would cut them in; they did and he did, to a modest percentage. Warner, in Welch's judgment, was a fine coach but a man with little principle.

The broad investigation charged Superintendent Moses Friedman with uneven disciplinary actions, linking a decline in conduct among the students with the special privileges given the football boys. The superintendent was accused of filing false travel vouchers to the government after his rail trips had already been paid for out of the handy athletic fund. Musical director Claude Stauffer was described as having autocratic control at the school second only to that of athletic director Warner. The joint commission, led by chairman Joe Robinson, found fault with the school's dormitory mattresses, dining hall rations, inflated attendance rolls, drinking among the football boys (Welch and Thorpe by mention) which brought no disciplinary action, the irregular manner of the flag salute by students and a drop in interest in the industrial trades. The long catalogue of criticism ended with the recommendation to the Department of the Interior that Superintendent Friedman, athletic director Warner, bandleader Stauffer, and the school clerk, S. J. Nori, who had entered Carlisle as a student at the age of six, be dismissed. Carlisle had obviously run its course; it had become too similar to the non-military, success-oriented, self-perpetuating private schools in the United States that were turning undisciplined white students into the world.

The hearings brought the most abrupt change in the attitude toward athletics at Carlisle. Pop Warner's extravagant quarters for athletes and the training table were closed. When Joel Wheelock eagerly suggested to the new superintendent that he

be sent rail fare so that he could come back and do some volunteer coaching at the school he was told: "Athletics are being conducted differently at Carlisle than has been the custom and no
inducements whatever can be held out to students who desire to
be enrolled or to former students who desire to return to school
for the purposes outlined in your letter."

Carlisle closed without ever approaching fulfillment of the am-
bitious dream that Richard Henry Pratt held onto for so many
years. The school did have its impact on each of the relatively
few Indian lives it touched, sending some out educated and well
motivated into the white world and providing others with disciplinary and vocational training that served mostly as an
interlude away from a barren existence on the reservation. Post-
graduate experience of the athletes, whose most intense education had come on Indian Field, was typical of the range of
"success" and "failure"—as measured by the society they had been
taught to live within.

There were the achievers among the football boys, such as Albert Exendine and Gus Welch, who went on achieving. Ex, a
commanding figure, carried the respect he had earned at Carlisle
through a coaching career at Otterbein, Occidental, George
Washington, the Oklahoma Aggies and a life span that lasted
eighty-eight years. Gus Welch stretched his wit and energy
through seasons of coaching at colleges and prep schools. In the
latter part of his life he returned to a wilderness environment,
such as he had known as a Chippewa boy, and he and wife,
Julia, settled high on a mountainside of the Virginia Blue Ridge.
(When the National Park Service took some of his land for a
highway extension and paid him less than the original price,
Gus fought against what he considered bureaucratic injustice.
The court ruled against him and Gus turned to the judge with a
last word: "The white man has been taking land from the Indian
for so long that it has become a habit with him. There's nothing
an Indian man can do about changing the white man's habits.")

Henry Roberts, one of the football boys who never went back
to the game, epitomized the success story Carlisle cared to boast
of: a business career with an oil firm in Oklahoma, a home on a
hilltop in Pawnee not far from the reserve where he was born, a
happy marriage with the girl he had met at Carlisle. Everyone's

"best man," Sam Burd turned to ranching in the valleys of his native Montana, and Alex Arcasa took the enthusiasm he had showed at Carlisle for mechanics and carpentry into the railroad boiler shops of Altoona. Isaac Seneca, the dynamic pre-Thorpe ball carrier, became a master blacksmith, teaching the trade to other Indians. Charles Dillon, who embarrassed Harvard, went into the familiar Indian Service, and Bill Hodge returned to Oregon to become a logger on the Klamath River. For Possum Powell, Louis Tewanima and others there was a headlong flight to obscurity after the public attention that focused on them at Carlisle. Tewanima went back to the sun in Second Mesa, on the Hopi Reserve, tending his fruit trees and occasionally running and hitching his way to Winslow sixty miles away to watch the trains go by. Late one evening in 1969 the elderly little priest of the Antelope clan took a wrong turn on his way home from a religious ceremony and fell over a cliff to his death. Bill Newashe found unwanted anonymity with industrial and minor-league baseball teams in the Midwest, occasionally sending clippings to the Sac and Fox Agency from hotels in Sioux City, Wichita and Peoria if he had had a good game at bat. When Newashe had grown too old for the trade he had learned best at Carlisle, he quietly returned to his Sac and Fox land, surfacing publicly once after his friend Jim Thorpe had been named "Athlete of the Half Century" by the Associated Press with the soft-spoken words of admiration he had always had when they were early teammates.

Of all the football boys it was Thorpe, of course, who found it hardest to shed the past and reach fresh success, or much contentment, in the future. His passage through three marriages and a series of jobs that ran a demeaning scale, his bouts with drinking and ill health, always seemed to be within public attention. The wondrous "horse" of the 1912 Olympics became "Poor Jim" as the newspapers provided irregular traces of his troubles: He was photographed in his job digging ditches at the Los Angeles County Hospital site. A few months later he was signed for his first role by Universal Studios as Chief Black Crow in *Battling With Buffalo Bill*. At the age of fifty-one he was rescued by lifeguards at Hermosa Beach after developing leg cramps while trying to qualify for a bit part in *Too Hot to Han-*

dle. In 1941 his second wife and mother of four sons, Freeda Kirkpatrick, whom he married in 1926, sued for divorce. Two years later Thorpe was stricken with a heart attack while working as a gate guard at the River Rouge plant of the Ford Motor Company. A Los Angeles judge fined him fifty dollars for drunken driving and, in his reprimand, reminded him he was "a legend to our youth." He sold the film rights to his life story for a few thousand dollars. His third wife, the former Patricia Askew, announced plans in 1950 for a "make-a-million" campaign and said that Thorpe would take over as manager and second for Sunny War Cloud, a West Coast wrestler. He became part owner of the Jim Thorpe All-American Café in Sacramento and the Bank Café in San Pedro, where he spent a lot of his time. There seemed no end to the misadventures or the failing efforts to trade on the past.

Thorpe could have made it easier on himself, the people who knew and admired him and the world who knew only of his fame and his middle-aged problems if he had managed to change that Indian-Irish Thorpe personality that was set so firmly in his childhood. He was forever caught between moody gentleness and irascibility. His returns to Shawnee, where acceptance of him dimmed over the years, often left a wake of bruises and broken bottles in the back saloons on East Main Street where Indians could do their drinking. Once the police had to rope and tie him to get him into jail and when brother Frank came to release him the officers cleared out, fearful of another exhausting round. (Such is the legacy of the battling Thorpes in the area along the North Canadian—handed down from Hiram to Frank to George to Jim and others in line—that Richard and Jack Thorpe, the two youngest sons who have returned to live in Shawnee, sense there is a fight waiting for them in any beer joint they choose to enter. Like their father, they prefer not to be provoked but are capable of handling matters when they are.) In Hollywood's Palm Grove Bar, W. C. Fields and other celebrities tried to edge Thorpe toward action. Sometimes he would crush a beer glass in his hands while trying to control himself. He enjoyed attending the boxing and wrestling matches in Los Angeles, but he could count on being challenged to a little arm-wrestling in a bar afterwards. A wrestler on the program one evening made a bar bet that he could throw the aging and overweight Thorpe with one move. He did, and made the mistake of bragging about it later. Thorpe listened for a while and then walked over and clipped the wrestler on the chin with the point of his elbow, dropping him cold by the bar stool. Thorpe could least tolerate any damage to the pride he took in his fishing and hunting, much as he once regarded his ability to run with and kick a football. He stood on a California fishing pier with his sons one afternoon and listened to a fellow fisherman kid him about his empty pail. Suddenly Thorpe grabbed the man in a bear hug and silently dropped him over the side and into the water.

Saloons had a tendency to expose Thorpe's streak of gullibility and softness, leaving him an easy mark for a loan if he happened to have money with him. At Dearborn, Michigan, where Thorpe had taken all four of his sons—Carl, William, Dick and Jack—and was trying clumsily to take care of them by himself on his gate tender's pay, he once took the $250 he had received for appearing on a radio show into a bar after telling the boys to wait for him in the car. Carl, the oldest at fourteen, finally went into the bar to get his father and found him in a conversation with a man who was explaining why he was about to lose his property if he didn't come up with a few hundred dollars. Carl watched in dismay as his father reached into his pocket and pulled out several large bills and handed them to the stranger. Back in the car, the boy nervously pressed him, "Did you get his name? Do you know who he is?" Thorpe refused to discuss it.

His careless way with money, which had come and gone easily enough ever since his first annuity payment, and his lack of steady employment beyond baseball and football plunged him frequently enough into financial distress. It became his custom to solve the problem by wiring collect to his old roommate Gus Welch. Once Gus took over eight hundred dollars in unpaid hotel bills after Jim had walked out on his wife following an argument. Counting on Gus was as easy and natural as drinking with him.

Thorpe's later years may have appeared as a dismal stretch of odd jobs, unpaid bills, bar fights, broken homes, but he never really lost his capacity for the enjoyment of things that always appealed to him. He took his sons rabbit and coon hunting in

the Santa Ana hills when they were so young they would fall
asleep and he would carry them on his back for miles. There
were long days on charter boats fishing for bonita, yellow-tail
and mackerel. He was a strong swimmer and liked to put Richard or Jack on his back and swim around the pier near his home
at Hawthorne. His cars, which he drove until they collapsed, always seemed to be stuffed with greyhounds and boys eating ice
cream cones. He held onto his urge to kick a football as long as
he could swing a leg above his sagging stomach, giving impromptu demonstrations on school playgrounds and football
fields. When, between marriages, he moved in with Indian
friends from Oklahoma, Lee and Celia Blanchard, he could occupy himself for nights at a bridge table playing "losers do the
dishes." The Blanchards knew that "few people in the world had
felt Thorpe's warmth or understood his enjoyment of being with
people he trusted as friends." He liked to joke and tease, to talk
of just about everything except the lost trophies and medals and
all the games he had won. He never mentioned them.

But Thorpe's past was kept up for barter as long as he lived
and, for a time, even after his death. Under the prodding and
direction of his third wife, he went back on the exhibition road
late in his life, seeking payment for personal appearances and
fronting for Indian dancers and singers on cross-country tours.
An operation for lip cancer and his wife's public revelation that
they were broke did not bring ease to this final passage. Two
years later, on March 28, 1953, he died of a heart attack in his
Lomita, California, trailer home.

His death, with all its newsmaking, brought public recognition again of how prominent he had been in football and track
during the early part of the century. But Thorpe was prevented
from reminding the world of his heritage as an Indian or of his
predominance in the unique Indian athletic emergence in America. There was a funeral in his native Oklahoma but no burial
as he had wished, no proper closing of the circle with a marker
along the North Canadian River. Private Sac and Fox funeral
rites were given Thorpe by the Thunderbird clan at the farm of
Ed Mack, whose wife is a descendant of Black Hawk, on the
edge of Shawnee. The following day a Catholic service in the
city brought family, old friends Joe Guyon, Albert Exendine, Bill

Newashe among the eight hundred people at St. Benedict's Church on North Kickapoo Street. Shawnee had raised the money to have Thorpe's body brought from California, but there was no start toward construction of a discussed $100,000 memorial or any follow-through on Mrs. Thorpe's large plans for an adjoining motel to be called Jim Thorpe Tepees or a site for her Jim Thorpe Memorial Cancer and Heart Foundation hospital. When the rent became overdue at the crypt where the Thorpe casket had been placed, the widow had it moved to Tulsa while she shopped for a town that would provide a burial site suitable to her conditions.

She found one along the Lehigh River valley in eastern Pennsylvania, a bizarre distance from any of the major milestones in Thorpe's life. Mauch Chunk and East Mauch Chunk, wedged in between mountain and river, agreed to use some $12,500 of its industrial development fund to build a marble tomb. Residents voted to merge and change the community's name to Jim Thorpe, Pennsylvania, in hopes of attracting both business and tourists.

Thorpe's final resting place, inscribed in red marble, is in a modest park just off North Street on the steep edge of town. It brought neither tourist volume nor a surge in commerce to the place which calls itself the "Switzerland of America," yet voters have defeated proposals to change the name back to Mauch Chunk. The tomb is off Route 903 just past the Mauch Chunk Trust Co. which competes for customers with the nearby Jim Thorpe National Bank. Farther up the hill stands a civilized "Deer Crossing" sign, the only suggestion on the landscape that America's most famous Indian athlete is not in completely alien ground.

Acknowledgments

The following individuals and agencies were of special help to me in the preparation of this book: John Taylor and Joe Walker of the Bureau of Indian Affairs, Shawnee Agency, Hugh and Guy Wakole, Ed Mack and Roy Angel of Shawnee, Oklahoma; Mrs. Rella Looney and Mrs. Martha Blaine of the Oklahoma Historical Society, Oklahoma City, Oklahoma; Dick Gallagher, Don Smith and Jim Campbell of Professional Football's Hall of Fame and Clem Mitchell of Canton, Ohio; Mrs. Samella Anderson, The National Archives, Washington, D.C.; Roger Todd, Roger Steck and Mrs. Florence Dupuis of the Hamilton Library and the Cumberland County Historical Society, Carlisle, Pennsylvania, and Mac Pittinger, Hyman Goldstein, Mrs. Verna Whistler, and James Wardecker also of Carlisle; Vic Frolund of Youngstown, Ohio; Homer Ray of Yale, Oklahoma; Mrs. Gus Welch of Bedford, Virginia; Mrs. Iva Davies of Los Angeles, California; and Bill Stancil of Rocky Mount, North Carolina.

Among the major sources of printed information, the following were of special interest to me: Report of the Joint Commission of Congress, 63rd Congress, Second Session, to Investigate Indian Affairs, February 6, 7, 8–March 25, 1914; *The Black Hawk War* by Frank E. Stevens; *Sac and Fox Indians* by William T. Hagan; *Great Indian Chiefs* by Albert Britt; Chronicles of Oklahoma; *The Life Story of Glenn S. (Pop) Warner* by Francis J. Powers; *A Course in Football for Players and Coaches* by Glenn S. Warner; *Jim Thorpe—Carlisle Indian* by Wilbur J. Obrecht and the Cumberland County Historical Society;

The Foreman Pioneer Collection; *A Localized History of Pottawatomie County to 1907* by Charles Mooney; *Pott County and What Has Come of It* by John Forston; Carlisle Indian School publications: *The Arrow, The Red Man; The Last Trek of the Indians* by Grant Foreman; *The Indian Industrial School—Its Origins, Purposes, Progress and the Difficulties Surmounted* by Brig. General R. H. Pratt; *Battlefield and Classroom* by Richard Henry Pratt; Jack Cusack's *Own Story of the Pro Football Period, 1912–17 and 1921.*